RESERVOIR ECOLOGY

RESERVOIR ECOLOGY

By

Dr. Ashwini Dnyandeo Chalak
Assistant Professor
Department of Zoology
Kai Shankarrao Gutte Mahavidyalaya
Dharmapuri - 431 515
Maharashtra (India)

&

Dr. Vishwas Balasaheb Sakhare
Head and Associate Professor
Post Graduate Department of Zoology
Yogeshwari Mahavidyalaya
Ambajogai - 431 517
Maharashtra
(India)

DPH

DISCOVERY PUBLISHING HOUSE PVT. LTD.
INDIA

Published by:
Namit Wasan
DISCOVERY PUBLISHING HOUSE PVT. LTD.
4383/4B, Ansari Road, Darya Ganj
New Delhi-110 002 (India)
Phone : +91-11-23279245, 43596064-65
Fax : +91-11-23253475
E-mail : discoverypublishinghouse@gmail.com
namitwasan9@gmail.com
sales@discoverypublishinggroup.com
web : www.discoverypublishinggroup.com

First Edition: **2018**

ISBN: 978-93-86841-21-6

Reservoir Ecology

Printed at:
Infinity Imaging Systems
Delhi

Acknowledgements

We are highly thankful to Dr. Balasaheb Chavan, Principal, Yogeshwari Mahavidyalaya Ambajogai for giving permission to conduct the research work and for laboratory and library facilities during the entire study period.

We are also thankful to Dr. T.L. Holambe, Principal, Kai. Shankarrao Gutte Mahavidyalaya, Dharmapuri for encouragement.

We record our gratitude to Shri Nandkishor Parikh Secretary of 'Shri Samarth Machhimar Utpadak va Vikri Sahakari Sanstha Maryadit Bhavthana' for providing background data regarding Bhavthana reservoir. We are very much thankful to the local fishermen and their children for such a voluntarily cooperation.

We thank to publisher Shri Namit Wasan of Discovery Publishing House Private Limited, New Delhi, for taking pains in bringing out this volume.

We are grateful to our family members for helping us by several ways and encouraging us for publication of this book.

We are thankful to each and every person who directly or indirectly motivated and helped us during entire study period. Thanks are to all those who have not mentioned by name but nevertheless played a significant role in different ways.

Dr. Ashwini D. Chalak

Dr. Vishwas B. Sakhare

Contents

Abbreviations and Notations

A.D.	In the year of our Lord (Anno Domini)
B.C.	Before Christ
D.O.	Dissolved Oxygen
0	Degree
e.g.	For example (exempli gratia)
ed.	Editor
et.al.	And others (et alii)
etc.	And so forth (et cetera)
Fig figs.	Figure(s)
F.R.L.	Full Reservoir Level
ft	Feet
i.e.	That is (id est)
Kg	Kilogram
Kg/ha/yr	Kilogram per hectare per year
,	Minute
m	Meter
mcft	Million cubic feet
Nos/lit	Numbers per liter
Rev.	Revised
TDS	Total Dissolved Solids
vol vols.	Volume (s)
viz.	Namely
yr	Year

1

Introduction

In India, there are 19,370 reservoirs, covering an area of 3.15 million ha. The area is expected to grow further to 6 million ha in due course of time of 25 years. Reservoirs are generally classified as small (<1000 ha), medium (1000-5000 ha) and large (>5000 ha), especially in the records of the Government of India. Unfortunately, majority of reservoirs are not being scientifically managed for fisheries. Only a handful of them have so far been harnessed along scientific lines, while the others are either half-heartedly managed or not managed at all. As compared to several developed countries, the per hectare fish production in Indian reservoirs is very poor, being only about 29.70 kg per year as against 88 kg in the Russia, 100 kg in Sri Lanka and 65 kg in large reservoirs of Thailand. The present low yield levels from the reservoirs is on account of many reasons such as lack of fish seed stocking, inappropriate gear and craft, poor landing and marketing channels, absence of closed season and other management bottlenecks such as weak cooperatives and stranglehold of middle-men.

Small reservoirs are managed like ponds and constitute a 'put and take' fishery. However, the medium and large sized reservoirs constitute a capture fishery resource but have to be managed through enhancement programmes. The hidden fish production potential of reservoirs has not so far been realized. So much so the yield gap continues to be large, the average productivity being only 20 kg/ha/yr against a possible yield of over 200 kg/ha/yr in the case of small reservoirs, 100 kg/ha/yr in the case of medium and 50 kg/ha/yr for large reservoirs.

The main problem in developing the fisheries of reservoirs has been stocking with inadequate numbers of advanced fingerlings, small size of fingerlings stocked, skewed proportion of species, release of fingerlings (truly speaking advanced fry) at a wrong place and at a wrong time.

Indian reservoirs are spread over various geoclimatic regions and their drainages represent different types of catchment areas. Besides, the varying design and purpose of dams make the reservoirs different in their hydrographic and morphoedaphic characteristics. All these diversities frustrate the efforts to evolve a common management strategy that can be universally applied to Indian reservoirs. Researches conducted in selected reservoirs, selected as types, help us in arriving at common strategies for a group of reservoirs. Bhavthana reservoir is one such water body that could represent several of small Indian reservoirs. Therefore, ecology based investigations were carried out on fish and fisheries of this reservoir and the package was evolved to manage its fisheries with a scientific basis.

A need has long been felt by those engaged in research, education, development and planning for consolidated information on reservoirs, which includes the reservoirs available, level of technologies and the extent of their utilization. A lot of literature has been generated on the ecology and fisheries of lakes and reservoirs from various parts of India, but very little attention has been given to the water bodies in Maharashtra in general and Marathwada region in particular. The present work is an attempt to study the fish and fisheries of Bhavthana reservoir in Beed district of Maharashtra. The work done purports to fill the void by bringing the up to date knowledge on fish and fisheries of Bhavthana reservoir. The research programme included:

1. Morphometry and hydrgraphy of Bhavthana reservoir;
2. Monthly physico-chemical analysis of water of Bhavthana Reservoir;
3. Monthly qualitative and quantitative analysis of phytoplankton and zooplankton;
4. Studies on various aspects of fish and fisheries of reservoir; and
5. Socio-economic status of fishermen community.

The results of the research work are organized under 6 chapters. In the first introductory chapter.

In chapter 2 details on meterology, morphometry and hydrography of Bhavthana reservoir are described. Bhavthana reservoir is located near village Bhavthana of Ambajogai tehsil in Beed district of Maharashtra. The reservoir was constructed about 15 km from Ambajogai. The reservoir site is located in longitude 76 17′ 29″ and latitude 18 48′ 33″. Bhavthana reservoir was constructed in the year 2004-2005, under Godavari Marathwada Patbandhare Vikas Mahamandal, Aurangabad. The reservoir was primarily constructed for irrigation. It has an opportunity to provide water for agriculture to villages like Bhavthana, Sonavala and Morafali. The water spread area of the reservoir is 70ha.

The fish and fisheries of Bhavthana reservoir are summarized in chapter 3.This chapter contains information of ichthyofauna, fish seed stocking and its composition, fish catch and catch composition, crafts and gears used for fishing and socio-economic status of fishermen. This chapter also contains introduction, result (tables and figures included) and discussion. During the present investigation a total of 33 species of fishes belonging to 5 orders, 11 families and 20 genera have been recorded from Bhavthana reservoir. The in depth survey and analysis revealed that order cypriniformes (45.45%) was dominated by 15 species which was followed by perciformes (27.27%) with 9 species, order siluriformes (18.18%) was represented by 6 species and order osteoglossiformes (6.06%) by 2 species and order cyprinodontiformes (3.03%) was represented by a single species.

The average fish production from the reservoir was 238.29 kg/ha/yr. It was 241.85 kg/ha/yr in 2012-13 and 234.74 kg/ha/yr in 2013-14. The carps dominated with 236 kg/ha/yr (97.46%) and 229 kg/ha/yr (97.37%) during 2012-13 and 2013-14 respectively. Local fishes (murrels, catfishes and others) occupied second position with 6.14 kg/ha/yr (2.53%) in 2012-13 and 617 kg/ha/yr in 2013-14.

During 2012-13 stocking of fry was done at 1786 nos/ha and 2500 nos/ha in 2013-14. This worked out to a mean of 2143 nos/ha. The composition of stocked seed included Indian major carps, common carp, silver carp and grass carp. Seed was stocked in the reservoir in the fry stage (20-25mm size). The natural recruitment of major carps is either absent or poor due to non-availability of suitable breeding grounds in lotic sector of the reservoir or on account of inadequacy of water inflow at the right time. Therefore, the reservoir needs regular stocking support.

The gears operated in Bhavthana reservoir are gill-net, cast net and hook and line. Maximum catch in the reservoir was performed by multifilament gill net. The mesh size of net shows variations and depend upon the species to be caught. Mesh size varies from 12-50 mm. Readymade gill nets are available in the local markets of Majalgaon and Beed from where the fishermen used to purchase them. Thermocol raft and tubes of wheels of motor cars are the commonly used crafts in reservoir. This study is based on the information collected from 35 fishermen who are the members of co-operative society, engaged in fishing of Bhavthana reservoir. Data was collected by interviewing method using a pre-tested questionnaire in vernacular language. The information collected was tabulated, analyzed and the results are presented below.

A co-operative society named "Shri Samarth Machhimar Utpadak va Vikri Sahakari Sansatha Maryadit Bhavthana" was established with registration number CHR/AJI/RSR/NC/542/1999 in December 1999. There are 35 co-operative members, out of which only 2 are female. The socio-economic analysis was carried out on different aspects such as age, education, family type, type of house, monthly income and other related parameters. The total fishermen population of Bhavthana reservoir is 35, out of which, there are 33 males (94%) and 2 females (6%). Most of the fishermen are part time operators, unskilled and they adopted only traditional methods of fish catching, restricted to holidays. Agriculture was main occupation of almost all fishermen. One of the most important reasons for the poor stage of agriculture is the lack of irrigation facilities. The rainfall is by and large, sufficient and fairly dependable. But no efforts were made in past to develop the irrigation potential.

The physico-chemical characteristics of the reservoir are presented in chapter 4. This chapter starts with an introduction, followed by results with corresponding tables, figures and discussion. Three sampling stations were selected from reservoirs to study physico-chemical parameters. The three sampling stations were at three different locations i.e. Ist at lentic, IInd at intermediate and IIIrd at lotic sector of reservoir. Monthly samples were collected from the above three stations for two years. Different physico-chemical parameters such as temperature, transparency, hardness, chlorides, total dissolved solids, pH, dissolved oxygen, free carbon dioxide, alkalinity etc were analyzed with the help of standard methods. The physico-chemical analysis of reservoir revealed that the water is suitable for fisheries.

The chapter 5 embodies the plankton diversity of Bhavthana reservoir. This chapter includes an introduction, results (with tables and figures) and discussion. The study of the phytoplankton sampled in Bhavthana reservoir showed 16 species. The phytoplankton assemblage was represented by three classes viz. bacillariophyceae, cyanophyceae and chlorophyceae. Microscopic examination of zooplanktons revealed that there were for groups consisting of 31 species of zooplankton and were represented by rotifers (13 species), cladocerans (8 species), copepods (6 species) and ostracods (4 species)

Chapter 6 embodies and conclusion and recommendations. Conclusion highlights the important results of the investigation. Based on the results of the study some recommendations were also framed and presented.

This chapter is followed by a list of literature consulted and cited, under the heading 'References'.

2

About Bhavthana Reservoir

The Bhavthana reservoir (Fig. 2.1, Fig. 2.2 and Fig. 2.3) is a small sized reservoir in Beed district of Maharashtra. This reservoir was constructed in year 2005 at village Bhavthana of Kaij tehsil, across a seasonal river known as Adas river to meet the water requirement for irrigational purposes. Reservoir was constructed by Godavari Marathwada Irrigation Development Corporation.

The reservoir is located at Longitude 76 17′ 29″ and Latitude 18 48′ 33″. The reservoir is having catchment area of 12.2 sq.miles. The maximum water level of Bhavthana reservoir is at 653 m. It is an earthen dam with height and length of 26.76 m and 434 m respectively. The water spread area of the reservoir is 70 ha.

As it is a small sized reservoir, no village was submerged under this reservoir. The villages such as Bhavthana, Sonvala and Morphali receive benefit due to the irrigation facilities under this reservoir. The initial estimated cost of the dam was Rs. 333,14000/- only. The final expenses incurred are Rs. 773,95000/-. The salient features of Bhavthana reservoir are depicted in Table 2.1.

The Bhavthana reservoir water is continuously drawn for irrigation and the major crops grown by the farmers include groundnut, soyabean, jowar, cotton, wheat, and sugarcane. Water from Bhavthana reservoir help farmers in keeping the water-guzzling sugarcane crop irrigated. Sugarcane, one of the most water-intensive crops grown, requires 10 times more water than groundnut or jowar. Besides, village panchyat also draws water regularly for drinking and other purposes. The continuous draw-down of reservoir water and the variation in the inflow from catchment areas seasonally results in wide fluctuations in water level in Bhavthana reservoir. The fluctuations in water level have been found to affect the fish catch considerably. The reservoir level increases from the month of August with onset of monsoon and reaches the highest level in September. From December, the level decreases and a lowest level was generally recorded in May.

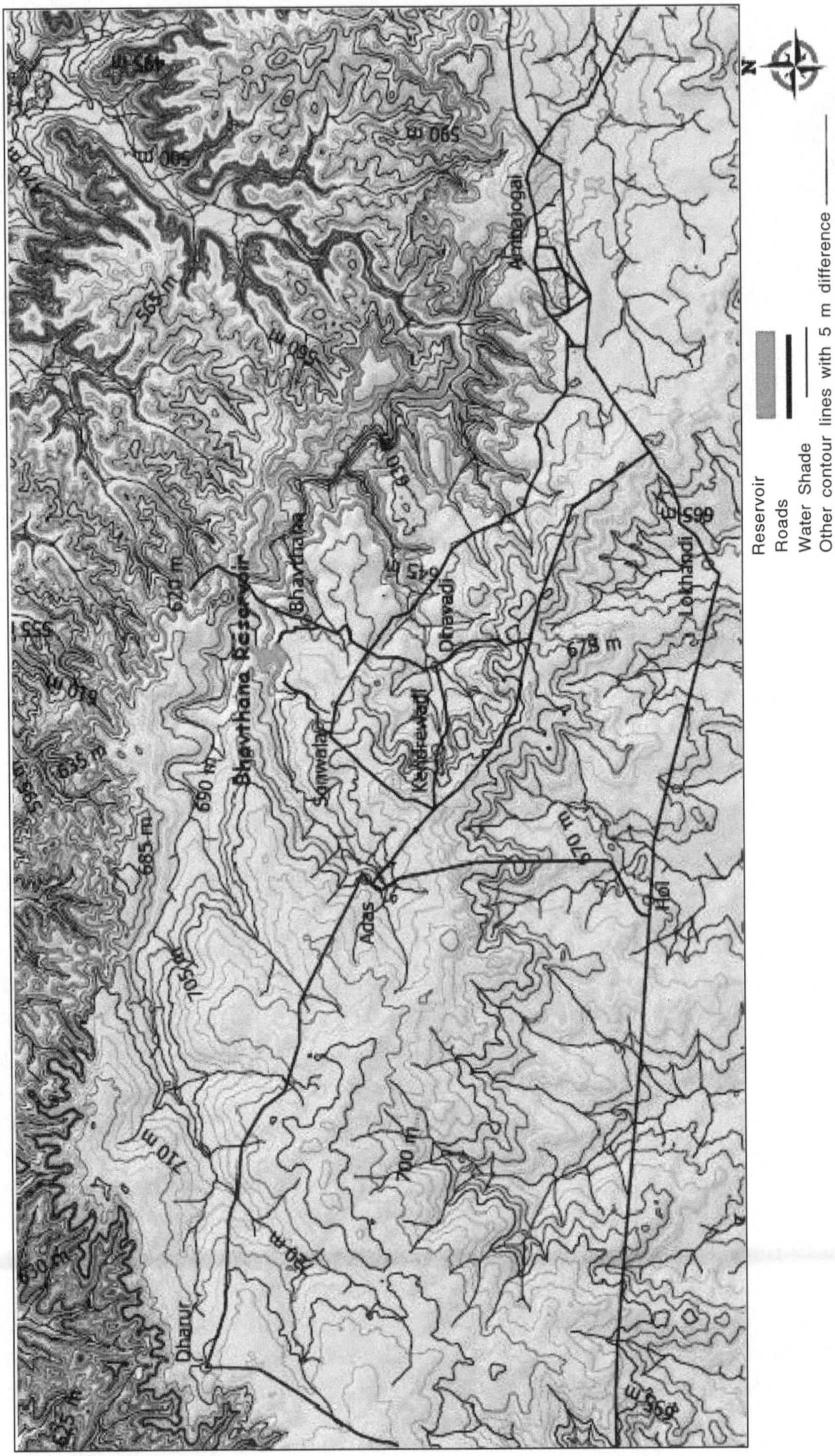

Fig. 2.1: Elevation Contour Line Map of Bhavthana Reservoir

Fig. 2.2: Satellite Image of Bhavthana Reservoir

Fig. 2.3: Panoramic view of Bhavthana Reservoir

The climate of reservoir area is semi-arid, hot and dry. Climate consists of three seasons. The rainy season starts from mid-June and remains till end of September. With onset of the rainy season there is an appreciable drop in temperature.

Table 2.1: Salient features of Bhavthana Reservoir in Beed district

1.	Name of River	Adas river
2.	Basin	Godavari
3.	Type of dam	Earthen
4.	Purpose of dam	Irrigation
5.	Year of completion	2005
6.	Gross storage capacity (mm^3)	5.274
7.	Live storage capacity (mm^3)	4.67
8.	Full tank level (m)	651
9.	Maximum water level (m)	653
10.	Minimum draw down level (m)	639.50
11.	Catchment area (sq.miles)	12.2
12.	Maximum height of dam (m)	26.76
13.	Length of earthen dam (m)	434
14.	Maximum flood discharge (cumecs)	553.3519
15.	River bed level (m)	627.74
16.	Length of waste weir (m)	99
17.	Area of submergence (ha)	70
18.	Gross command area (ha)	1100
19.	Culturable command area (ha)	1066.80
20.	Irrigation potential (ha)	889

From October to November the climate is humid. From mid-November to January it is winter. From February to March the climate is dry and from April to June it is summer. May is the hottest month. The average rainfall of area is 720.25 mm. Though the area is thought to belong to assured rainfall zone, the area has experienced moderate, severe and acute drought conditions for more than 35% of the last 80 years. Hence the entire area comes under the category of drought area.

3

Fish and Fisheries of Bhavthana Reservoir

INTRODUCTION

Inland fisheries in the world account for about 9% of total fish production, and of these, Asia accounts for nearly 60% of world production. In the light of stabilizing marine fish catches inland fisheries, in particular reservoir fishery potential, need to be exploited. In small reservoirs, culture based fisheries have been very effective.

India is one of the mega diversity countries with respect to freshwater fish species (Molur and Walker 1998). Nearly 2200 finfish species recorded from India, are widely distributed in the upland coldwater (3.32%), warm waters of the plain (24.73%), brackishwater (6.50%) and marine environment (65.45%). Of these, about 400 species are commercially important which are grouped as cultured, cultivable and wild (Pandey and Das, 2002).

India's inland resources are as diverse as they are plentiful. It is important source of food and provides employment and sustenance to sizeable sections of the society in rural area. At present, about 78% of the inland fish produced in India is derived from aquaculture and 22% from capture fisheries.

Rivers and reservoirs in country harbor a rich and varied spectrum exceeding 400 species, which include commercially important fishes such as Indian major carps, minor carps, mahseers, snow trouts, peninsular carps, catfishes, featherbacks, murrels and a number of exotic species.

The fish biodiversity in reservoirs is based on the biodiversity of the parent rivers. But in post impoundment period there are significant changes in fish fauna due to changes of the hydrobiological regime and biological conditions. The fish biodiversity is also influenced by fisheries management, particularly stocking, as well as their interaction.

The freshwater fish diversity of India is changing and depleting alarmingly as a result of extinctions is caused by a variety of reasons. Anthropogenic activities in the form of habitat destruction, pollution, introduction of foreign fish species and over exploitation are the main reasons for the extinction and endangerment of a number of fish species in

India. Fishery Survey of India has listed total 678 inland fish species in India. The dominant fish groups in the freshwaters are the cyprinids followed by siluroids and a few representatives of the perciformes and synbranchiform species.

Some of the important studies on fresh water fish fauna in India include the works of Karmarkar and Datta (1988), Sugunan (1995), Rao *et.al.* (1998), Khanna *et.al.* (1999), Menon (1999), Ponniah and Sarkar (2000), Piska *et.al.* (2000), Thomas (2002), Suresh (2002), Manoj kumar and Kurup (2002), Anna Mercy *et.al.* (2002), Radhakrishnan and Kurup (2002), Kurup (2002), Sekharan *et.al.* (2002, Jameela and Ramachandran (2002) Mahapatra (2003), Charak and Fayaz (2008), Kodarkar (2008), Dua and Prakash (2009), Rao *et.al.* (2010), Pari *et.al.* (2010), Thirumala *et.al.* (2011), Mali and Shaikh (2012), Laxmappa *et.al.* (2014) and Dhanalakshmi and Priyatharsini (2015).

In Maharashtra, the distribution of fresh water fishes from rivers, lakes and reservoirs have been investigated by CIFRI (1997), Sakhare (1999, 2001a, 2001b, 2007, 2008, 2012, 2014), Ahirrao and Mane (2000), Sakhare and Bidkar (2001), Sakhare and Joshi (2005), Joshi and Sakhare (2002), Lohar and Borse (2003), Wagh and Ghate (2003), Chandanshive *et.al.* (2006), Kamble *et.al.* (2006), Muley and Patil (2006), Mohite (2006) Battol *et.al.* (2007), Jaybhaye and Khedkar (2008), Shinde *et.al.* (2009), Jetithor (2010), Mali and Bondhare (2012), Ahirrao (2014), Niture and Chavan (2014) and Manjare (2015).

MATERIALS AND METHODS

Fishes for the purpose of study were collected with the help of local fishermen in spite of buying from the market. Three sampling sites were chosen for study; the outlet, the inlet and an approximate intermediate of the water body. The collected fishes were brought to the laboratory after noting their original colour and capturing photographs. The collected fishes were preserved in 5% formalin solution for further study. The identification of fishes was done with the help of standard keys (Talwar and Jhingran 1991 and Day 1967).

A questionnaire and interview method was applied to gather data on socio-economic status of fishermen community, fish catch, catching methods, monthly income of fishermen and problems in fishing. Questions in the questionnaire were so drafted to get three kinds of information from the fishermen viz. personal, social and economical.Personal contact method was also used to know better their problems and to establish free communication.

RESULTS

Fish Fauna

During the present investigation a total of 33 species of fishes belonging to 5 orders, 11 families and 20 genera have been recorded from Bhavthana reservoir (Table 3.1).Order cypriniformes (45.45%) was dominated by 15 species which was followed by perciformes (27.27%) with 9 species, order siluriformes (18.18%) was represented by 6 species and order osteoglossiformes (6.06%) by 2 species and order cyprinodontiformes (3.03%) was represented by a single species (Fig. 3.1).

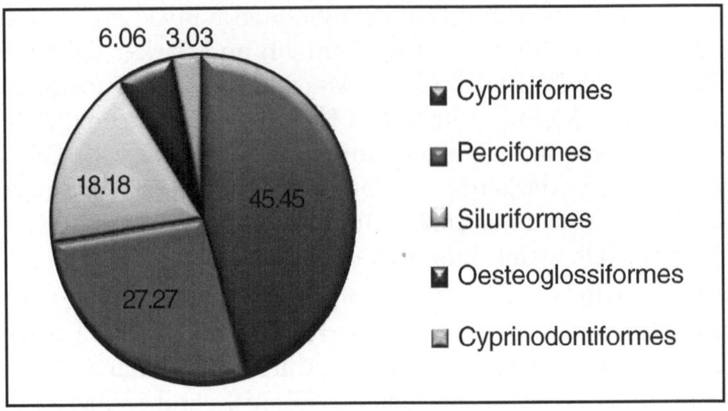

Fig. 3.1: Quantitative Occurance of Fish Fauna (Order wise) in Bhavthana Reservoir

Among order cypriniformes, the family cyprinidae contributed to 45.45% and represented with *Catla catla, Labeo rohita, Labeo calbasu, Labeo boggut, Cirrhinus mrigala, Osteobrama cotio, Osteobrama belkeri, Chela phulo, Puntius ticto ticto, Puntius chola, Puntius sophore, Ctenopharyngodon idella, Cyprinus carpio communis* and *Hypophthalmichthys molitrix*. The genus *Puntius* represented by 4 species and *Labeo* with 3 species (Table 3.1). The other families like channidae (12.12%), notopteridae (6.06%), siluridae (6.06%), bagridae (6.06%), ambassidae (6.06%), mastacembelidae (6.06%), poeciliidae (3.03%), clariidae (3.03%), heteropneustidae (3.03%), and gobiidae (3.03%).

In the present study an attempt is made to classify the fishes on the basis of their economic importance (Lagler, 1956). From Table 3.2, it is seen that, out of 33 fish species recorded, only 17 species are economically important. Species like *Channa punctatus, Channa striatus, Channa gachua, Gambussia affinis, Puntius sarana sarana, Puntius sophore, Puntius ticto, Puntius chola Chanda ranga, Chanda nama* are common in reservoir. These small sized fishes are larvivorous in nature.

The commercially important species of fishes from culture as well as dietary point of view are *Catla catla, Cirrhinus mrigala, Ctenopharyngdon idella, Cyprinus carpio, Hypophthalmichthys molitrix, Labeo rohita* and *Labeo calbasu.* Total 22 species among 33 species are evaluated as fine food fishes which has good consumer demand and nutritive value. While assessing the potential utilization of the collected fishes, it is revealed that 2% species have ornamental value.

Table 3.1: Checklist of Fishes from Bhavthana Reservoir

Class	Pisces
Subclass	**Teleostei**
Order	**Osteoglossiformes**
Family	**Notopteridae**
	1. *Notopterus notopterus* (Pallas)
	2. *Notopterus chitala* (Hamilton)
Order	**Cypriniformes**
Family	**Cyprinidae**
	3. *Catla catla* (Hamilton)
	4. *Labeo rohita* (Hamilton)
	5. *Labeo calbasu* (Hamilton)
	6. *Labeo boggut* (Sykes)
	7. *Cirrhinus mrigala* (Hamilton)
	8. *Osteobrama cotio* (Hamilton)
	9. *Osteobrama belkeri* (Sykes)
	10. *Chela phulo* (Hamilton)
	11. *Puntius ticto ticto* (Hamilton)
	12. *Puntius sarana sarana* (Hamilton)
	13. *Puntius chola* (Hamilton)
	14. *Puntius sophore* (Hamilton)
	15. *Ctenopharyngodon idella* (Valenciennes)
	16. *Cyprinus carpio communis* (Linnaeus)
	17. *Hypophthalmichthys molitrix* (Valenciennes)
Order	**Cyprinodontiformes**
Family	**Poeciliidae**
	18. *Gambusia affinis* (Baird and Girard)
Order	**Siluriformes**
Family	**Siluridae**
	19. *Ompak bimaculatus* (Bloch)
	20. *Wallago attu* (Schneider)
Family	**Bagridae**
	21. *Mystus seenghala* (Sykes)
	22. *Mystus cavasius* (Hamilton)
Family	**Clariidae**
	23. *Clarius batrachus* (Linnaeus)

(Table Contd...)

Class	Pisces
Family	**Heteropneustidae**
	24. *Heteropneustes fossilis* (Bloch)
Order	**Perciformes**
Family	**Channidae**
	25. *Channa marulius* (Hamilton)
	26. *Channa punctatus* (Bloch)
	27. *Channa striatus* (Bloch)
	28. *Channa gachua* (Bloch)
Family	**Ambassidae**
	29. Chanda nama (Hamilton)
	30. Chanda ranga (Hamilton)
Family	**Gobiidae**
	31. Glossogobius giuris (Hamilton)
Family	**Mastacembelidae**
	32. Mastacembelus armatus (Lacepede)
	33. Mastacembelus pancalus (Hamilton)

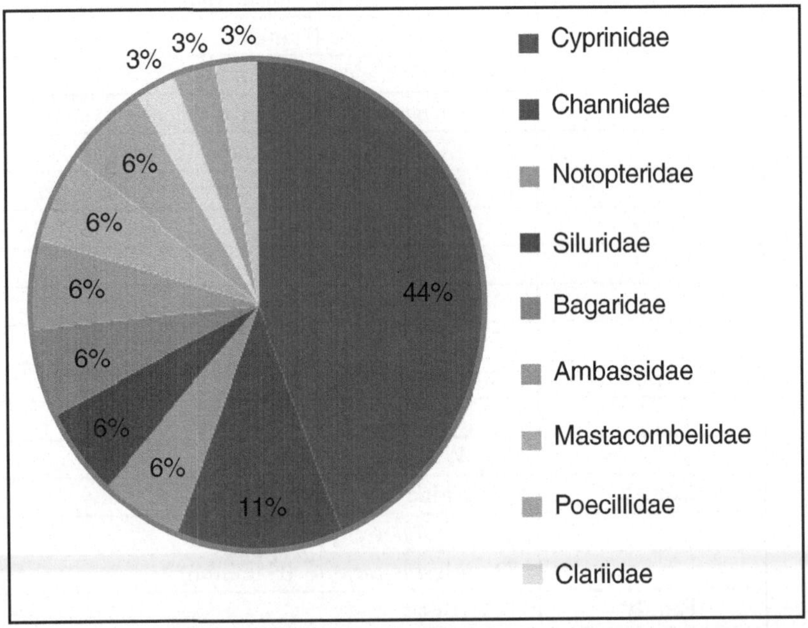

Fig. 3.2: Quantitative Occurance of Fish Fauna (Family wise) in Bhavthana Reservoir

Table 3.2: Economic Importance of Fishes recorded from Bahvthana Reservoir

Species	Commercial	Fine Food	Coarse Food	Aquarium Fishes	Others
1. *Notopterus notopterus*			√	√	MD
2. *Notopterus chitala*			√	√	MD
3. *Catla catla*	√	√			
4. *Labeo rohita*	√	√			
5. *Labeo calbasu*	√	√			
6. *Labeo boggut*	√	√			
7. *Cirrhinus mrigala*	√	√			
8. *Osteobrama cotio*		√			
9. *Osteobrama belkeri*		√			
10. *Chela phulo*			√		Lv
11. *Puntius ticto ticto*			√	√	Lv, Bt, Wf
12. *Puntius sarana sarana*			√	√	Lv, Bt, Wf
13. *Puntius chola*			√	√	Lv, Bt, Wf
14. *Puntius sophore*			√	√	Lv, Bt, Wf
15. *Ctenopharyngdon idella*	√	√			
16. *Cyprinus carpio*	√	√		√	
17. *Hypophthalmichthys Molitrix*	√	√			
18. *Gambusia affinis*			√	√	Lv
19. *Ompak bimaculatus*	√	√		√	Pf
20. *Wallago attu*		√			Pf
21. *Mystus seenghala*	√	√		√	Pf
22. *Mystus cavasius*	√	√		√	Pf
23. *Clarius batrachus*		√		√	Pf
24. *Heteropneustus fossilis*		√		√	Pf
25. *Channa marulius*	√	√			MD, Lv, Pf
26. *Channa punctatus*	√	√		√	MD, Lv, Pf
27. *Channa striatus*	√	√		√	MD, Lv, Pf
28. *Channa gachua*	√	√		√	MD, Lv, Pf
29. *Chanda nama*				√	Lv
30. *Chanda ranga*				√	Lv
31. *Glossogobius giurius*		√		√	Lv
32. *Mastacembelus armatus*	√	√		√	MD, Pf
33. *Mastacembelus pancalus*	√	√		√	MD, Pf

Lv= Larvivorous fishes, Bt= Bait, MD= Medicinal vslue, Wf= Weed fishes, Pf= Predatory food fishes

Plate 3.1: Common Fishes recorded in Bhavthana Reservoir

Catla catla (Hamilton)

Ctenopharyngodon idella (Valenciennes)

Plate 3.2: Common Fishes recorded in Bhavthana Reservoir

Hypophthalmichthys molitrix (Valenciennes)

Cyprinus carpio (Linnaeus)

Plate 3.3: Common Fishes recorded in Bhavthana Reservoir

Channa punctatus (Bloch)

Mystus seenghala (Sykes)

Plate 3.4: Common Fishes recorded in Bhavthana Reservoir

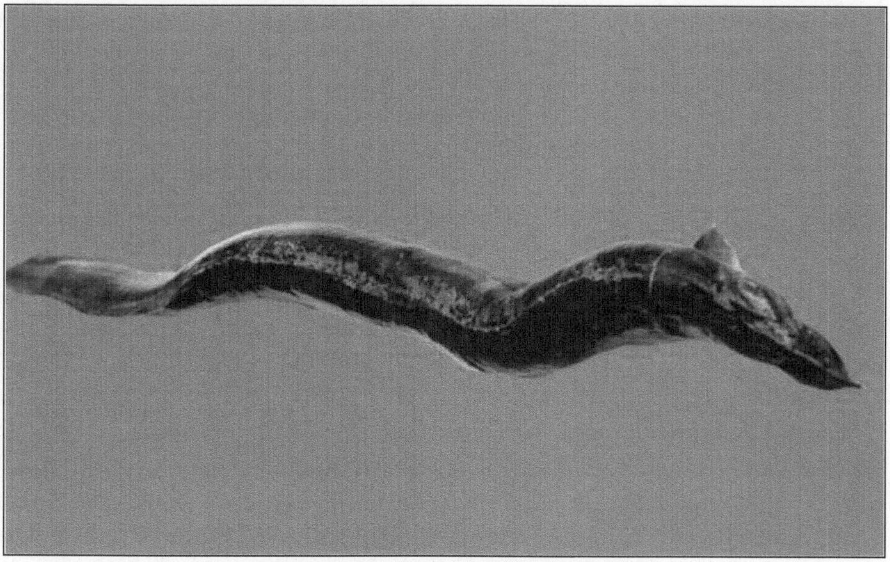

Mastacembelus armatus **(Lacepede)**

Notopterus notopterus **(Pallas)**

Fish Production

The details of fish production for the period of two years 2012-13 and 2013-14 are furnished in Table 3.3. The average fish production from the reservoir was 238.29 kg/ha/yr. It was 241.85 kg/ha/yr in 2012-13 and 234.74 kg/ha/yr in 2013-14. The carps dominated with 236 kg/ha/yr (97.46%) and 229 kg/ha/yr (97.37%) during 2012-13 and 2013-14 respectively. Local fishes (murrels, catfishes and others) occupied second position with 6.14 kg/ha/yr (2.53%) in 2012-13 and 617 kg/ha/yr in 2013-14.

Table 3.3: Fish Catch in Bhavthana Reservoir

Year	Carps (kg)	Local Fishes (kg)	Total Catch (kg)	Fish Catch (kg/ha/yr)
2012-13	16500	430	16930	241.85
2013-14	16000	432	16432	234.74

The variations in fish landings seem to be largely related to the fluctuation in water levels. The highest water level was recorded during the lean months viz; August, September and October. Generally the lowest water levels in reservoir were recorded during the peak fishing months viz; April, May and June. In certain years due to draught the draw-down crossed the limits of dead storage level to meet the pressing irrigation demands which had adversely affected fish.

The common species in the catches were *Catla catla, Labeo rohita, Cirrhinus mrigala, Cyprinus carpio, Ctenopharyngodon idella,* among carps, *Mystus cavassius* and *Wallago attu*. Species like *Osteobrama cotio, Channa marulius* and *Channa gachua* were also recorded in small quantities. Except for carps, which are introduced, all other species are native to this region.

The fish catch of the individual fisherman is handed over to the co-operative society, which in turn sells it to fish traders. Besides a small percentage of catch being sold locally, a sizeable quantity is dispatched to nearby markets like Adas, Kaij, Kille Dharur and Ambajogai.

Seed Stocking

The details of fish seed stocking in the reservoir for the period of 2012-2013 and 2013-2014 are furnished in Table 3.4. During 2012-13 stocking of fry was done at 1786 nos/ha and 2500 nos/ha in 2013-14. This worked out to a mean of 2143 nos/ha.

The composition of stocked seed included Indian major carps, common carp, silver carp and grass carp. Seed was stocked in the reservoir in the fry stage (20-25mm size). The natural recruitment of major carps is either absent or poor due to non-availability of suitable breeding grounds in lotic sector of the reservoirs or on account of inadequacy of water inflow at the right time. Therefore, the reservoir needs regular stocking support.

Table 3.4: Composition of Seed Stocked in Bhavthana Reservoir

Year	Catla	Rohu	Mrigal	Silver carp	Grass carp	Common carp	Total
2012-13	40,000	20,000	20,000	5000	20,000	20,000	1,25000
Percentage	32%	16%	16%	4%	16%	16%	100%
2013-14	50,000	30,000	30,000	25,000	20,000	20,000	1,75000
Percentage	28.58%	17.14%	17.14%	14.29%	11.42%	11.42%	100%

Among the varieties, catla seed was stocked in large number, when compared to the seed of others. Maximum amount of catla seed was stocked during 2013-14. Catla seed, constituting 32% of the total seed stocked in 2012-13 and a marginally lower quantity in 2013-14 (28.58%). Maximum rohu seed was stocked during 2013-14 (17.14%), mrigal seed during 2013-14 (17.14%), silver carp during 2013-14 (14.29%), grass carp seed during 2012-13 (16%), and common carp during 2012-13 (16%).

Gears and Crafts used for Fishing

The gears operated in Bhavthana reservoir are gill-net, cast net, drag net and hook and line. Maximum catch in the reservoir was performed by multifilament gill net. The mesh size of net shows variations and depend upon the species to be caught. Mesh size varies from 12-50 mm. Readymade gill nets are available in the local markets of Majalgaon and Beed from where the fishermen used to purchase them. The price of gill net ranges between Rs. 1000-1200 per kg of webbings. Small meshed gill-nets were found to be an effective technique for exploitation small sized uneconomical fishes like

Chanda spp and *Gambussia affinis*. It is interesting to note that the use of gill-nets and hook and line is increasing. Very few fishermen use cast net for fishing. Cast net, also known as 'chatri jal' or 'fek jal' in vernacular language, is commonly used for the capture of small sized fishes.It is a circular net of different mesh sizes. Hook and line are mostly used to catch murrels and catfishes. In this method, different numbered hooks with baits are tied to the line to catch different varieties of fish. Single man can operate this line. This net is operated by a single fisherman and can carry 10-15 operations within a day. On an average the catch obtained by cast net is about 0.2 to 4 kg. Using tiny creatures like earthworms, grasshopper, small prawns and cockroach as bait, most fishermen used to catch murrels and catfishes. The advantage of this gear is that it can be used in areas where other fishing gears are difficult to be employed due to submerged obstruction.

Thermocol raft and tubes of wheels of motor cars are the commonly used crafts in reservoir. Thermocol raft is prepared by slices of thermocols tied together with rope to make a bundle of length 0.5 m with a diameter of 0.3 m. Two bundles are tied together with the help of rope on which fishermen used to sit and go for fishing in reservoir (Fig. 3.3).

Fig. 3.3: Craft use at Bhavthana Reservoir

In Bhavthana reservoir, the fishermen were observed to rely on another type of improvised materials. They showed considerable ingenuity in fabricating make shift rafts out of discarded old rubber tubes of vehicles. A wooden platform was placed over for laying and hauling of gill-nets and angling.

Clearance of Tree Trunks

With the formation of Bhavthana reservoir, the trees growing along the banks of the river get submerged under water and remain as tree trunks. These tree trunks obviously become obstructions for effective operation of encircling gill nets. The submerged obstructions render certain areas of the reservoir as non-fishing territory providing shelter to many species of fishes.

Siltation

In Bhavthana reservoir excessive siltation resulted in the reduction of water holding capacity. Siltation also hampered the reservoir productivity by affecting the life process of biotic communities. Siltation in reservoir, apart from diminishing the quantum of water flow, resulted in destruction of spawning grounds of fishes and badly affected the benthic population of the reservoir. Extensive siltation has, however, eased the operation of dragged gear in some areas of the reservoir.

Fishing Days and Closed Season

In Bhavthana reservoir fishing is carried out throughout the year. No 'closed season' has been declared by the co-operative society or distirct fisheries department. Breeding of the Indian major carps, catla (*Catla catla*), rohu (*Labeo rohita*) and mrigal (*Cirrhinus mrigala*) has not so far been noticed in the Bhavthana reservoir. This seems to be for the reason that upstreams of this reservoir are having steeper slopes, rocky beds and are prone to flash floods. They do not provide favourable habitat for spawning of the economically important fishes. On the other hand, trash and carnivorous fishes are most self-generating and prolific breeders.

The Bhavthana reservoir water is continuously drawn for irrigation and other purposes. The continuous draw-down of reservoir water and the fluctuation in the inflow from the catchment aeras also not providing favourable habitat for carp spawning.

Socio-economic Status of Fishermen

This study is based on the primary data collected from 35 fishermen who are the members of co-operative society, engaged in fishing of Bhavthana reservoir. Data was collected by interviewing method using a pre-tested questionnaire in vernacular language.

The information collected was tabulated, analyzed and the results are presented below.

A co-operative society named "Shri Samarth Machhimar Utpadak va Vikri Sahakari Sanstha Maryadit Bhavthana" was established with registration number CHR/AJI/RSR/NC/542/1999 in December 1999. There are 35 co-operative members, out of which only 2 are female. The socio-economic analysis was carried out on different aspects such as age, education, family type, type of house, monthly income and other related parameters. The total fishermen population of Bhavthana reservoir is 35, out of which, there are 33 males (94%) and 2 females (6%). There are 6 (17%) unmarried males. Likewise there are 28 married males and 2 married females. Early marriages are generally held. The total number of educated fishermen is about 32 numbers, out of which 4 fishermen studied up to primary standard, 5 up to upper primary, 5 up to intermediate 17 and 9 up to higher education (up to 12th). The total illiterate were 3, out of which 2 are males and one is female. The illiterate were more in number in fishermen's family due to lack of communication in the village. The female illiterate are more in the families as compared to the male. Due to lack of education females have not been able to contribute much to the family

Karmarkar and Dutta (1988) reported 100 species belonging to 45 genera and 19 families from Bastar district of Madhya Pradesh.

Rao *et. al.* (1998) recorded 24 fish species belonging to 18 genera falling in 4 orders from freshwater ponds of Amalapuram, Andhra Pradesh. Of the 24 species, 7 were the cultivable and commercially important.

Sakhare (2001) reported 23 fish species from Jawalgaon reservoir in Solapur district and identified 9 commercially important, 4 ornamental fishes, 6 coarse food fishes, 6 larvivorous fishes and 3 fish species with medicinal value. On similar lines Rao *et al.* (1998) identified 24 fish species from ponds of Andhra Pradesh, of which 7 were commercially important, 12 species with food value, 8 species as trash fishes, 4 species suitable for aquarium and one with medicinal value.

Kumar (1990) reported 51 species belonging to 4 families from Govindsagar reservoir of Himachal Pradesh.

Hiware (2006) described 66 fish species belonging to 33 genera, 16 families and 8 orders from four districts of Marathwada region of Maharashtra. The fish fauna consisted of carps, catfishes and trash fishes. The carps dominated overall over the groups.

Telkhade (2007) described 39 fish species belonging to 6 orders and 17 families from Tadoba Lake of Chandrapur, Maharashtra.

Vyas *et.al.* (2009) recorded 52 species belonging to 28 genera, 13 families and 7 orders from Indira Sagar reservoir and confirmed the region as hotspot of fish biodiversity.

Kharat *et.al.* (2012) studied freshwater fish fauna of the Krishna River at Wai and Dhom reservoir and recorded 51 species belonging to 14 families and 33 genera.

Dubey *et.al.* (2012) identified 32 fish species belonging to eleven families in seven orders from Banisagar Dam of Chhatarpur, Madhya Pradesh. Family cyprinidae was most dominant.

Sakhare (2012) worked on ecology and ichthyofauna of Ekruk reservoir near Solapur city, Maharashtra and listed 34 species of fishes belonging to 24 genera falling under 7 orders. Of the 7 orders, order cypriniformes dominated with 17 species falling under 12 genera of which genus *Puntius* is abundant with 4 species of them dominating the catch. Next in abundance are the fishes coming under the order siluriformes in which *Mystus* is dominant with 2 species, while the order anguilliformes has only one dominant species.

Sanap *et.al.* (2012) confirmed the occurrence of 23 fish species belonging to 7 orders from water bodies around Ambajogai, Maharashtra. In the present investigation species occurrence is very much similar to Sakhare

(2001, 2006) and Sanap *et.al.* (2012). The observed similarity could be due to the presence of water bodies in the same geographic and climatic regions of Maharashtra.

Kamble and Mudkhede (2013) recorded 15 species of fishes from Loni reservoir of Nanded district and reported fish production at 8.82 kg/ha/yr.

Ridhi *et.al.* (2013) reported 72 species of fishes belonging to 9 orders, 20 families and 43 genera from Gandhisagar reservoir of Madhya Pradesh. They revealed that order cypriniformes (59.72%) was dominated by 43 species which was followed by Siluriformes (18.05%) with 13 species, order perciformes (12.5) represented by 9 species and order beloniformes, clupeiformes, mugiliformes, osteoglossiformes and synbranchiformes were also represented by each of one species (1.3%).

Khan and Nagma (2013) recorded 36 fish species belonging to 6 orders, 11 families and 23 genera from Bijnor district of Uttar Pradesh. The order cypriniformes was dominant with 18 species, followed by siluriformes 10 species, perciformes 4 species, osteoglossiformes 2 species synbranchiformes and clupeiformes 1 species each.

Kumar Naik *et.al.* (2013) found 64 species of fishes belonging to 37 genera, 10 families and 5 orders from Karanja reservoir of Karnataka. Among them order cypriniformes represented 31 fish species followed by siluriformes 20, perciformes 10, osteoglossiformes 2 and order synbranchiformes 1 fish species.

Vasanthkumar *et.al.* (2013) reported on the fin fish diversity of Tungabhadra reservoir (Karnataka) and listed 36 species of fishes. More than 75% of the total catch comprised *Aorichthys seenghala, Wallago attu, Silonia children* and *Pseudeutropius taakree.*

Sakhare (2014) described reservoir fisheries of Satara district of Maharashtra and listed 22 fish species from Shivajisagar reservoir (Koyna reservoir), one of the largest reservoirs in the state.

Niture and Chavan (2014) reported 41 species of fishes belonging to 8 orders and 15 families from Siddheshwar reservoir of Hingoli district Maharashtra.

The productivity of the reservoir is determined by total area and total fish production. The average fish productivity in Indian reservoirs is only 14.5 kg/ha/yr. In Uttar Pradesh the fish productivity is only 4.5 kg/ha/yr; Tamil Nadu -32 kg/ha/yr; Punjab-less than 100 kg/ha/yr; Madhya Pradesh-8.6 kg/ha/yr; Andhra Pradesh-37 kg/ha/yr;Gujarat-32.5 kg/ha/yr; Haryana 97.3 kg/ha/yr; Himachal Pradesh and Rajasthan have good productivity (Agarwal,1990).

By adopting improved management measures the Central Inland Fisheries Institute (CIFRI), Barrackpore has been able to increase the fish yield of Gularia (150ha) and Bachhra (140ha) reservoirs in Uttar Pradesh to 100 kg/ha and 139 kg/ha respectively. Similarly the fish production from Aliyar reservoir (646 ha) in Tamil Nadu has increased from 27 kg/ha to 202 kg/ha (Sugunan, 1990). These are reservoirs where natural breeding of Indian Major Carps is reported. In comparison, Bhavthana reservoir fares better in per hectare yield, even without autostocking of the Indian Major Carps. However, small reservoirs in China under intensive management generally yield 0111 kg/ha/yr (Tapiadar *et.al.* 1977).

Bhavthana reservoir is a typical example for put and takes system of culture-based fisheries. In the absence of natural breeding and autostocking of Indian major carps fish stock can be enhanced only through regular stocking. In Bhavthana there is a direct relationship between stocking and yield rates. Piska (2000) observed gradual increase in fish production with the increase of stocking density. Devi (1991) and Piska (1999) also reported an increase of fish production with increase of stocking in Ibrahimbagh reservoir.

In Kovilar and Periyar reservoirs of Tamil Nadu high yields of 736 kg/ha and 582 kg/ha were achieved (Sreenivasan, 2001).

Bhaumik *et.al.* (2009) carried out systematic investigation on ecology and management of the Dhaura reservoir of Tarai region (Uttaranchal) and reported the fish production at 106.6 kg/ha/yr.

The fish production noted in the present study is much higher than the average fish production of 49.90 kg/ha/yr in minor reservoirs of India (Piska, 1998). The present productivity of Bhavthana reservoir is higher than other reservoirs like Baghla (106 kg/ha/yr), Bachhra (139 kg/ha/yr), Gularia (100 kg/ha/yr, which were managed with the application of scientific management (Jhingran and Sugunan, 1990).

The fish production in Bhavthava reservoir is much higher than other small Indian reservoirs like Chulliar (275 kg/ha/yr) in Kerala, Meenkara (105 kg/ha/yr) in Uttar Pradesh, Thirumoorthy (200 kg/ha/yr) of Tamil Nadu and Aliyar (215 kg/ha/yr) of Tamil Nadu which were scientifically managed (Doddamani *et.al.* 2011).

Sakhare (2001) estimated 37.43 kg/ha/yr, 69.84 kg/ha/yr, 48 kg/ha/yr and 72 kg/ha/yr fish yield in Jawalgaon, Hingni (Pangaon), Ekruk and Pathri reservoirs of Solapur district of Maharashtra. All these reservoirs are small reservoirs. When compared to above reservoirs, the present productivity of Bhavthana reservoir is much higher.

The development of reservoir fisheries is closely linked with an assessment of their seed stocking needs and actual stocking from year to year with advanced fingerlings of fast growing fish species. The assessment of stocking requirements is connected with the present status of fisheries of a given reservoir, the existing fishing efforts and the type of fishery to be promoted, consistent with the conditions of existence and the types of fishing that are suitable for the waters.

Mostly small reservoirs fall in the category where extensive aquaculture practice is followed. Such impoundments are developed through 'put and take' system, where the fish production is augmented through large scale stocking and allowing grow-out period of 8 to 9 months before harvesting. These shallow reservoirs, getting dried up during summer season, allow complete harvesting of fish leaving no brood stock for succeeding fishery through natural recruitment and therefore their population has to be built up through regular stocking. Stocking policy is to be evaluated on biogenic capacity of the reservoir concerned, giving allowance for escapement of brood fishes and young ones through spillways and irrigation canals. Absence of predators in such reservoirs encourages early stocking of late fry instead of fingerlings to give maximum grow-out period. The main management parameters for culture based fisheries are species selection, stocking rate, size of stocking, size of harvesting and growing time.

Thus the stocking supports, stocking monitoring and effort monitoring are the three cardinal principles of ecosystem-oriented reservoir management. The commercial fish species should share the ecological niches in such a way that trophic resources are utilized to the optimum. The stocked fish seed should be of short food chain to obtain maximum efficiency in converting the primary food resources in to harvestable materials. But this situation seldom exists in medium and large reservoirs and in this respect small reservoirs are more rewarding than medium and large ones (Desai, 2013).

Stocking has been more effective in improving the yield from small reservoirs since success of their management depends on recapturing the stocked fish rather than on their building up population. The smaller reservoirs have advantage of easy stock monitoring and manipulation. Accordingly, the success recorded in managing fisheries of small reservoirs in India is excellent. The small reservoir, Aliyar (646 ha) of Tamil Nadu is a standing testimony of this management based on staggered stocking to yield 215 kg/ha (Desai, 2013).

To meet financial need of State Fisheries Departments, the National Fisheries Development Board (NFDB) with its office at Hyderabad, constituted in 2006, has come up as a boom to reservoir fisheries development to help the State Fisheries Departments in financial matters. The impediments felt into this integrated effort of increasing fish production from reservoir due to inadequate management practices, have thus motivated NFDB to come forward to help state fisheries development to optimize national reservoir fish production with their significant role in partnership.

Accordingly, NFDB has started working under the reservoir fisheries development scheme, as a flagship activity to stock reservoirs of 8.5 lakh ha with an advanced fish fingerlings in 17 states of the country. The scheme has been evaluated by CIFRI. It is stated that the stocking programme had a positive effect on the productivity of the reservoirs, with increased fish production of 50-174 kg/ha/yr and 11-33 kg/ha/yr in small, medium and large reservoirs respectively. It is really a welcoming achievement.

Small irrigation impoundments which dry up in summer have much more production potential per unit area, compared to the larger ones. These water bodies are intensively stocked and harvested completely in summer. Proper stocking and harvesting schedules are the key to small reservoir management where it has to be ensured that the fish stock is not lost through the overflowing spillways and allowing a reasonable grow out period.

India needs nearly 10 million tons of fish annually to bring up per capita consumption of the people of the country (presently 9 kg against 12 kg of the world). With this objective, the country was heading well to achieve annual total fish production of 7.7 million tones with inland production of 4.6 million tone a few years back, to be in the second rank globally. However, all of a sudden, there seed med to be a crunch in fish production of the country. As per FAO's report published in 2012, in global fish production of 2010, China ranked first (15.66 million tonnes), followed by Indonesia (5.38 million tonnes) and India (4.69 million tonnes). Similarly, in aquaculture production of 2010, China was at top (47.83 million tonnes) followed by Indonesia (6.27 million tonnes) and India (4.65 million tonnes). Thus, at a time when India was heading towards second rank in global fish production it dropped down to third rank. The declining trend in country's fish production could be the impact of climatic change when the year 2010 was declared as the world's warmest year by WMO and the warmest decade by Indian metrologista (Sharma and Das, 2012). Pillai (2012) has also observed that erratic monsoon in India with E1-Nino effect during the year 2010 resulted in deficient rain fall thereby impacting the fish production adversely. It is also reflected from low fish production of open waters (particularly reservoirs), subduedly recorded at 0.04 million tone in 2010. Further, some management lapses in exploitation of open waters like overfishing and environmental reasons may also be responsible for low fish production. Therefore, the fishery resources of open waters, particularly reservoirs and flood plain lakes,have to be developed and tapped up to increase the annual fish yield of the country in the years to come. The highly discouraging shape of reservoir fisheries development was likely to be brought to the notice of standing committee of Loksabha.

Stocking of appropriate quantity and quality of fish seed is pre-requisite for reservoir fisheries development. The rate of stocking seed in production units, considered in terms of fry stage. The different rates of stocking intensity in different categories of water bodies are different in the different states. Stocking density is an important factor that determines the success or failure of the whole programme and hence this needs to be assessed carefully. Very often too many fish are stocked leading to deterioration of the existing fishery. To determine the optimum stocking density, factors such as ecological characteristics and existing biomass should also be considered.

Seed stocking in to small reservoirs has proved to be a useful tool for developing fisheries potential of such small aquatic systems. Introduction of economically important fast growing fish from outside is aimed at colonizing all the diverse niches of the biotope for harvesting maximum sustainable crop from them. This widespread management practice has been shown to be highly remunerative in small water bodies where almost complete annual harvesting is possible. This has amply been demonstrated in Gularia and Bachhra reservoirs of Uttar Pradesh and Aliyar reservoir of Tamil Nadu.

Stocking has proved more effective in small reservoirs. It is because of the following factors:

1. In large reservoirs, competition and predation will be greater resulting in reduced survival;
2. Aspects of enhancement such as fertilization, control of undesirable species are more manageable in small reservoirs; and
3. Large reservoirs are difficult to manage socially and may have a high probability of losses through poaching and unreported catch.

There exists a very high complexity of factors for deciding on the most appropriate size or age of the fish to be stocked. The reason is that these are known to vary from species to species and place to place. Paucity of information in this regard is one of the main factors, leading to the complexity referred to the optimal size of stocking is mainly chosen by considering two factors, viz; cost and survival (Lalrinsanga *et.al.* 2006). Stocking of fish at very small sizes leads to risks associated with high mortality even though the cost of stocking material increases exponentially with length. This mortality size relationship also provides the basis for a quantitative assessment of stocking density. However, other factors such as biology and life history traits of the species are also vital tools to be considered. It is known that fishes stocked as fry are more prone to density-dependent mortality than those stocked at fingerlings or juvenile stage.

The time of stocking also plays an important role and determines the success or failure of the whole programme. In general, it is perceived that stocking in spring is more suitable than during the winter season. It should also be noted that fish are to be stocked when the rate of water flow and water temperature is low so as to minimize the displacement and stress respectively. Stocking should also be carried out when the system shows high productivity. Generally, fish should be stocked in the morning or evening hours when the oxygen concentration is considered to be optimal (Lalrinsanga *et.al.* 2006).

Stocking of reservoirs with fast growing species based on the biogenic capacity and food spectrum available is one of the most important management measures for the reservoir. However, this principle of massive stocking with fast growing carps in inadequately followed in India and the reservoirs are often stocked arbitrarily based on the availability of the stocking material rather than the biogenic production potentiality of the ecosystem (Jhingran, 1986). Besides, the stocking density is also often very low (Natarajan, 1976).

The stocking programme in the reservoir has been generally devoid of any rationale behind them and consequently, no discernible impact is visible in most of the cases. In many reservoirs, stocking programmes on scientific basis are impaired due to lack of seed availability. Stocking becomes necessary to enlarge spectrum and to correct the imbalances in utilization of different ecological niches by the species.

Selection of fishes for stocking is based on an assessment of existing biotic communities and their efficiency in converting primary trophic resource to harvestable products. Our country is bestowed with a variety of fast growing fishes like catla, rohu and mrigal feeding at different trophic niches that can be suitably employed for reservoir fisheries management. The introduction of exotic fishes in Indian reservoirs is still a subject of controversy due to possible deleterious effects on indigenous population (Jhingran, 1988).

The rate of stocking and species ratio has conspicuous bearing on the ecological conditions of the reservoir, growth potential of the stocked species and the overall biogenic capacity of the reservoir.

Jhingran (1990), after considering the potential yield from various categories of reservoirs, suggested that with scientific management the fish yield from small reservoirs could be enhanced to the tone of 200-300 kg/ha/yr. Bhavthana could well conform to this norm of small reservoirs for the adoption of scientific fisheries management.

With a view to exploiting diverse niches of this reservoir, stocking with quality fish seed was initiated by the fishermen's co-operative society. The regular fishing of the reservoir was started by the society during.

Quality fish seed stocking in adequate numbers is one of the pre-requisites in reservoir fishery management. Different stocking rates have been suggested by various authers. Mathew and Mohan (1990) suggested a stocking rate of 2000 fingerlings/ha for optimum production. The Indian Institute of Management, Ahmedabad (1983) suggested stocking with advanced fingerlings (12.5 cm size) at 1000 nos/ha taking 60% of FRL area in to account. In Bhavthana reservoir annual average stocking was 2143 nos/ha. Thus fairly good rate of stocking has resulted in significant improvement in fish catch.

The optimum size of the fish seed is an important factor in the management of small reservoirs (Lorenzen, 1994). According to Velayudhan and Sidharthan (1998) stocking with fish seed of varying size in adequate numbers can be an option for thedevelopment of small reservoirs particularly when the area of seed farms to rear advanced fingerlings is limited.

The species composition of fish seed stocked showed wide variations over the period under study on an average. Indian major carps accounted for 63.43% of the total fish seed stocked followed by chinese carps 36.56%.

Sreenivasan (1984) has made a critical observation on the influence of stocking on fish production in some South Indian reservoirs. The analysis of stocking as well as landing data of Bhavthana reservoir indicates that continuous stocking of major carps seed has been instrumental in raising fish production to an average level of 238 kg/ha/yr. The share of carps in the landings is good.

The term 'fishing gear' refers to all those implements and devices used for fishing, which employ gears ranging from simple metallic hook and line to the modern fish pumps. The type of gears depends on size of fish to be caught, construction material, operation method and area of operation. Every water body has its unique pattern of crafts and gear. It also gives indication about the economic condition of the fisher community where they use locally available less costly materials to make substances of technological delight giving maximum return. Some earlier records on fishing crafts and gears from freshwater sector of India are well deserved to be mentioned (Joseph and Narayanan 1965, Vijay Anand 1996, Varghese *et.al.* 1982, Sharma 2001, Sheshappa 2002, George 2002, Baiju and Haridayanathan 2002, Bhattacharjya *et.al.* 2005, Ramesan 2006, Mansi *et.al.* 2009, Gurumayum and Choudhary 2009, Pravin *et.al.* 2011, Manna *et.al.* 2011, Subenthung and Nagesh 2012, Kumar and Kumar 2013, Baruah *et.al.* 2013, and Purkayashtha and Gupta 2014). But the information available on types of fishing gears and crafts in freshwater sector of Maharashtra is scanty (Sakhare, 2007; Niture and Chavan, 2009; Mali and Bhandare, 2012 Sakhare and Jetithor, 2013).

The gears operated in Bhavthana reservoir are gill-net, cast net, drag net and hook and line. Small meshed gill-nets were found to be an effective technique for exploitation small sized uneconomical fishes like *Chanda spp* and *Gambussia affinis*. It is interesting to note that the use of gill-nets and hook and line is increasing. Very few fishermen use cast net for fishing.

Mann *et.al.* (2011) reported gill net, cast net, drag net, push net, scoop net, ring net, hook and line, lantern net, box-trap and cradle trap from river Krishna. They also accounted different crafts such as coracle, plank-built boat, palme-canoe, thermocol raft, banana stem raft and rubber tube platform from same river.

Subenthung and Nagesh (2012) reported gill nets from Doyang reservoir of Nagaland where gill-nets account for 80% of the fish catch followed by hook and line (9%), traps (8%) and cast nets (3%).

The fishing gear normally employed for harvesting the vast fishery resources of the Indian reservoirs are traditional gill nets, entangling nets, lines and shore seines (Percy, 2002).

In Yeldari reservoir of Maharashtra primitive type of crafts are used, which is a platform of 6×3 feet size with a depth of 5 to 8 inches. It is constructed from the thermocol and covered by a plasting covering (Sakhare, 2007). In Bhavthana reservoir similar type of craft is used for fishing. Sakhare and Jetithor (2013) and Mali and Bhandare (2012) also reported such type of thermocol crafts from different parts of Maharashtra.

Ahirrao and Mane (2000) accounted indigenous crafts and Ratnagiri type of boats from rivers and reservoirs of Parbhani district.

Devi (1997) mentioned use of traditional catamaran with thermocol and coracle from Ibrahimbagh and Shathamraj reservoirs of Hyderabad.

Dubey (2008) described gill nets, drag nets and long lines and Bengal type dingy boats and mechanized boats from Gandhisagar reservoir.

Due to diversity of fish population in the Hirakud reservoir of Orissa, different types of gears are operated by the fishermen from various sectors of the reservoir and in different seasons. The important gears are gill nets and long line. Hook and line are mostly used to catch catfish and Indian major carps. Very few fishermen use cast net and rod-line for fishing (Mahapatra, 2003).

Khan *et.al.* (1991) enumerated the various crafts and gear systems deployed for judicious exploitation of fishery resources.

The available information confirms that in Indian reservoirs gill-nets are the common gears (Khan *et.al.* 1991; Ahirrao and Mane, 2000; Sakhare, 2007, 2014; Sakhare and Jetithor 2013; Subenthung and Nagesh, 2012; Mahapatra, 2003; Dubey, 2008; CIFRI 1997; Sakhare and Joshi, 2011; Pau *et.al.* 2009; Das *et.al.* 2001; Kumar and Kumar 2013).

Gill nets in almost all Indian reservoirs require improvements in respect of design, rigging and other parameters like mesh-size and twine size in order to increase its efficiency. The introduction of synthetic fibres like nylon in place of natural fibre enhanced the catch efficiency of gill nets used in reservoirs to nine times (Khan *et.al.* 1991).

Fishing craft is a floating plate from by which fishermen go to the fishing grounds with suitable gear along with the catches to the shore. Cataloguing of the fishing technique of rivers and reservoirs of India was undertaken by George (2002). According to him traditional building materials for coracles prevalent in peninsular reservoirs have been completely replaced by synthetic materials. Wooden canoes and rafts are being replaced by tin canoes or fiber glass canoes. The floating rafts of migrating fishermen have been replaced by compact, easy to transport buoy and foam plastic rafts. Fishing gear material is changed from time to time, as the industry is in the lookout for newer and efficient materials available in the market. There is a gradual shift from polyamide multifilament to polyamide monofilament, polyethylene twisted monofilament and polyethylene yarn.

Mansi *et.al.* (2009) reported two main types of fishing nets across the Tungabhadra basin i.e; Alivi nets and gill-nets. Licensed Alivi nets contribute to about 88.92% of fish catch and the nets have proved economically profitable. Gill-nets are generally used to caught all types of fishes small-scale fishermen usually own nets from 3-10 inches. Surface gill-nets, bottom set gill-nets, small shore drag nets, cast nets and hook and line are the common gears used for fishing in Tungabhadra basin.

Deforestation of standing trees in Bhavthana reservoir has always remained neglected. Sakhare (2007) also reported problems of standing trees in Yeldari reservoir, Maharashtra where the submerged trees and shrubs remained permanent obstacles for fishing which cause loss or damage through the entanglement, prevent fishing operations and also provides fish with hideouts. This also reduces the area available for fishing. Once submerged, the standing forest turns an eternal problem for fishing. Hence these tree trunks should be removed by using mechanized power winches, saws and grabbers. Apart from these mechanical devices, fishermen should also be told to cut the tree trunks for possible use by them as fuel. This work can be done during summer when the tree trunks get exposed with the reduced water level of the reservoir (Desai, 2008).

Parihar (1999) suggested that the bottom of reservoir should be cleared from the obstruction such as aquatic vegetation, weeds and other submerged objects like stones, plant stem and debris finding access through inflowing water of river.

Excessive siltation is a serious problem in Bhavthana reservoir. Many of the reservoirs recorded siltation rates, much in excess of what was envisaged during the planning stage of the project (Sugunan, 1995; Gupta, 1975). Khan (1990) reported heavy siltation @23.14 mm^3yr^{-1} due to erosion in Hirakud reservoir of Orissa where siltation has changed the basin topography and spawning ground has been lost.

Siltation in reservoirs and rivers, apart from diminishing the quantum of water flow, results in destruction of breeding grounds of fishes, migration of fishes and overall productivity of the reservoirs. Siltation also affects the benthic population and the natural recruitment of fishes in the impounded waters such as lakes and reservoirs (Joshi, 1990).

Erosion of topsoil in the catchment area is the main man-made factor the leads to increased sediment load in rivers. The Indian rivers carry about 2,050 million t of silt, of which nearly 480 million t is deposited in the reservoirs and 1572 million t is washed away into the sea every year.

In almost all states of India, some form of fishery regulations is being followed. They basically pertain to minimum mesh size of the net, closed season of fishing during spawning season of carps and prohibition of illegal fishing. The regulations vary from state to state and even from reservoir to reservoir to suit the local situations. While most of the regulations are backed by biological reasoning, some of them are conspicuously based on economic considerations.

Indian major carps and most of the other economically important fishes breed during monsoons. This period when fishes breed, is generally observed as a 'closed season' in respect of most of the Indian reservoirs and during this period fishing is prohibited. But in the Bhavthana reservoir, fishing is carried out throughout the year and no 'closed season' for fishing has been observed. Breeding of Indian major carps was not observed in Bhavthana reservoir.

Socio-economic indicators form a base for social or technological interventions by the government or any development organizations. Factual variations in the social status of a community clearly indicate the level of growth and development. In general, the fishermen are considered to be encoded with low economic backgrounds. Since they are fully occupied with fishing activities, their migration to other fields of work is rather difficult. Limited access to land based activities also hinders their economic progress. In addition, they also face complex interplay of a number of factors such as inadequate infrastructure facilities, low profitability and other factors which ultimately affect their performance and involvement. Moreover, the socioeconomic status of the fishermen play important role in their day to day activities and it also influences their involvement in their occupation. Therefore, it is important to examine the socio-economic status of fishermen.

Ekka *et.al.* (2012) documented socio-economic status of fishermen of Indian reservoirs and concluded that the literacy rate of fishermen was less than the average national literacy of the country. Low income from fisheries, combined with high labour and risk, compelled the young working group to shift occupation towards non-fishing activities. The average monthly expenditure of households was also too low to sustain livelihood of the household.

Madhyastha and Murugan (1993) studied socio-economic status of fishermen in relation to fish and fisheries of Hemavathy reservoir (Karnataka) and reported 60% migratory fishermen which live in huts. About 70% migratory fishermen were illiterate which could be attributed to their unsettled life and periodic movement. The economic condition of the fishermen was below average. This is mainly due to the lack of guidance to utilize the available facilities and the poor support given by the state government.

Several studies exist on the economic and social status of marine fishermen (Prasada Rao and Kumar 1984, Sathiadhus and Venkitaraman 1981, OMCAR 2013, Madhyastha and Murugan 1993,Shiyani 2003, Balasubramaniam *et.al.* 2001, Bhattacharya 2011, Jha *et.al.* 2003, Kalvathy 1985, Ali 1996, Ekka *et.al.* 2012 Nayak *et.al.* 2012, Devaraj and Smita 1988, Ramchandra 2003 and Sahu 2000).However, such studies are limited in case of inland fishermen (Nandeesha *et.al.* 1986;Choudhary 1989; Minimol 2001; Balasubramaniam and Bihari 2002; Braj Mohan 2002; Jha *et.al.* 2004; Beegum 2006; Sakhare 2007; Devi 1997; Sharma *et.al.* 2010; Jetithor 2010; Mukharjee and Praharaj *2009*, Basavaraja *et.al.* 2011; Lanka and Khabade 2012).

A detailed survey of the fishermen communities operating around Hemavathy reservoir in Karnataka was made by Devaraj and Mahadeva (1990). Majority of the fishermen were illiterate and has no exposure to modern fishing practices. Literacy rate was as low as 15.7% and not more than 10% fisher children attended the schools. About 76.85% fishermen had a per capita income range of only Rs. 500-1000/- and came under the income group of Rs. 1000 to 5000/- per family. Those who had income from both agriculture and fishing earned more than Rs. 10,000/- per annum with a per capita income higher than Rs. 1500/-.

In Hirakud reservoir of Orissa the average income per fisherman per day varied from Rs. 7.68 to 14.51 (Khan, 1990). The members of the co-operative societies fail to cantain the influence of rich middlemen on the fishery, who sieves away juveniles and brooders from the reservoirs with nets having no mesh regulation. The most of the fishermen are unable to come above poverty line. Fluctuation of income to the fishermen is mainly due to the seasonality and unstable fish catch composition.

The fishermen play a major role in fish marketing. The actual involvement of the fisherwoman starts right from the fish landing at the fishing harbor, followed by the related activities such as sorting out the fish either for supplying to processing industries or for carrying to the fish market. In Maritime states like Maharashtra, the fisherwomen are involved in fish selling in daily and weekly fish markets. They also undertake door-to-door vending and are also involved in drying, salting and other ways of curing of fishes and in the production of a few value-added fish products like papads, chutney and pickles. Many researchers have stated that economic empowerment of women can be achieved through entrepreneurship development (Purshan 2001; Patra *et.al.* 2002; Nakhwa 2003; Kamalkannan and Namasivayam 2005, Kokate and Upare 2005 and Rabeem 2005; Mohite and Mohite 2009).

Because they market the fish, the fisherwomen exercise rather more power, and play a more important economic role. The women sell the fish and receive the money; they are therefore in a strong position to decide whether the money is to be saved or spent, and for what. Women infact participate in decision making on the buying of nets and other fishing equipment as well as on the handling of domestic purchases.

Socio-economic indicators form a base for social or technological interventions by the government or any developmental organizations. Factual variations in the social status of a community clearly indicate the level of growth and development. In general, the fishermen are considered to be encoded with low economic backwardness. Since they are fully occupied with fishing activities, their migration to other fields of work is rather difficult. Limited access to land based activities also hinders their economic progress. In addition, they also face complex interplay of a number of factors such as inadequate infrastructure facilities, low profitability and other factors which ultimately affect their performance and involvement. Moreover, the socio-economic status of the fishermen play an important role in their day to day activities and it also influences their involvement in their occupation. Therefore, it is important to study the socio-economic conditions, living status and constraints faced by fishermen and suggest suitable strategies for improving their socio-economic status.

The government has undertaken responsibility of raising the status of the fishermen community. There are so many programmes through which state and central government attempt to help this weaker section of the rural society. Concrete steps for their upliftment have been taken up in all the five year plans.

Co-operatives are the shield of weak and in India fishermen are among the weakest sections of the society. Illiteracy, poverty, and lack of knowledge of latest fisheries technology are contributing factors. This vicious circle is further strengthened by lack of institutional support, both in finances and infrastructure. Consequently, fishermen are subjected to exploitation by middlemen, who act as money lenders, traders and contractors.

Fishermen discovered co-operatives could spare them from exploitation and improve their socio-economic conditions. Efforts made in this direction have yielded good results in some areas, but the overall picture of fishery co-operatives is not encouraging.

A number of fishery co-operatives in India are helping their members and their family members to the extent of providing complete marketing infrastructure for the sale of the catch at remunerative prices.

To market fish profitability, ensuring a fair price for producers and consumers, co-operative marketing of Shri Samarth Machhimar Utpadak va Vikri Sahakari Sanatha society must be strengthened. For this purpose, marketing infrastructure must be developed. Financial assistance for infrastructure should be provided by state, central and local bodies, and then handed over for management to fisheries co-operative society.

The economic standard of the fishermen of Bhavthana reservoir remained very low. Socially and economically they belong to one of the most depressed classes. Their annual income and land ownership and housing facilities are very low. Out of 35 respondents, 2 of them have one child, 9 of them have two children and 24 of them have three or more than three children contributing to 5.7%, 26% and 68% of the total respectively. Majority of the respondents (52%) have 3 children. About 5.7% of the respondents have less than 5 family members in their house, 9% represents have 5-7 members in their family, a majority of 24% represents 7-10 family members.

Income is an important variable that is always considered in any study. Respondents were asked to indicate their monthly family income by selecting the range provided from less than Rs. 3000 to above 12000.

Children are commonly affected by skin diseases and frequent exposure to water born diseases. No fisherman is using toilet and bathrooms on personal hygiene has to start from school children and adults.

The overall assessment of the present investigation is that the society has failed to implement the developmental and management programmes of the Bhavthana reservoir on scientific lines and no improvement of socio-economic conditions of its members could be made. There is an urgent need to reorganize the entire functioning of the co-operative society. For this, the state fisheries department should come forward and help the society by providing necessary technical personnel and financial assistance to it so that approximate developmental programmes could be chalked out and launched for the improvement of the fisheries of the Bhavthana reservoir as well as the socio-economic conditions of its members.

The membership of the co-operative society comprises middle age and elderly men. Efforts should be done to provide membership to the young persons and fishermen training programmes should be organized with the help of district fisheries department. The programmes will be helpful to train fishermen on techniques and skills necessary to approach fishing as a business. The co-operative society should initiate to join the youngsters in the co-operative society good results in some areas, but the overall picture of fishery co-operatives is not encouraging.

A number of fishery co-operatives in India are helping their members and their family members to the extent of providing complete marketing infrastructure for the sale of the catch at remunerative prices.

To market fish profitability, ensuring a fair price for producers and consumers, co-operative marketing of Shri Samarth Machhimar Utpadak va Vikri Sahakari Sanatha society must be strengthened. For this purpose, marketing infrastructure must be developed. Financial assistance for infrastructure should be provided by state, central and local bodies, and then handed over for management to fisheries co-operative society.

The economic standard of the fishermen of Bhavthana reservoir remained very low. Socially and economically they belong to one of the most depressed classes. Their annual income and land ownership and housing facilities are very low. Out of 35 respondents, 2 of them have one child, 9 of them have two children and 24 of them have three or more than three children contributing to 5.7%, 26% and 68% of the total respectively. Majority of the respondents (52%) have 3 children. About 5.7% of the respondents have less than 5 family members in their house, 9% represents have 5-7 members in their family, a majority of 24% represents 7-10 family members.

Income is an important variable that is always considered in any study. Respondents were asked to indicate their monthly family income by selecting the range provided from less than Rs. 3000 to above 12000.

Children are commonly affected by skin diseases and frequent exposure to water born diseases. No fisherman is using toilet and bathrooms on personal hygiene has to start from school children and adults.

The overall assessment of the present investigation is that the society has failed to implement the developmental and management programmes of the Bhavthana reservoir on scientific lines and no improvement of socio-economic conditions of its members could be made. There is an urgent need to reorganize the entire functioning of the co-operative society. For this, the state fisheries department should come forward and help the society by providing necessary technical personnel and financial assistance to it so that approximate developmental programmes could be chalked out and launched for the improvement of the fisheries of the Bhavthana reservoir as well as the socio-economic conditions of its members.

The membership of the co-operative society comprises middle age and elderly men. Efforts should be done to provide membership to the young persons and fishermen training programmes should be organized with the help of district fisheries department. The programmes will be helpful to train fishermen on techniques and skills necessary to approach fishing as a business. The co-operative society should initiate to join the youngsters in the co-operative society.

4 Physico-chemical Environment of Bhavthana Reservoir

INTRODUCTION

Water, the unique component of nature has played a crucial role in life from molecule to man. For any nation, its aquatic ecosystems; rivers, lakes, reservoirs and coastlines are national wealth and constant efforts are made to exploit them for the benefit of its population.

Freshwater has become a critical natural resource due to a number of reasons, important among which are unprecedented population growth, man-induced interruptions and modifications in the global energy and material cycles, deforestation on massive scale and industrialization linked population of air, water and soil.

Fresh water habitats are the potential source for mankind. They are the primary source of water for drinking, agriculture, aquaculture, transport, bathing and other purposes.

Water quality is the summation of all physical, chemical, biological and aesthetic characteristics of water that influence its beneficial use. Any characteristic of water in production system that effects survival, growth, reproduction and production of aquaculture species, influences management decisions, causes environmental impacts, or reduces product quality and safety can be considered a water quality variable. Knowledge of water quality principles will help aquaculturists to determine the potential of water body to produce aquaculture species, to minimize problems of fish stress and fish health, to produce higher quality aquaculture products to reduce environmental impacts of effluents, and to realize more efficient production and great profits (Boyd and Tucker, 2009).

Water quality is determined by different variables, but fortunately, only a few normally play a decisive role. Some variables such as water temperature and salinity are important when assessing the suitability of a site for the culture of a particular species. Other parameters, such as turbidity, alkalinity, suspended and dissolved solids, and compounds of phosphorous and nitrogen are also important. Dissolved oxygen, carbon-dioxide, ammonia and other factors come in to play during the grow-out period because they are potential stressors of the animal under culture (Boyd and Tucker, 2009). Successful reservoir fisheries management operations mainly depend on maintenance of a healthy aquatic environment.

Water is the primary requisite to support aquatic flora and fauna. Physical, chemical and biological properties of water play an important role in governing production of fish. Water not only plays an important role in the fish production, but also it helps in the survival and growth of the fish. If the water quality is maintained, the fish also have a good taste.

The physico-chemical methods give information about the type of substance or pollutant and its concentration. With the help of physico-chemical parameters of water, a better understanding of the effects of pollution is obtained and an integrated picture of water body is furnished.

In this connection details of limnological investigation in relation to productivity of Indian reservoirs have been worked out. The notable studies on physico-chemical environment of Indian reservoirs are those of Alam (1980), Kaul *et.al.* (1980), Khatri (1984, 1985), Bagde and Varma (1985), Singhai *et.al.* (1990), Malhotra *et.al.* (1991), Kulshrestha *et.al.* (1992), Sharma *et.al.* (1992), Trivedy (1993), Kataria and Jain (1995), Chandrasekhar (1996), Jain *et.al.* (1996), CIFRI (1997), Hazarika and Datta (1998), Mani and Gaikwad (1998), Krishna Rao *et.al.* (1999), Thomas and Aziz (2000), Sharma (2000, 2001), Bahura (2001a), Gupta and Mathur (2001), Adak *et.al.* (2002), Khabade *et.al.* (2002), Sakhare and Joshi (2002), Siddiqi and Khan (2002), Chatterjee and Raziuddin (2003), Srivastava *et.al.* (2003), Awasthi and Tiwari (2004), Anita *et.al.* (2005), Singh and Mathur (2005) Sachidanandamurthy and Yajurvedi (2006), Sakhare (2005, 2007, 2012), Rajashekhar *et.al.* (2007), Garg *et.al.* (2008), Koliyar and Rokade (2008), Mishra *et.al.* (2008), Bade *et.al.* (2009), Khabade and Mule (2009), Sakhare and Jetithor (2009), Agarwal and Rajwar (2010), Jetithor (2010), Kiran and Puttaiah (2010), Sawant *et.al.* (2011), Shinde (2011), Thirumala *et.al.* (2011), Medudhula *et.al.* (2012), Mushtaa *et.al.* (2012), Pawar and Shembekar (2012), Vasanthkumar and Vijaykumar (2012), Ingole (2013) etc.

For scientific management and development of the reservoir fisheries, a correct understanding of the water quality of reservoir is a must. However, a good deal is still to be known about the water quality of fresh water reservoirs in Beed district of Maharashtra. Therefore, present work was undertaken to evaluate the physico-chemical environment of Bhavthana reservoir in relation to fisheries.

The work on physico-chemical environment of Bhavthana reservoir can provide valuable information to the planners, scientists and fishing authorities to chalk out strategies for the development of fisheries. However, in literature there is no record of limnological studies of Bhavthana reservoir.

Total hardness (mg/l)

50 ml of water sample was taken in conical flask in to which 1ml of ammonia buffer and a pinch of NaCN (inhibitor) was added. A pinch of erichrome black T indicator was added to develop wine red colour. The sample was then titrated against 0.01m EDTA solution to end point wine red to blue.

$$\text{Total hardness (mg/l) } (CaCo_3) = \frac{T \times 1000}{v}$$

Where

T = Titrant (ml)

v = sample (ml)

Chlorides (mg/l)

The chloride concentration was analyzed in the laboratory. 10 ml of water sample was taken in a conical flask and few drops of K_2CrO_4 were added in to it. The sample was titrated with 0.02 $AgNO_3$ to the end point from yellow to brick red.

$$\text{Chlorides (mg/l)} = \frac{V \times N \times 35.45 \times 1000}{v}$$

Where

V = Volume of titrant (ml)

N = Normality of $AgNO_3$ (0.02)

v = Volume of sample in ml.

Salinity (mg/l)

Calculation of the salinity from chloride value:

Salinity (mg/l) = 0.03 + 1.805 X chloride value

RESULTS

Atmospheric Temperature (°C)

Seasonal variations in atmospheric temperature at three sampling sites along Bhavthana reservoir are presented in Table 4.1 and 4.2 and graphically represented in Figs. 4.1 and 4.2.

Table 4.1: Monthly values of Atmospheric Temperature (°C) (Year 2012-2013)

Site	June	July	Aug.	Sept.	Oct.	Nov.	Dec.	Jan.	Feb.	Mar.	Apr.	May
I	37	32	29	32	32	32	32	34	36	38	37	39
II	34	29	30	32	32	32	33	35	38	39	38	40
III	32	29	29	30	34	32	33	35	38	38	36	37

Table 4.2: Monthly values of Atmospheric Temperature (°C) (Year 2013-2014)

Site	June	July	Aug.	Sept.	Oct.	Nov.	Dec.	Jan.	Feb.	Mar.	Apr.	May
I	39	31	29	31	32	30	32	34	36	38	39	41
II	34	29	30	33	34	30	30	35	37	39	39	40
III	33	28	31	29	34	32	32	33	36	40	40	37

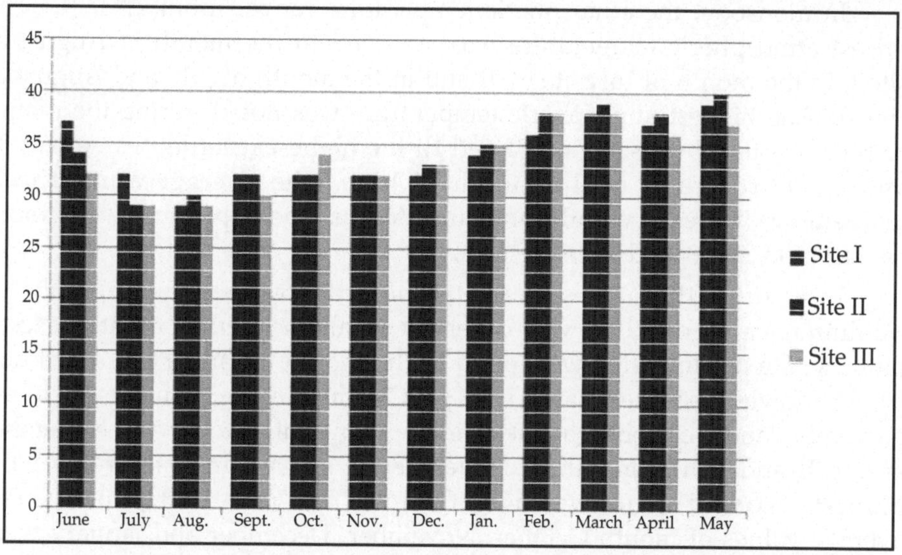

Fig. 4.1: Monthly Fluctuations of Atmospheric Temperature (°C) (Year 2012-2013)

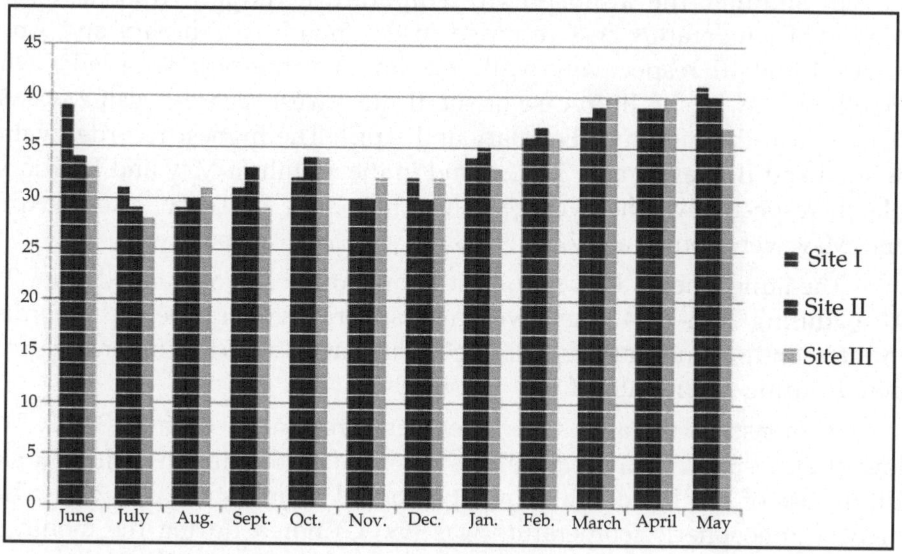

Fig. 4.2: Monthly Fluctuations of Atmospheric Temperature (°C) (Year 2013-2014)

The temperature of Bhavthana reservoir followed a pattern of change being low in monsoon and winter and higher during summer. The atmospheric temperature of Bhavthana reservoir ranged from 29-40 °C during 2012-2013. The lowest atmospheric temperature was recorded in the month of July (at site III) and during the month of August (at site I and III). The highest atmospheric temperature was noted during the month of May at site II.

In monsoon, the atmospheric temperature ranged from 29-37 °C. The lowest atmospheric temperature was recorded in the month of August at site I, in the month of July at site II and in the month of July and August at site III. The highest atmospheric temperature was noted during the month of June at site I. In case of site II and III the highest recorded value was 34 and 32 °C recorded in the month of June. The average atmospheric temperature values of month June, July, August and September were found as 34.33, 30, 29.33 and 31.33 respectively.

In winter, the atmospheric temperature ranged from 32-35 °C. Minimum value of 32 °C was observed in all the winter months except January. Maximum value was found in the month of January at site II and III. The lowest recorded value was 32 °C found in the month of October, November and December (at site I), in the month of October and November at site II and in the month of November at site III. In case of site I the highest recorded value was 34°C found in the month of January. The average values of month October, November, December and January were found as 32.66, 32 32.66 and 34.66 respectively.

In summer the atmospheric temperature ranged from 36-40 °C. Minimum temperature was recorded in the month of February and April at site I and III respectively while maximum value was recorded in the month of May at site II. In case of site II the lowest recorded value was 38 °C found in the month of February and April. The highest recorded value at site I and III was 39 and 38 °C found in the month of May and February-March respectively. The average values of month February, March, April and May were found as 37.33, 38.33, 37 and 38.66 respectively.

The atmospheric temperature of Bhavthana reservoir ranged from 28-41 °C during 2013-2014. The lowest atmospheric temperature was recorded in the month of July (at site III). The highest atmospheric temperature was noted during the month of May at site I.

In monsoon, the atmospheric temperature ranged from 28-39 °C. The lowest atmospheric temperature was recorded in the month of July at site III. In case of site I and II the lowest recorded temperature was 29 °C. The highest atmospheric temperature was (39 °C) noted during the month of June at site I. In case of site II and III the highest recorded value was 34 and 33 °C found the month of June. The average atmospheric temperature values of month June, July, August and September were found as 35.33, 29.33, 30 and 31 respectively.

In winter, the atmospheric temperature ranged from 30-35 °C. Minimum value of 30 °C was observed in the month of November and December at site I and II. Maximum value was found in the month of January at site II. The lowest recorded value at site III was 34 °C recorded in the month of October. In case of site I and III the highest recorded value was 34 °C found in the month of January and October. The average values of month October, November, December and January were found as 33.33, 30.66, 31.33 and 34 respectively.

In summer the atmospheric temperature ranged from 36-41 °C. Minimum temperature was recorded in the month of February at site I and III while maximu was recorded in the month of May at site I. In case of site II the lowest recorded value was 37 °C found in the month of February. The highest recorded value at site II and III was 40 °C found in the month of May and March-April respectively. The average values of month February, March, April and May were found as 36.33, 39, 39.33 and 39.33 respectively.

Water Temperature (°C)

Seasonal variations in water temperature at three sites in Bhavthana reservoir are presented in Table 4.3 and 4.4 and graphically represented in Figs. 4.3 and 4.4.

Table 4.3: Monthly Values of Water Temperature (°C) (Year 2012-2013)

Site	June	July	Aug.	Sept.	Oct.	Nov.	Dec.	Jan.	Feb.	Mar.	Apr.	May
I	30	28	28	29	29	26	24	24	29	32	36	38
II	32	30	29	32	29	28	22	28	29	33	35	36
III	31	31	27	30	27	28	26	25	29	35	36	37

Table 4.4: Monthly Values of Water Temperature (°C) (Year 2013-2014)

Site	June	July	Aug.	Sept.	Oct.	Nov.	Dec.	Jan.	Feb.	Mar.	Apr.	May
I	31	28	27	29	29	24	22	28	33	32	33	36
II	32	23	24	30	32	24	24	25	31	31	35	37
III	32	24	25	30	30	23	24	26	31	31	37	37

The water temperature of Bhavthana reservoir ranged from 22-38 °C during 2012-2013. The lowest atmospheric temperature was recorded in the month of August at site III and the highest during the month of May at site I.

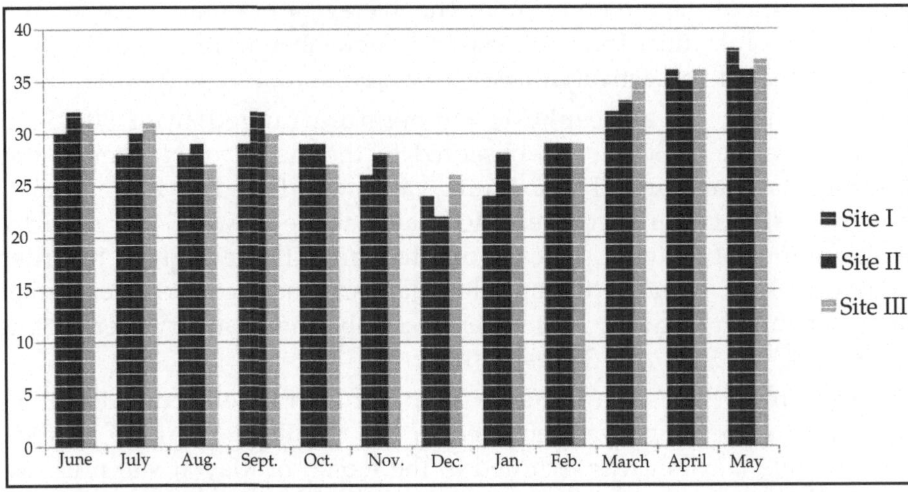

Fig. 4.3: Monthly Fluctuations of Water Temperature(°C) (Year 2012-2013)

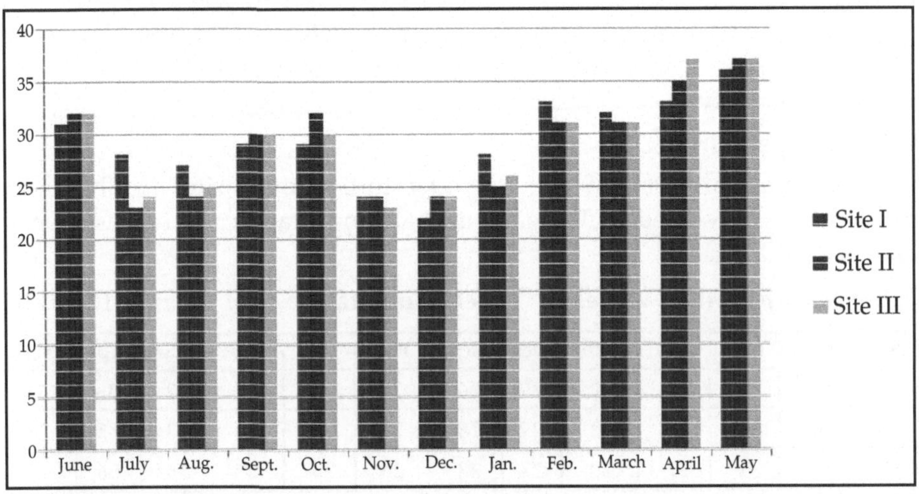

Fig. 4.4: Monthly Fluctuations of Water Temperature(°C) (Year 2013-2014)

In monsoon, the water temperature ranged from 27-32 °C. The lowest water temperature was recorded in the month of August at site III. The highest water temperature was noted during the month of June at site II. In case of site I and III the highest recorded value was 30 and 31 °C recorded in the month of June and June-July. The average water temperature values of month June, July, August and September were found as 31, 29.66, 28 and 30.33 respectively.

In winter, the water temperature ranged from 22-29 °C. Minimum value of 22 °C was noted in December at site II while maximum in the month of October at site I and II. At site I and III the lowest recorded value was 24 and 25 °C found in the month of December-January and

January respectively. In case of site III the highest recorded value was 28 °C found in the month of November. The average values of month October, November, December and January were found as 28.33, 27.33, 24 and 25.66 respectively.

In summer the water temperature ranged from 29-38 °C. Minimum water temperature was recorded in the month of February at all the three sites while maximum value was recorded in the month of May at site I. The highest recorded value at site II and III was 36 and 37 °C respectively found in the month of May. The average values of month February, March, April and May were found as 29, 33.33, 35.66 and 37 respectively.

The water temperature of Bhavthana reservoir ranged from 22-37 °C during 2013-2014. The lowest atmospheric temperature was recorded in the month of December at site I and the highest during the month of May and April-May at site II and III respectively.

In monsoon, the water temperature ranged from 23-32 °C. The lowest water temperature was recorded in the month of July at site II. The highest water temperature was noted during the month of June at site II and III. In case of site I and III the lowest recorded value was 27 and 24 °C recorded in the month of August and July. The average water temperature values of month June, July, August and September were found as 31.66, 25, 25.33 and 29.66 respectively.

In winter, the water temperature ranged from 22-32 °C. Minimum value of 22 °C was noted in December at site I while maximum in the month of October at site II. At site II and III the lowest recorded value was 24 and 23 °C found in the month of November-December and November respectively. In case of site I and III the highest recorded value was 29 and 30 °C found in the month of October. The average values of month October, November, December and January were found as 30.33, 23.66, 23.33 and 26.33 respectively.

In summer the water temperature ranged from 31-37 °C. Minimum water temperature was recorded in the month of February and March at sites II while maximum value was recorded in the month of May at site II and in the month of April-May at site III. The highest recorded value at site I was 36 found in the month of May. The average values of month February, March, April and May were found as 31.66, 31.33, 35 and 36.66 respectively.

Transparency (cms)

Observed seasonal variations in transparency expressed in centimeters for the two years study period are presented in Table 4.5 and 4.6 and graphically represented in Figs.4.5 and 4.6.

Table 4.5: Monthly values of Transparency (cm) (Year 2012-2013)

Site	June	July	Aug.	Sept.	Oct.	Nov.	Dec.	Jan.	Feb.	Mar.	Apr.	May
I	72	78	69	58	69	84	97	102	120	127	129	130
II	74	78	67	57	65	89	97	100	122	118	127	125
III	71	77	67	58	67	83	98	102	119	121.5	128	122

Table 4.6: Monthly Values of Transparency (cm) (Year 2013-2014)

Site	June	July	Aug.	Sept.	Oct.	Nov.	Dec.	Jan.	Feb.	Mar.	Apr.	May
I	72	58	69	78	71	84	102	118	121	120	118	128
II	70	57	70	78	76	89	101	116	119	118	120.2	127
III	75	58	66	77	75	88	102	119	115	127	126	123

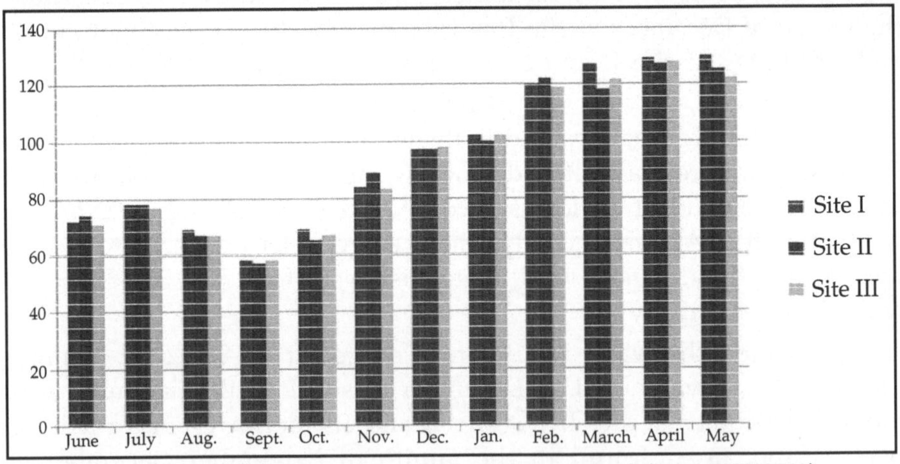

Fig. 4.5: Monthly Fluctuations of Transparency (cm) (Year 2012-2013)

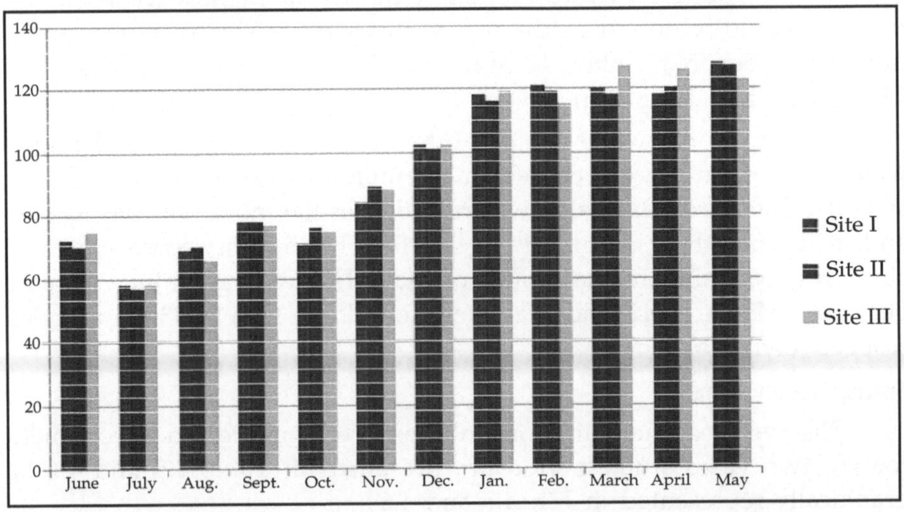

Fig. 4.6: Monthly Fluctuations of Transparency (cm) (Year 2013-2014)

The water was colorless, odorless and transparent during the whole period of study. The transparency of Bhavthana reservoir ranged from 57-130 cm during entire period of study. The minimum value (57cm) was recorded in the month of September and July respectively at site II during 2012-13 and 2013-14. The highest value was recorded in the month of May during 2012-2013 while during 2013-2014 the highest value was 128 cm found in the month of May at site I.

During 2012-2013 in monsoon the transparency ranged from 57-78 cm. Minimum value was observed in the month of July at site II while maximum value was recorded in the month of September at site I and II. In case of site I and III the lowest recorded value was 58cm observed in the month of July. In case of site III the highest recorded value was 77cm found in the month of September. The average transparency values of month June, July, August and September were found as 72.33, 77.66, 67.66 and 57.66 respectively.

In winter the transparency ranged from 65-102 cm. Minimum value was observed in the month of October at site II while maximum in the month of January at site I and III. The lowest recorded values at site I and III were 69 and 67 cm observed in the month of October.In case of site II the highest recorded value was 102 cm found in the month of January. The average values of month October, November, December and January were found as 67, 85.33, 97.33 and 101.33 respectively.

In summer the transparency ranged from 118-130cm. Minimum value was recorded in the month of May at site I and III and in the month of April at site III while maximum value (260) was recorded in the month of February at site II. In case of site I and III the highest recorded value was 250 cm found in the month of February. The average values of month February, March, April and May were found as 253.33, 200.3, 190 and 176.66 respectively.

During 2013-2014, in monsoon the transparency ranged from 57-78cm. Minimum value was observed in the month of July at all the three sites with slight fluctuations while maximum value was recorded in the month of September. The average transparency values of month June, July, August and September were found as 72.33, 57.66, 68.33 and 77.66 respectively.

In winter the transparency ranged from 71-119 cm. Minimum value was observed in the month of October at all the three sites with slightly fluctuating values viz. 71cm, 76 cm and 75 cm at site I, II and III respectively. The highest recorded value was 119 found in the month of January at site III. The average values of month October, November, December and January were found as 74, 87, 101.66 and 117.66 respectively.

In summer the transparency ranged from 115-128 cm. Minimum value was recorded in the month of February at site III while maximum value was recorded in the month of May at site I. In case of site I and II the lowest recorded value was 118 cm found in the month of April and March. The highest recorded value at site II and III was 127 cm found in the month of May and March respectively. The average values of month February, March, April and May were found as 118.33, 121.66, 121.4 and 126 respectively.

pH

Seasonal alterations in pH concentration at three experimental sites along Bhavthana reservoir are presented in Table 4.7 and 4.8 and graphically represented in Figs.4.7 and 4.8.

Table 4.7: Monthly Values of pH (Year 2012-2013)

Site	June	July	Aug.	Sept.	Oct.	Nov.	Dec.	Jan.	Feb.	Mar.	Apr.	May
I	8.2	8.3	8.2	7.9	7.8	8.1	8.3	7.7	8.5	8.3	7.9	7.7
II	8.1	7.9	7.6	8.2	7.7	8.0	8.4	7.8	7.6	8.0	8.2	7.8
III	7.9	8.1	8.2	7.7	8.0	8.5	7.6	7.8	8.2	8.1	8.0	7.8

Table 4.8: Monthly Values of pH (Year 2013-2014)

Site	June	July	Aug.	Sept.	Oct.	Nov.	Dec.	Jan.	Feb.	Mar.	Apr.	May
I	8.2	7.9	8.2	8.5	8.1	7.6	8.0	8.3	8.3	7.8	7.9	8.3
II	8.0	7.7	8.3	8.4	8.3	7.8	7.6	7.9	8.2	7.8	7.6	8.0
III	8.1	7.9	8.1	8.2	8.5	7.9	8.0	8.1	8.7	7.6	7.9	8.3

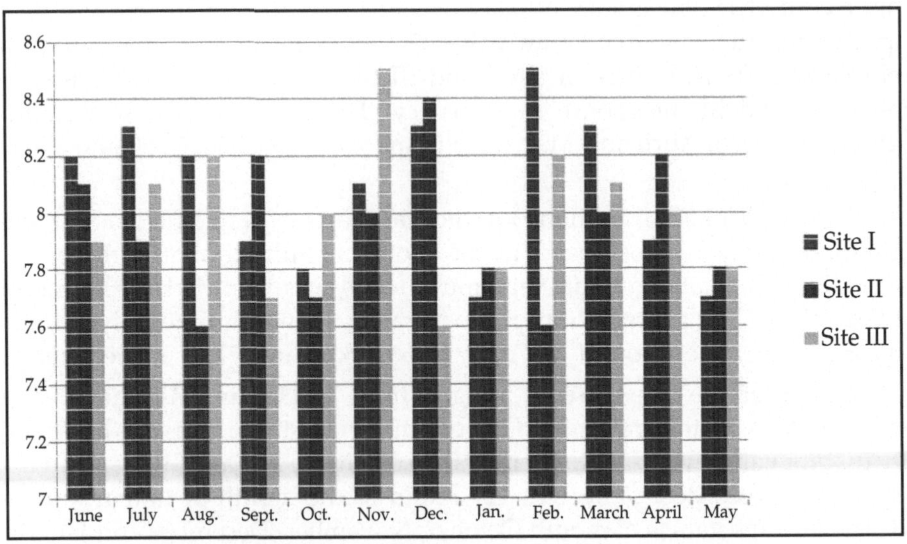

Fig. 4.7: Monthly Fluctuations of pH (Year 2012-2013)

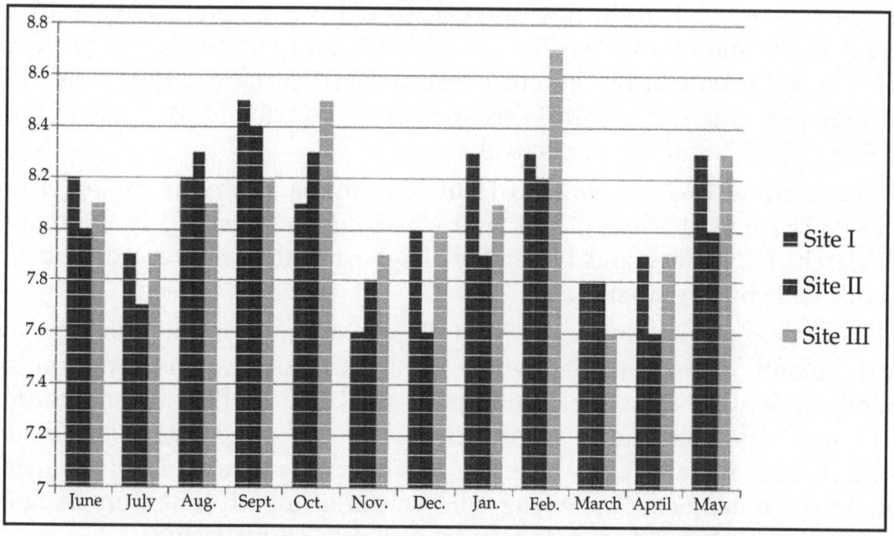

Fig. 4.8: Monthly Fluctuations of pH (Year 2013-2014)

The pH of Bhavthana reservoir ranged from 7.6-8.7 during entire study period. The water was alkaline throughout the study period.

During 2012-2013, water pH of Bhavthana reservoir ranged from 7.6-8.5. The lowest value of pH (7.6) was recorded at site II in the month of August and February and in the month of December at site III. At site I, the lowest recorded value of pH was 7.7. pH value was highest in the month of February (8.5), December (8.4) and November (8.5) at site I, II and III respectively.

In monsoon the pH ranged from 7.6-8.3.Its minimum value was observed in the month of August at site II while maximum value was recorded in the month of July at site I. In case of site I and III the lowest recorded pH value was 7.9 and 7.7 respectively found in the month of September. In case of site II and III the highest recorded pH value was 8.2 in the month of September and August. The average pH values of month June, July, August and September were found as 8.06, 8.1, 8 and 7.9 respectively.

In winter the pH ranged from 7.6-8.4. Both minimum and maximum values were observed in the month of December at site III and II respectively. In case of site I and II the lowest recorded pH was 7.7 found in the month of January and October respectively. In case of site I and III the highest recorded pH was 8.1 and 8.5 respectively found in the month of November. The average pH values of month October, November, December and January were found as 7.8, 8.2, 8.1 and 7.7 respectively.

In summer the pH ranged from 7.6-8.5. Both minimum and maximum values were recorded in the month of February at site II and I respectively.

In case of site I and III the lowest recorded pH was 7.7 and 7.8 respectively found in the month of May. In case of site II and III the highest recorded pH was 8.2 found in the month of April and February respectively. The average pH values of month February, March, April and May were found as 8.1, 8.03, 7.7 and 8.0 respectively.

During 2013-2014, water pH of Bhavthana reservoir ranged from 7.6-8.7. The lowest value of pH (7.6) was recorded at site II in the month of March, November and December. Highest value was recorded in the month of February at site III.

In monsoon the pH ranged from 7.7-8.5. Minimum value was observed in the month of July at site II while maximum value was recorded in the month of September at site I. In case of site I and III the lowest recorded pH value was 7.9 found in the month of July. In case of site II and III the highest recorded pH value was 8.4 and 8.2 respectively observed in the month of September. The average pH values of month June, July, August and September were found as 8.1, 7.8, 8.2 and 8.3 respectively.

In winter the pH ranged from 7.6-8.5. Minimum value was observed in the month of November and December at site I and II respectively. In case of site II and III the lowest recorded pH was 7.6 and 7.9 recorded in the month of December and November respectively. The maximum values were observed in the month of December at site III and II respectively. The average pH values of month October, November, December and January were found as 8.3, 7.7, 7.8 and 8.1 respectively.

In summer the pH ranged from 7.6-8.3. Minimum value was recorded in the month of March and April at site III while maximum values were recorded in the month of May at site I and III. In case of site I and II the lowest recorded pH was 7.7 and 7.6 found in the month of March and April respectively. In case of site II the highest recorded pH was 8.2 found in the month of February. The average pH values of month February, March, April and May were found as 7.7, 7.8, 7 and 8.04 respectively.

Total Dissolved Solids (mg/l)

Monthly variations in TDS values at three sampling sites in Bhavthana reservoir are depicted in Table 4.9 and Table 4.10 and graphically represented in Figs. 4.9 and 4.10.

Table 4.9: Monthly Values of Total Dissolved Solids (mg/l) (Year 2012-2013)

Site	June	July	Aug.	Sept.	Oct.	Nov.	Dec.	Jan.	Feb.	Mar.	Apr.	May
I	120	120	180	120	170	170	210	210	220	260	120	190.8
II	160	210.5	170	140	170.5	190	200	160	180	260	120.2	180.7
III	150	230	170	160.2	175	190	198	160	180	250	190	210

Table 4.10: Monthly Values of Total Dissolved Solids (mg/l) (Year 2013-2014)

Site	June	July	Aug.	Sept.	Oct.	Nov.	Dec.	Jan.	Feb.	Mar.	Apr.	May
I	160	180	190.5	180	170	190.5	200	190.8	250	220	210	170
II	180	170	190.4	180.5	190	180.9	210	230	260	190	180	190
III	170	170	210	170.8	190	169.8	210.1	240	250	190.9	180	170

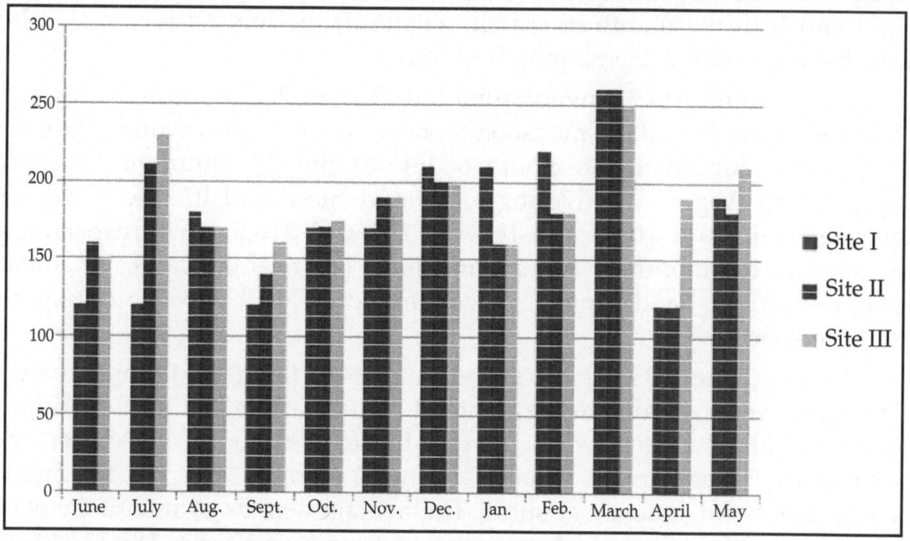

Fig. 4.9: Monthly Fluctuations of Total Dissolved Solids (mg/l) (Year 2012-2013)

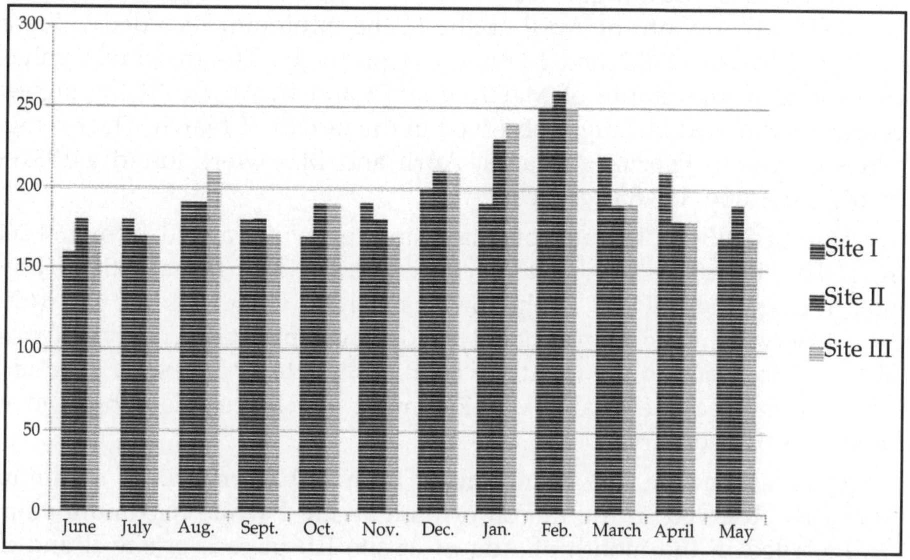

Fig. 4.10: Monthly Fluctuations of Total Dissolved Solids (mg/l) (Year 2013-2014)

The total dissolved solid content of Bhavthana reservoir ranged from 120-260 mg/l during entire study period.

During 2012-2013, water TDS of Bhavthana reservoir water ranged from 120-260 mg/l. The lowest value of TDS (120) was recorded at site I in the month of June, July, September and April. In case of site II and III the lowest recorded value was 120.2 and 150 mg/l recorded in the month of April and June respectively. The highest value (260 mg/l) was recorded at site I and II in the month of March. At site III the highest recorded value was 250 mg/l found in the month of March.

In monsoon TDS ranged from 120-230 mg/l. Minimum value was observed at site I in all the monsoon months except August while maximum value was recorded in the month of July at site III. Minimum observed value during August was 170 mg/l found at site II and III. The maximum recorded values at site I and II were 180 and 210.5 mg/l respectively recorded in the month of August and July. The average values of month June, July, August and September were found as 143.33, 186.83, 173.33 and 140.06 respectively.

In winter the TDS values ranged from 160-210 mg/l. Minimum values (160 mg/l) were recorded in the month of January at site II and III. Minimum observed value at site I was 170 recorded in the month of October and November. The maximum values (210 mg/l) were observed in the month of December and January at site I. The average values of month October, November, December and January were found as 171.83, 183.33, 202.66 and 176.66 respectively.

In summer the ranged from 120-260 mg/l. Minimum values were recorded in the month of April at site I. The minimum recorded value at site II and III was 120.2 and 180 mg/l respectively. The maximum values were found in the month of March at site I and II. At site III the highest recorded value was 250 mg/l observed in the month of March. The average values of month February, March, April and May were found as193.33, 256.66, 143.4 and 193.83 respectively.

During 2013-2014, water of Bhavthana reservoir ranged from 160-260 mg/l. The lowest value of was recorded at site I in the month of June only. In case of site II and III the lowest recorded value was 170 and 169.8 mg/l observed in the month of July and November respectively. Highest value was recorded in the month of February at site II. In case of site I and II the highest recorded value was 250 mg/l which was also observed in the month of February.

In monsoon the TDS value ranged from 160-210 mg/l. Its minimum value was observed in the month of June at site I while maximum value was recorded in the month of August at site III. In case of site II and III the lowest recorded value was 170 and 170.8 mg/l observed in the month of July and September respectively. In case of site I and II the highest recorded value was 190.5 and 190.4 mg/l respectively found in the month of August. The average TDS values of month June, July, August and September were 170, 173.33, 196.96 and 177.1 respectively.

In winter the TDS value ranged from 169.8-240 mg/l. Minimum value was observed in the month of November at site III. The lowest recorded values at site I and II were 170 mg/l and 180.9 mg/l observed in the month of October and November. The maximum value was observed in the month of January at site III. In case of site I and II the highest recorded value was 190.8 mg/l and 230 mg/l respectively found in the month of January. The average values of month of October, November, December and January were 183.33, 180.4, 206.7 and 220.26 respectively.

In summer the TDS value ranged from 170-260 mg/l. Minimum value was recorded in the month of May at site I and III and in the month of April at site III while maximum value (260) was recorded in the month of February at site II. In case of site I and III the highest recorded value was 250 found in the month of February. The average values of month February, March, April and May were found as 253.33, 200.3, 190 and 176.66 respectively.

Dissolved Oxygen (mg/l)

Dissolved oxygen content observed at three sites during 2012-2013 and 2012-2013 is presented in Table 4.11 and 4.12 and graphically represented in Figs. 4.11 and 4.12.

Table 4.11: Monthly Values of Dissolved oxygen (mg/l) (Year 2012-2013)

Site	June	July	Aug.	Sept.	Oct.	Nov.	Dec.	Jan.	Feb.	Mar.	Apr.	May
I	9.4	7.6	6.8	6.5	9.2	9.3	9.0	9.2	5.0	5.3	6.4	7.3
II	10.6	7.8	7.9	6.2	10.5	9.1	9.2	10.5	9.1	5.8	6.8	7.8
III	9.7	7.4	8.8	6.3	11.3	9.4	9.8	10.3	6.1	5.6	6.5	6.9

Table 4.12: Monthly Values of Dissolved Oxygen (mg/l) (Year 2013-2014)

Site	June	July	Aug.	Sept.	Oct.	Nov.	Dec.	Jan.	Feb.	Mar.	Apr.	May
I	8.2	7.5	9.9	9.1	12.2	9.0	9.1	8.7	6.5	5.3	5.9	5.2
II	7.5	7.8	9.7	9.7	9.2	9.1	9.2	9.5	6.2	5.9	5.9	5.8
III	7.9	8.1	9.6	8.3	11.1	9.2	9.2	9.3	6.3	6.0	6.0	5.9

The concentration of dissolved oxygen during 2012-2013 was 5-11.3mg/l. The lowest value was observed in the month of February at site I and highest value was observed in the month of October at site III. In monsoon the dissolved oxygen ranged from 6.2-10.6 mg/l. Minimum value was observed in the month of September at site II while maximum value was recorded in the month of June at site II. In case of site I and III the lowest recorded value was 6.5 and 6.3 respectively observed in the month of

September. In case of site I and III the highest recorded value was 9.4 and 9.7 respectively found in the month of June. The average dissolved oxygen values of month June, July, August and September were 9.9, 7.6, 7.8 and 6.3 respectively.

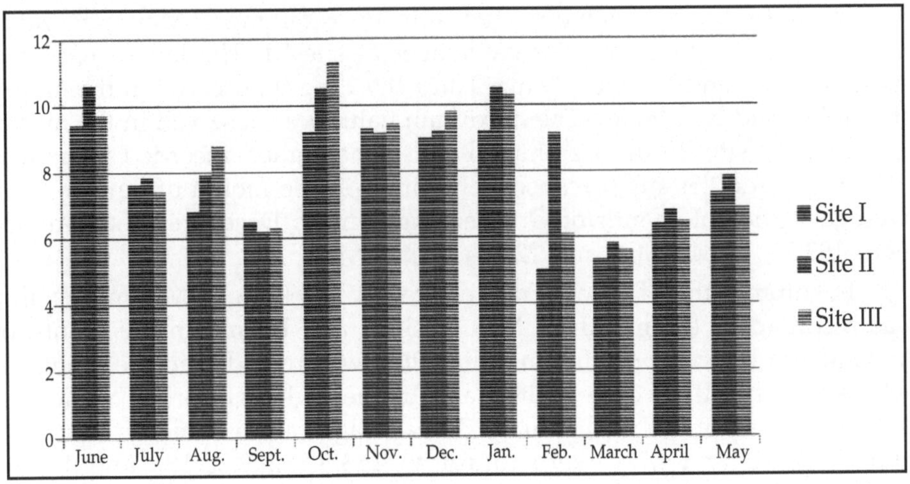

Fig. 4.11: Monthly Fluctuations of Dissolved Oxygen (mg/l) (Year 2012-2013)

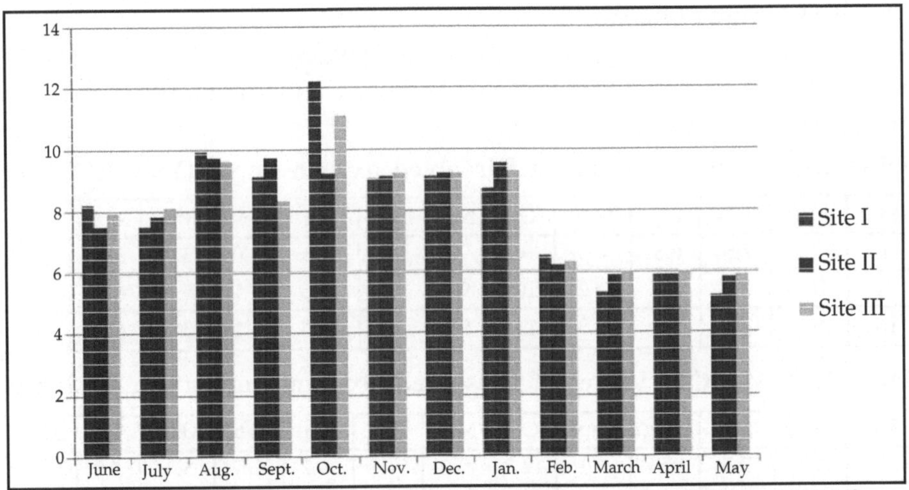

Fig. 4.12: Monthly Fluctuations of Dissolved Oxygen (mg/l) (Year 2013-14)

In winter the dissolved oxygen ranged from 9-11.3mg/l. Minimum value was observed in the month of December at site I while maximum in the month of October at site III. The lowest recorded values at site II and III was 9.1 and 9.4 respectively observed in the month of November. In case of site I and II the highest recorded value was 9.3 and 10.5 found in the month of November (site I) and October and January (site II). The average values of month October, November, December and January were found as10.33, 9.26, 9.33 and 10 respectively.

In summer dissolved oxygen ranged from 5 to 9.1 mg/l. Minimum value was recorded in the month of February at site I while maximum value was recorded in the month of May at site II. In case of site II and III the lowest recorded value was 5.8 and 5.6 found in the month of March. The highest recorded value at site I and III was 7.3 and 6.9 respectively found in the month of May. The average values of month February, March, April and May were found as 6.7, 5.56, 6.56 and 7.33 respectively.

The concentration of dissolved oxygen during 2013-2014 was 5.2-12.2 mg/l. The lowest value was observed in the month of May at site I and highest value was observed in the month of October at site I.

In monsoon the dissolved oxygen ranged from 7.5 to 9.9 mg/l. Its minimum value was observed in the month of July and June at site I and II respectively while maximum value was recorded in the month of August at site I. In case of site III the lowest recorded value was 7.9 mg/l observed in the month of June. In case of site II and III the highest recorded value was 9.7 and 9.6 mg/l found in the month of August-September and August respectively. The average dissolved oxygen values of month of June, July, August and September were 7.86, 7.8, 9.73 and 9.03 respectively.

In winter dissolved oxygen ranged from 9-12.2 mg/l. Its minimum value was observed in the month of November at site I while maximum in the month of October at site I. The lowest recorded value at site II and III was 9.1 and 9.2 observed in the month of November and November-December respectively. In case of site II and III the highest recorded value was 9.5 and 11.1 mg/l found in the month of January and October. The average values of month October, November, December and January were found as 10.8, 9.1, 9.16 and 9.16 respectively.

In summer dissolved oxygen ranged from 5.2 to 6.5 mg/l. Minimum value was recorded in the month of May at site I while maximum value was recorded in the month of February at site I. In case of site II and III the lowest recorded value was 5.8 and 5.9 found in the month of May. The highest recorded value at site II and III was 6.2 and 6.3 mg/l respectively found in the month of February. The average values for month of February, March, April and May were found as 6.33, 5.73, 5.93 and 5.63 respectively.

Free Carbon dioxide (mg/l)

Monthly values of free carbon dioxide are shown in Table 4.13 and 4.14 and graphically represented in Figs. 4.13 and 4.14.

Free carbon dioxide in reservoir water was recorded only in the month of October (0.2 mg/l) at site II, in 2012-2013 and in the month of February (0.3 mg/l) at site III, during 2013-2014.It was completely absent in eleven months of each year of investigation.

Table 4.13: Monthly values of Free CO_2 (mg/l) (Year 2012-2013)

Site	June	July	Aug.	Sept.	Oct.	Nov.	Dec.	Jan.	Feb.	Mar.	Apr.	May
I	–	–	–	–	–	–	–	–	–	–	–	–
II	–	–	–	–	0.2	–	–	–		–	–	–
III	–	–	–	–	–	–	–	–	–	–	–	–

Table 4.14: Monthly Values of Free CO_2 (mg/l) (Year 2013-2014)

Site	June	July	Aug.	Sept.	Oct.	Nov.	Dec.	Jan.	Feb.	Mar.	Apr.	May
I	–	–	–	–	–	–	–	–	–	–	–	–
II	–	–	–	–	–	–	–	–	–	–	–	–
III	–	–	–	–	–	–	–	–	0.3	–	–	–

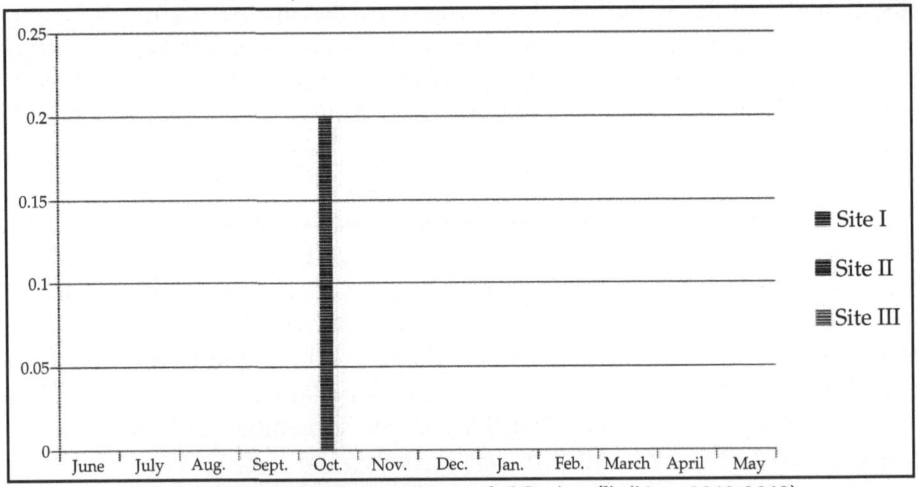

Fig. 4.13: Monthly Fluctuations of CO_2 (mg/l) (Year 2012-2013)

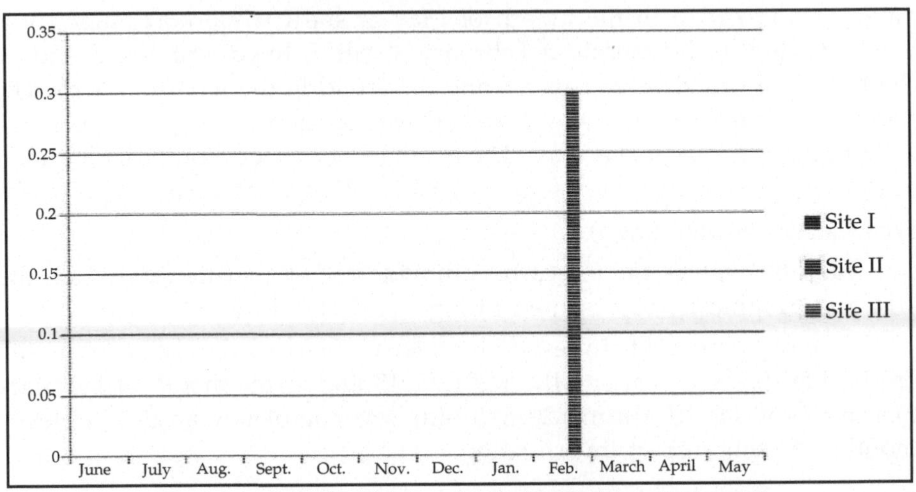

Fig. 4.14: Monthly Values of CO_2 (mg/l) (Year 2013-2014)

Phenolphthalein Alkalinity (mg/l)

Monthly values of phenolphthalein alkalinity are expressed in Table 4.15 and Table 4.16 and graphically represented in Figs. 4.15 and 4.16.

During 2012-2013 the phenolphthalein alkalinity of Bhavthana reservoir ranged from 28.36-63.81 mg/l. Its minimum concentration was observed in the month of January at all the three sites while maximum in the month of October at site I.

In monsoon the phenolphthalein alkalinity of Bhavthana reservoir ranged from 29.7-41.5 mg/l. The lowest concentration was observed in the month of June at site III while highest in the month of September at site III. In case of site I and II the lowest concentration of 30 and 29.9 mg/l respectively was observed in the month of June. In case of site I and II the highest concentration of 38.7 mg/l and 40.1 mg/l respectively was observed in the month of September. The average phenolphthalein alkalinity values of month June, July, August and September were 30, 29.8, 35.2 and 40.1 respectively.

Table 4.15: Monthly Values of Phenolphthalein Alkalinity (mg/l) (Year 2012-2013)

Site	June	July	Aug.	Sept.	Oct.	Nov.	Dec.	Jan.	Feb.	Mar.	Apr.	May
I	29.7	29.5	32.7	38.7	40	38.6	37.8	29.6	28.4	28.6	28.6	29
II	30.2	29.7	34.3	40.1	40	36.3	38.5	28.8	28.6	28	28	29.5
III	30.1	30.2	38.6	41.5	40	39.2	38	29.4	28.6	27.9	28	29.5

Table 4.16: Monthly values of Phenolphthalein Alkalinity (mg/l) (Year 2013-2014)

Site	June	July	Aug.	Sept.	Oct.	Nov.	Dec.	Jan.	Feb.	Mar.	Apr.	May
I	30	30.2	38	38.7	42	39.8	36.8	28.2	25.4	27.7	29.9	29.3
II	29.9	30.5	39.1	40.1	41.5	38.7	36.9	28.2	25.6	28.6	29.9	29.2
III	29.7	30.5	40.5	41.5	42	39.7	36	28.6	26.7	27.9	29.2	30

In winter the phenolphthalein alkalinity of Bhavthana reservoir ranged from 28.36 mg/l to 63.81mg/l. The lowest concentration was observed in the month of January at site II and III while highest in the month of October at site I. In case of site I the lowest concentration of 29.36 mg/l was observed in the month of January. In case of site II and III the highest concentration of 61.22 and 58.66 mg/l respectively was observed in the month of October. The average phenolphthalein alkalinity values of month October, November, December and January were 40, 38.03, 38.1 and 29.26 respectively.

In summer the phenolphthalein alkalinity of Bhavthana reservoir ranged from 27.9 to 29.5mg/l. Minimum concentration was observed in the month of March at sites III while maximum value was recorded in the month of May at site II and III. The highest recorded value at site I was 29 mg/l which was also found in the month of May. The lowest observed value at site I and II was 28.4 and 27.9 mg/l found in the month of March-April and March respectively. The average phenolphthalein alkalinity values of month February, March, April and May were 28.53, 28.16, 28.2 and 29.33 respectively.

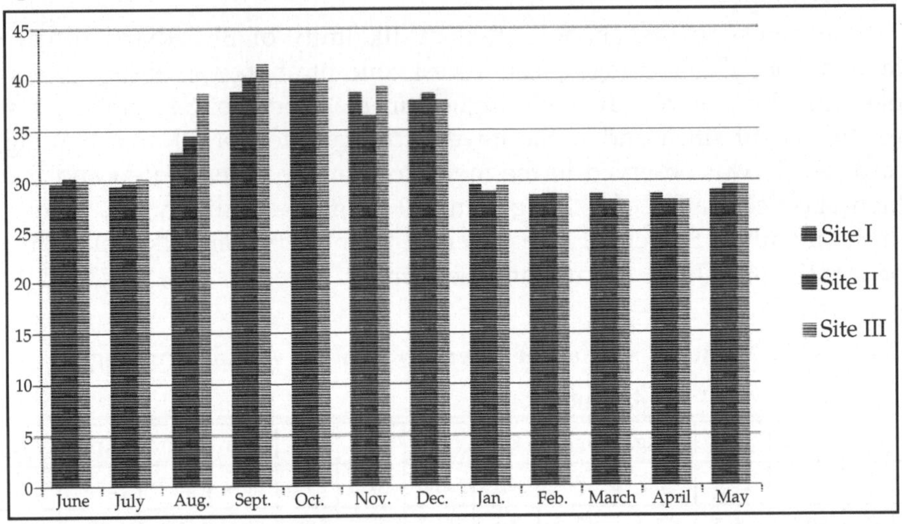

Fig. 4.15: Monthly Fluctuations of Phenolpthalein Alkalinity (mg/l) (Year 2012-2013)

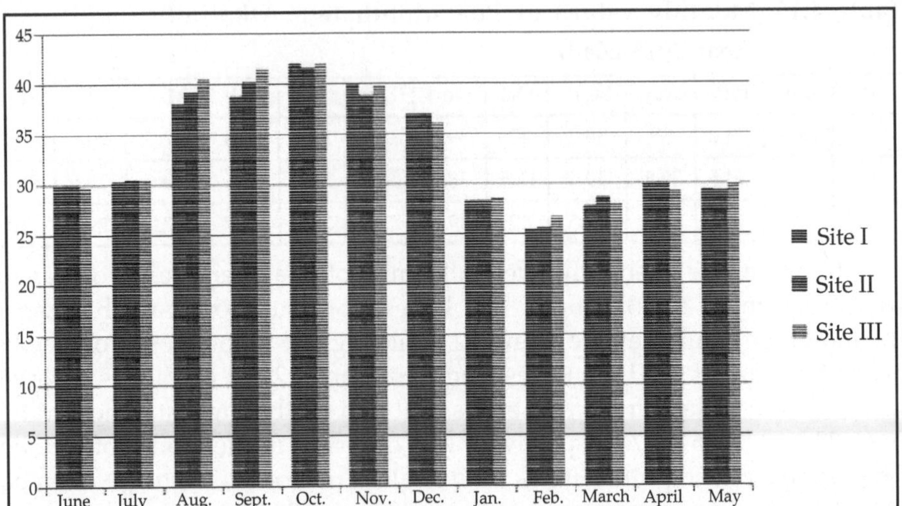

Fig. 4.16: Monthly Fluctuations of Phenolpthalein Alkalinity (mg/l) (Year 2013-2014)

During 2013-2014 the phenolphthalein alkalinity of Bhavthana reservoir ranged from 25.4-41.5 mg/l. Its minimum value was observed in the month of February at site I while maximum in the month of September at site III.

In monsoon the phenolphthalein alkalinity of Bhavthana reservoir ranged from 29.5-41.5 mg/l. The lowest value was observed in the month of July at site I while highest in the month of September at site III. In case of site II and III the lowest concentration of 29.7 and 30.1mg/l respectively was observed in the month of July. In case of site I and II the highest concentration of 38.7 and 40.1mg/l respectively was observed in the month of September. The average phenolphthalein alkalinity values for the month of June, July, August and September were 29.86, 30.4, 39.2 and 40.1 respectively.

In winter the phenolphthalein alkalinity of Bhavthana reservoir ranged from 28.8 to 40 mg/l. The lowest concentration was observed in the month of January at site II while highest in the month of October at all the three sites. In case of site I and III the lowest concentration of 29.6 and 29.4 mg/l was observed in the month of January. The average phenolphthalein alkalinity values of month October, November, December and January were found as 41.83, 39.4, 36.56 and 28.33 respectively.

In summer the phenolphthalein alkalinity of Bhavthana reservoir ranged from 25.4 mg/l to 30 mg/l. Minimum concentration was observed in the month of February at site I while maximum value was recorded in the month of May at site III. The highest recorded value at site I and II was 29.9 mg/l found in the month of April. The lowest observed value at site II and III was 25.6 and 26.7 mg/l found in the month of February. The average phenolphthalein alkalinity values for month of February, March, April and May were 25.9, 28.06, 29.66 and 29.5 respectively.

Total Alkalinity (mg/l)

Monthly fluctuations in total alkalinity are shown in Table 4.17 and Table 4.18 and graphically represented in Figs.4.17 and 4.18.

Table 4.17: Monthly values of Total Alkalinity (mg/l) (Year 2012-2013)

Site	June	July	Aug.	Sept.	Oct.	Nov.	Dec.	Jan.	Feb.	Mar.	Apr.	May
I	276.5	249	262.2	281	384	360	205.06	279	197	166	256	254.2
II	279	252.5	264	288	384	265	205	298	210	239	239	255
III	272.8	256	268	283	384	369	209	299.5	202	186	239	265

Table 4.18: Monthly Values of Total Alkalinity (mg/l) (Year 2013-2014)

Site	June	July	Aug.	Sept.	Oct.	Nov.	Dec.	Jan.	Feb.	Mar.	Apr.	May
I	277	177.2	250	279	263	380	284	310	205.08	176	250	217
II	292.3	178	264	270	270	378	278	289	205	168	250	165.5
III	310	178	270.5	262	263	383	283	290	209.5	210	249.2	162

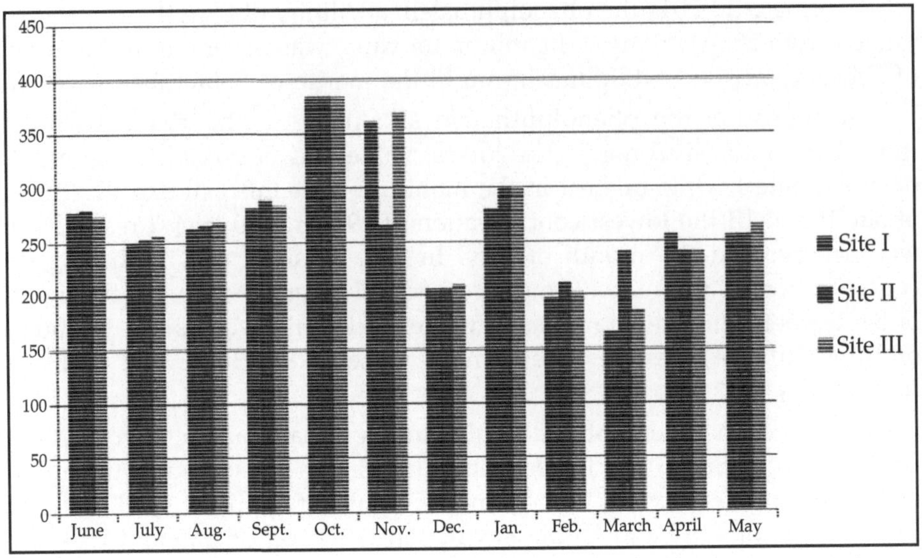

Fig. 4.17: Monthly Fluctuations of Total Alkalinity (mg/l) (Year 2012-2013)

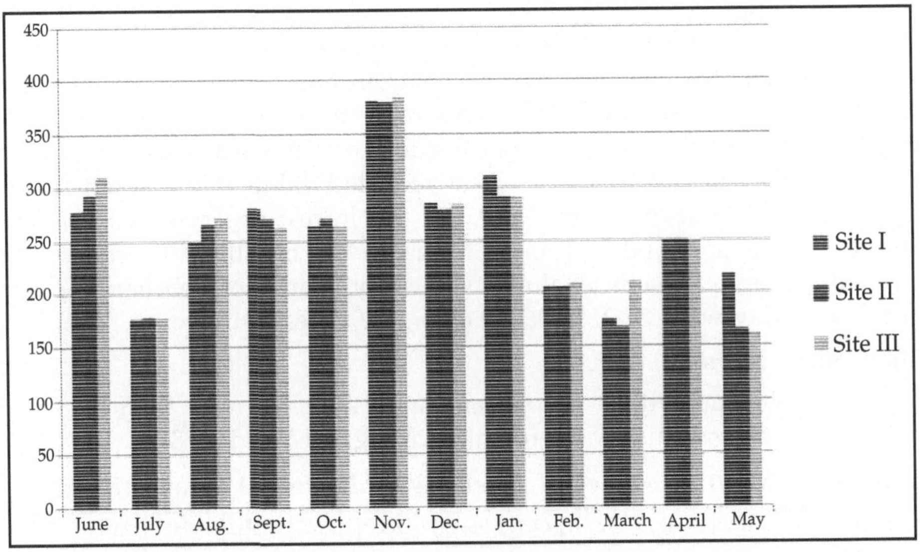

Fig. 4.18: Monthly Fluctuations of Total Alkalinity (mg/l) (Year 2013-2014)

During 2012-2013 the total alkalinity of Bhavthana reservoir ranged from 166mg/l to 384 mg/l. Its minima was observed in the month of March at site I while maxima in the month of October at all the sites.

In monsoon the total alkalinity of Bhavthana reservoir ranged from 249 to 288 mg/l. The lowest value was observed in the month of July at site I while highest in the month of September at site II. In case of site II and III the lowest concentration of 252.5 and 256 mg/l respectively was observed in the month of July. In case of site I and III the highest concentration of 281and 283 mg/l respectively was observed in the month of September. The average total alkalinity values of month June, July, August and September were found as 276.1, 252.5, 264.73 and 284 respectively.

In winter the total alkalinity of Bhavthana reservoir ranged from 205 to 384 mg/l. The lowest concentration was observed in the month of December at site II while highest in the month of October at all the three sites. In case of site I and III the lowest concentration of 205.05 and 209 mg/l was observed in the month of December. The average total alkalinity values for month of October, November, December and January were 384, 331.33, 206.35 and 292.16 respectively.

In summer the total alkalinity of Bhavthana reservoir ranged from 166 mg/l to265 mg/l. Its minimum value was observed in the month of March at sites I while maximum value was recorded in the month of May at site III. The highest recorded value at site I and II was 256 and 255 mg/l which were found in the month of May. The lowest observed value at site II and III was 210 and 186 mg/l found in the month of February and March respectively. The average total alkalinity values of month February, March, April and May were found as 203, 197, 244.66 and 258.06 respectively.

During 2013-2014 the total alkalinity ranged from 162 mg/l to 383 mg/l. Its minimum concentration was observed in the month of January at all the three sites while maximum in the month of October at site I.

In monsoon the total alkalinity of Bhavthana reservoir ranged from 177.2 to 310 mg/l. The lowest concentration was observed in the month of July at site I while highest in the month of June at site III. In case of site II and III the lowest concentration of 178 mg/l was observed in the month of July. In case of site I and II the highest concentration of 279 and 292.3 mg/l was observed in the month of September and June respectively. The average total alkalinity values of month June, July, August and September were found as 293.1, 177.73, 261.5 and 270.33 respectively.

In winter the total alkalinity of Bhavthana reservoir ranged from 263mg/l to 383 mg/l. The lowest concentration was observed in the month of October at site I and III while highest in the month of November at site III. In case of site II the lowest concentration of 270 mg/l was found in the same month. The average total alkalinity values of month October, November, December and January were found as 265.33, 380.33, 281.66 and 296.33 respectively.

In summer the total alkalinity of Bhavthana reservoir ranged from 168 mg/l to 250 mg/l. Minimum concentration was observed in the month of March at sites II while maximum value was recorded in the month of

April at site I and II. The highest recorded value at site III was 249.2 mg/l also found in the month of April. The lowest observed value at site I and III was 176 and 209.5 mg/l found in the month of March and February respectively. The average total alkalinity values for months of February, March, April and May were 206.52, 184.66, 249.73 and 181.5 respectively.

Total Hardness (mg/l)

Seasonal variations in total hardness at three sites in Bhavthana reservoir are presented in Table 4.19 and Table 4.20 and graphically represented in Figs.4.19 and 4.20.

Table 4.19: Monthly values of Total Hardness (mg/l) (Year 2012-2013)

Site	June	July	Aug.	Sept.	Oct.	Nov.	Dec.	Jan.	Feb.	Mar.	Apr.	May
I	149.5	150	95.8	180	113	138.2	145	98	167.4	190.5	200	210
II	149.2	152	99	164	143	139.4	141	128.2	200	198.7	204.5	220
III	151	153	110	159	112	140	138.4	128.2	167.2	192.3	168.4	225

Table 4.20: Monthly Values of Total Hardness (mg/l) (Year 2013-2014)

Site	June	July	Aug.	Sept.	Oct.	Nov.	Dec.	Jan.	Feb.	Mar.	Apr.	May
I	179.5	152	98.6	185	113	120	138.2	110	158.6	145	175.5	224
II	152.2	152	100	161.2	113	131.6	129.4	99	129.9	147.8	192.2	249
III	151.4	153	110	159	112	139.4	139.4	120	165.6	138.4	206.5	239

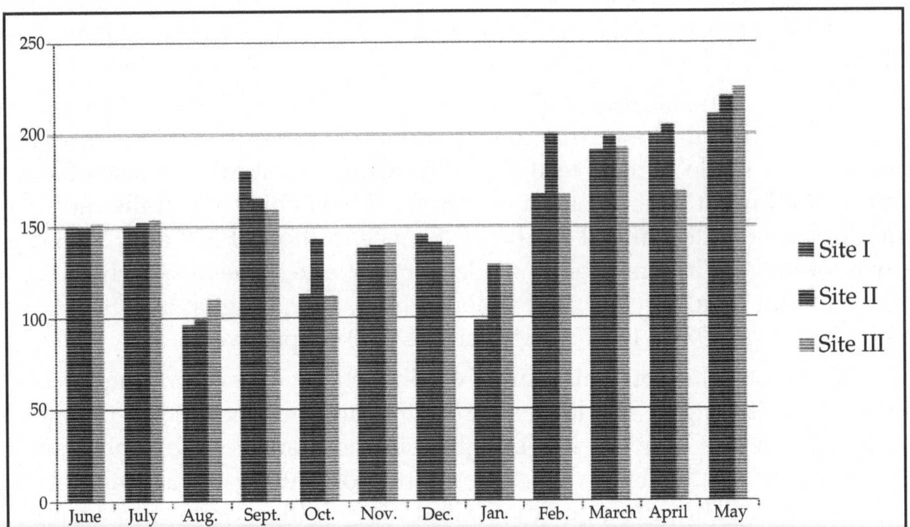

Fig. 4.19: Monthly Fluctuations of Total Hardness (mg/l) (Year 2012-2013)

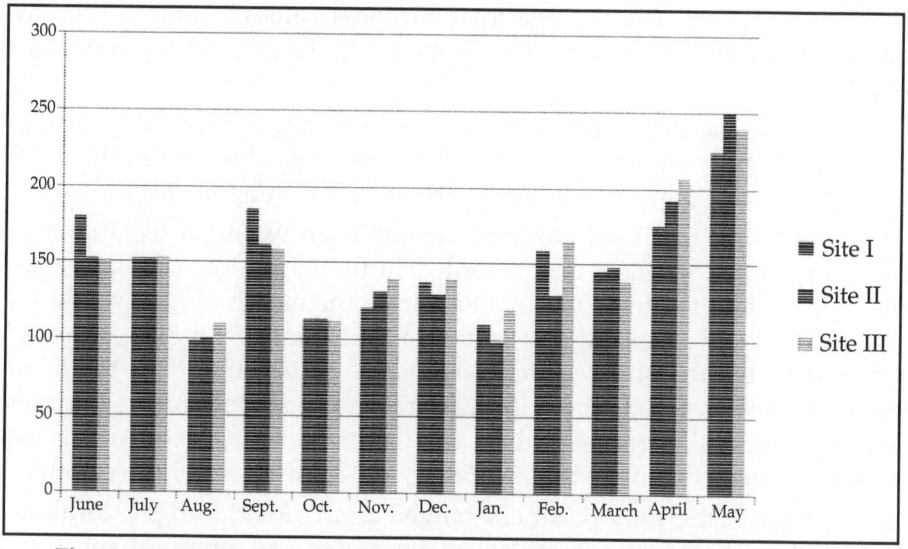

Fig. 4.20: Monthly Fluctuations of Total Hardness (mg/l) (Year 2013-2014)

The total hardness of Bhavthana reservoir ranged from 95.8mg/l to 225 mg/l during 2012-2013. The minimum total hardness was observed in the month of August at site I and maximum in the month of May at site III.

In monsoon, the total hardness ranged from 95.8 mg/l to 153 mg/l. The lowest total hardness was recorded in the month of August at site I. The highest total hardness was noted during the month of July at site III. In case of site II and III the lowest recorded value was 99 and 110 mg/l recorded in the month of August. The average total hardness values of month June, July, August and September were found as 149.9, 151.66, 101.6 and 167.66 respectively.

In winter, the total hardness ranged from 98mg/l to 145 mg/l. Its minimum value was noted in the month of January at site I and maximum in the month of December at site I. At site II and III the lowest recorded value was 128.2 and 112 mg/l found in the month of January and October respectively. In case of site II and III the highest recorded value of total hardness 143 and 140 was found in the month of October and November respectively. The average values of total hardness month October, November, December and January were found as 122.66, 139.2, 141.46 and 118.13 respectively.

In summer the total hardness ranged from 167.2 mg/l to 225 mg/l. Minimum value of total hardness was recorded in the month of February at sites III while maximum value was recorded in the month of May at site III. The highest recorded value at site I and II was 210 and 220 respectively found in the month of May. The lowest value of total hardness was observed at site I and II was 167.4 and 198.7 found in the month of February and

March respectively. The average total hardness values of month February, March, April and May were found as 178.2, 193.83, 190.96 and 218.33 respectively.

The total hardness of Bhavthana reservoir ranged from 98.6-249 mg/l during 2013-2014. The minimum total hardness was observed in the month of August at site I and maximum in the month of May at site II.

In monsoon, the total hardness ranged from 98.6mg/l to 179.5 mg/l. The lowest total hardness was recorded in the month of August at site I. The highest total hardness was noted during the month of June at site I. In case of site II and III the highest value was 161.2 and 159 mg/l respectively observed in the month of September. In case of site II and III the lowest recorded value was 100 and 110 mg/l recorded in the month of August. The average total hardness values for month of June, July, August and September were found as 161.03, 152.33, 102.86 and 168.4 respectively.

In winter, the total hardness ranged from 99-139.5 mg/l. Minimum value of total hardness was noted in the month of January at site II and maximum in the month of November and December at site III. At site I and III the lowest recorded value was 110 and 112 mg/l found in the month of January and October respectively. In case of site I and II the highest recorded value of total hardness 138.2 and 131.6 mg/l was found in the month of October and November respectively. The average total hardness values of month October, November, December and January were found as 112.66, 130.33, 135.66 and 109.66 respectively.

In summer the total hardness ranged from 129.9-249 mg/l. Minimum total hardness was recorded in the month of February at sites II while maximum value was recorded in the month of May at site II. The highest recorded value at site I and III was 224 and 239 mg/l respectively found in the month of May. The lowest total hardness observed at site I and III was 145 and 138.4mg/l respectively found in the month of March. The average total hardness values of month February, March, April and May were found as 151.36, 143.73, 191.4 and 237.33 respectively.

Chlorides (mg/l)

Monthly fluctuations in chlorides are shown in Table 4.21 and Table 4.22 and graphically represented in Figs. 4.21 and 4.22.

Table 4.21: Monthly Values of Chlorides (mg/l) (Year 2012-2013)

Site	June	July	Aug.	Sept.	Oct.	Nov.	Dec.	Jan.	Feb.	Mar.	Apr.	May
I	21.27	21.27	28.28	28.36	29.36	30.36	38.99	35.45	40.23	45.45	46.50	40.28
II	21.27	21.27	28.39	28.36	28.36	23.46	38.99	35.42	45.45	45.42	45.45	40.23
III	14.18	28.28	28.28	30.36	28.28	33.46	36.52	36.52	40.23	44.42	30.36	40.28

Table 4.22: Monthly Values of Chlorides (mg/l) (Year 2013-2014)

Site	June	July	Aug.	Sept.	Oct.	Nov.	Dec.	Jan.	Feb.	Mar.	Apr.	May
I	29.36	29.36	14.18	28.28	30.36	30.36	33.28	36.52	35.25	45.45	46.50	40.28
II	21.27	28.36	28.39	28.39	28.36	28.36	35.32	38.99	36.60	45.42	45.45	40.23
III	28.28	28.36	29.36	28.28	28.36	28.36	34.42	38.99	38.42	46.50	45.46	40.28

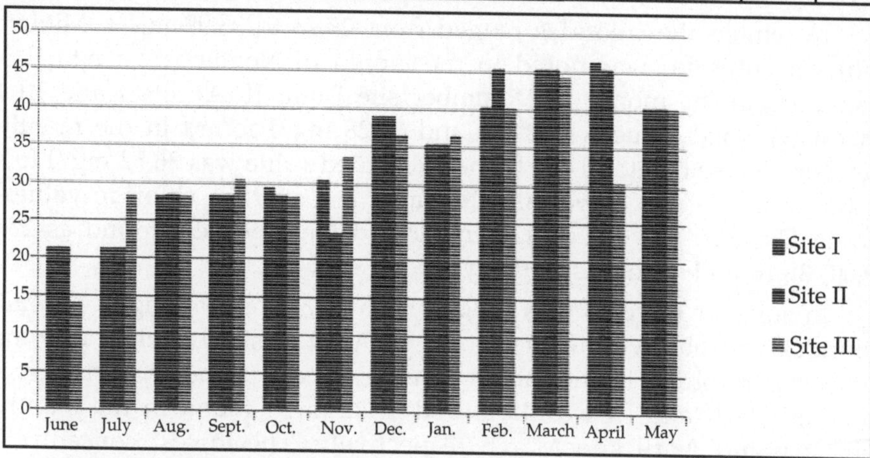

Fig. 4.21: Monthly Fluctuations of Chlorides (mg/l) (Year 2012-2013)

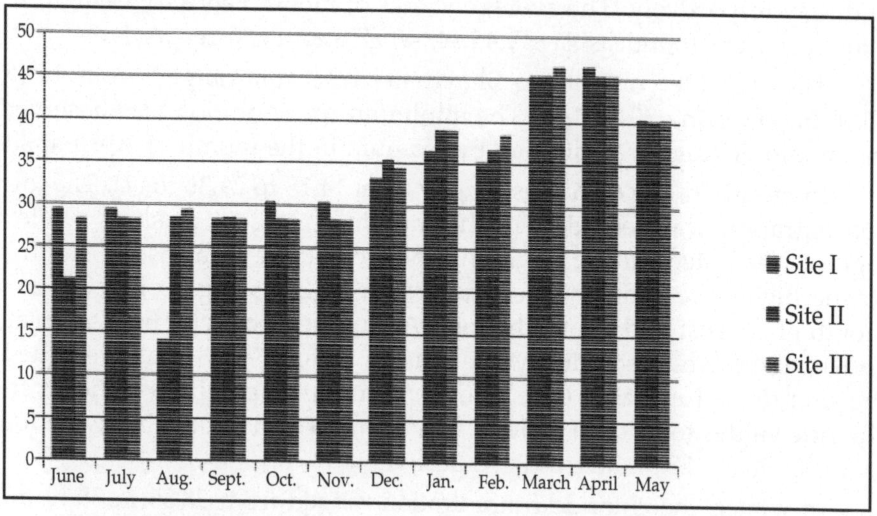

Fig. 4.22: Monthly Fluctuations of Chlorides (mg/l) (Year 2013-2014)

The chloride concentration of Bhavthana reservoir ranged from 14.18 to 46.50 mg/l during 2012-2013. The minimum concentration was observed in the month of June at site III and maximum in the month of April at site I.

In monsoon, the chlorides ranged from 14.18 to 30.36 mg/l. The lowest concentration was observed in the month of June at site III while the highest was noted during the month of September at site III. In case of site I and II the lowest recorded value was 21.27 mg/l recorded in the month of June and July. In case of site I and II the highest recorded value was 28.36 and 28.39mg/l recorded in the month of September and August respectively. The average chloride values of month June, July, August and September were found as 18.90, 23.60, 28.31 and 29.06 respectively.

In winter, the chlorides ranged from 23.46 to 38.99 mg/l. Minimum value of chlorides was noted in the month of November at site II and maximum in the month of December site I and II. At site I and III the lowest recorded value was 29.36 and 28.28 mg/l found in the month of October. In case of site III the highest recorded value was 36.52 mg/l found in the month of December and January. The average chloride values of month October, November, December and January were found as 28.66, 29.09, 38.16 and 35.79 respectively.

In summer the chlorides ranged from 30.36 to 46.50 mg/l. Minimum chlorides was observed in the month of April at site III while maximum value was recorded in the month of April at site I. The highest recorded value at site II and III was 45.45 and 44.42 mg/l found in the month of February and April and March respectively. The lowest concentration observed at site I and II was 40.23 mg/l found in the month of February and May respectively. The average values of month February, March, April and May were found as 41.97, 45.44, 40.77 and 40.26 respectively.

The chloride contents of Bhavthana reservoir ranged from 14.18 to 46.50 mg/l during 2013-2014. The minimum concentration was observed in the month of August at site I and maximum in the month of April at site I.

In monsoon, the chlorides ranged from 14.18 to 29.36 mg/l. The lowest concentration was recorded in the month of August at site I while the highest was noted during the month of June at site I. In case of site II and III the highest recorded value was 28.39 and 29.36 mg/l observed in the month of August and September and August respectively. In case of site II and III the lowest recorded value was 21.27 and 28.28 mg/l recorded in the month of June and June and September respectively. The average chloride values for month of June, July, August and September were found as 26.30, 28.69, 23.97 and 28.31respectively.

In winter, the chloride concentration ranged from 28.36 to 38.99 mg/l. Minimum value was noted in the month of October and November at site II and III while maximum in the month of January at site II and III. At site I the lowest recorded value was 30.36 mg/l found in the month of October and November. In case of site I the highest recorded value of chlorides was 36.52 mg/l found in the month of January. The average values of total hardness for October, November, December and January were 29.02, 29.02, 34.34 and 38.16 respectively.

In summer the chloride concentration was comparatively high and ranged from 35.25 to 46.50 mg/l. Minimum concentration was observed in the month of February at sites I while maximum value was recorded in the month of March and April at site III and I respectively. The highest recorded value at site II was 45.45 mg/l found in the month of April. The lowest observed value at site II and III was 36.6 and 38.42 mg/l respectively found in the month of February. The average values of month February, March, April and May were found as 36.75, 45.79, 45.80 and 40.25 respectively.

Salinity (mg/l)

Monthly values of Salinity for the study period of two years are expressed in Table 4.23 and Table 4.24 and graphically represented in Figs.4.23 and 4.24.

During 2012-2013, the salinity of Bhavthana reservoir ranged from 25.62 to 83.96 mg/l. Its minimum concentration was observed in the month of June at site III while maximum in the month of April at site I.

In monsoon the salinity of Bhavthana reservoir ranged from 25.62 to 54.82 mg/l. The lowest concentration was observed in the month of June at site III while highest in the month of September at site III. In case of site I and II the lowest concentration of 38.42 mg/l was observed in the month of June and July. In case of site I and II the highest concentration of 51.21 and 51.27 mg/l respectively was observed in the month of September and August respectively. The average salinity values for June, July, August and September were 34.15, 42.63, 51.13 and 52.41 respectively.

Table 4.23: Monthly values of Salinity (mg/l) (Year 2012-2013)

Site	June	July	Aug.	Sept.	Oct.	Nov.	Dec.	Jan.	Feb.	Mar.	Apr.	May
I	38.42	38.42	51.07	51.21	53.02	54.82	70.40	60.01	72.64	82.06	83.96	72.73
II	38.42	38.42	51.27	51.21	51.21	42.37	70.40	63.96	73.04	82.01	82.06	72.64
III	25.62	51.07	51.07	54.82	51.07	60.42	65.94	65.94	72.64	80.20	54.82	72.73

Table 4.24: Monthly Values of Salinity (mg/l) (Year 2013-2014)

Site	June	July	Aug.	Sept.	Oct.	Nov.	Dec.	Jan.	Feb.	Mar.	Apr.	May
I	53.02	53.02	25.62	51.07	54.82	54.82	60.10	65.94	63.65	82.06	83.96	72.73
II	38.42	51.21	51.27	51.27	51.21	51.21	70.40	70.40	66.09	82.01	82.06	72.64
III	51.07	51.21	53.02	51.07	51.21	51.21	62.15	70.40	69.37	83.96	82.08	72.73

In winter the salinity of Bhavthana reservoir ranged from 42.37 to 70.40 mg/l. The lowest concentration was observed in the month of November at site II while the highest concentration of salinity was also observed in the same month of December at site I and II. In case of site I and III the lowest concentration of 53.02 and 51.07 mg/l was found in the month October. In case of site III the highest concentration of 65.94 mg/l was found in the month of December and January. The average total alkalinity values of October, November, December and January were 51.76, 52.53, 68.91 and 63.30 respectively.

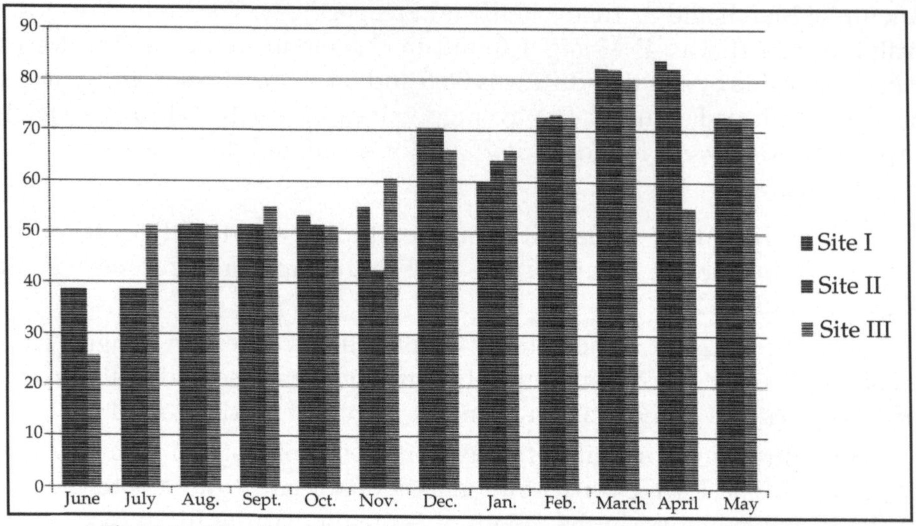

Fig. 4.23: Monthly Fluctuations of Salinity (mg/l) (Year 2012-2013)

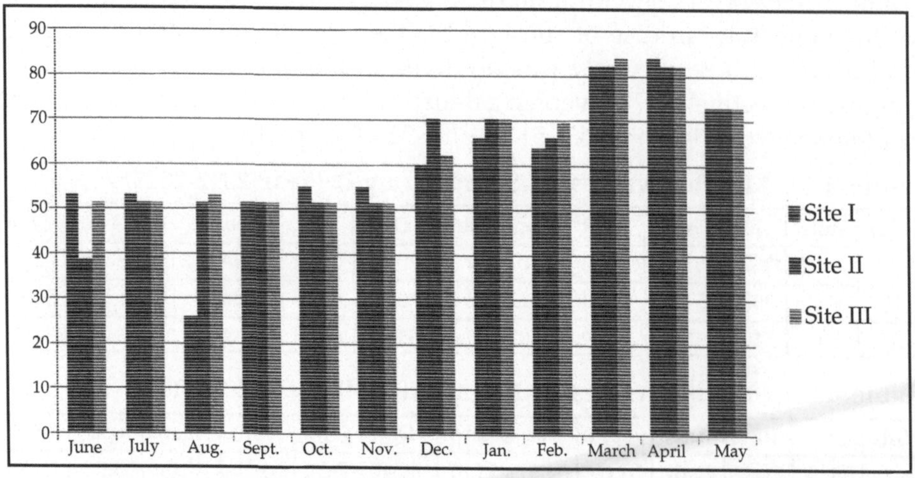

Fig. 4.24: Monthly Fluctuations of Salinity (mg/l) (Year 2013-2014)

In summer the salinity of Bhavthana reservoir ranged from 54.82 to 83.96 mg/l. Its minimum concentration was observed in the month of April at site III while maximum value was recorded at site I in the same month. The highest recorded value at site II and III was 82.06 and 80.20 mg/l found in the month of April and March respectively. The lowest observed value at site I and II was 72.64 mg/l found in the month of February and May. The average salinity values of month February, March, April and May were 72.77, 81.42, 73.61 and 72.70 respectively.

During 2013-2014, the salinity of Bhavthana reservoir ranged from 25.62 to 83.96 mg/l. Its minimum concentration was observed in the month of August at site I while maximum in the month of April at site I.

In monsoon the salinity of Bhavthana reservoir ranged from 25.62 to 53.02 mg/l. The lowest concentration was observed in the month of August at site I while highest in the month of June, July at site I and August at site III. In case of site II and III the lowest concentration of 38.42 and 51.07 mg/l was observed in the month of June and June and September respectively. In case of site II the highest concentration of 51.27 mg/l was observed in the month of August and September respectively. The average salinity values for month of June, July, August and September were 47.50, 51.81, 43.30 and 51.13 respectively.

In winter the salinity of Bhavthana reservoir ranged from 51.21 to 70.40 mg/l. The lowest concentration was observed in the month of October and November at site II and III while highest in the month of December and January at site II and III respectively. In case of site I the lowest concentration of 54.82 mg/l was recorded in the months of October and November respectively. In case of site I the highest concentration of 65.94 mg/l was found in the month of January. The average salinity values of month October, November, December and January were found as 52.41, 52.41, 64.21 and 68.91 respectively.

In summer the salinity of Bhavthana reservoir ranged from 63.65 to 83.96 mg/l. Its minimum concentration was observed in the month of February at site I while maximum value was recorded in the month of April at site I and March at site III. The highest recorded value at site II was 82.06 mg/l found in the month of April. The lowest observed value at site II and III was 66.09 and 69.37 mg/l respectively recorded in the months of February. The average salinity values for February, March, April and May were 66.37, 82.67, 82.7 and 72.7 respectively.

DISCUSSION

Temperature is one of the key factors that accelerate the rate of physical, chemical and biological reactions in an ecosystem. The atmospheric temperature and water temperature have direct impact on the aquatic life as well as they influence the rate of evaporation, relative humidity and wind speed and direction. In the entire study period, the atmospheric temperature ranged from 29 to 41°C. Rowland (1986) stated that many aquaculture species can survive over a wide range of temperatures but will better grow only at a specific temperature range. Small reservoirs react quickly with the change in the atmospheric temperature. High summer temperature and bright sunshine accelerate the process of decay of organic matter resulting into liberation of large quantities of carbon dioxide and nutrients. In tropical countries a direct relationship between the duration of bright sunshine and temperature has been observed. During year 2012-13, the average values at sampling sites I, II, and III were 34.16, 30.72 and 33.58 respectively. During 2013-2014 the atmospheric temperature ranged from 28 to 41°C and the average values of the three sampling sites I, II, and III were 34.33°C,34.16 °C and 33.75°C respectively.

During first year of investigation (2012-2013), the atmospheric temperature ranged from 29 to 39 °C at site I. The minimum value was recorded during the month of August while maximum during the month of May. At the site II, the minimum value (29 °C) was recorded during the month of July while maximum (40 °C) during the month of May. At the site III the minimum value (29 °C) was recorded during two months July and August while maximum (38 °C) during the months of February and March.

During second year of study (2013-2014) temperature ranged from 29 to 41°C. Minimum value of temperature was recorded in the month of August (29°C), July (29°C) and July (28°C) at site I, II and III respectively. The maximum value of temperature was recorded in the month of May at site I (41°C) and II (40°C). At site III highest value (40°C) was recorded in the months of March and April.

Temperature has its prominent effect on oxygen utilization of fish. Rate of metabolic activities increases continuously with the increase in temperature till the attainment of lethal temperature limit. Each species displays its own characteristic rate of increase at a given range of temperature. The fluctuations in water temperature as compared to the atmospheric temperature are less as water takes more time to heat. Water has several unique properties that influence temperature like high specific heat, high latent heat of fusion and highest known latent heat of evaporation.

The water temperature of Bhavthana reservoir ranged from 22 to 38°C during the entire study period with average values of 29.41, 30.25 and 30.16 and 28.72, 28.27 and 28.45°C at site I, II and III during 2012-2013 and 2013-2014 respectively.

During first year of study the water temperature ranged from 22-38°C. The lowest value was recorded in the month of December, January (24°C), December (22°C) and January (25°C) at site I, II and III respectively. The highest values was recorded in the month of May at site I (38°C), II (36°C) and III (37°C).

During second year of study the water temperature ranged from 22 to 37°C. The lowest value was recorded in the month of December (22°C), July (23°C) and November (23°C) at site I, II and III respectively. The highest value was recorded in the month of May at site I (36°C), II (37°C) and III (37°C).

Transparency is a physical variable significant to production. Water sample in general was clear, less turbid and transparent. Transparency of water depends on various factors like dissolved soil particles, pollutants, depth of water body, wind flow and sources of water from where the water merges into water body etc. Transparency is an optical property of water that affects the penetration of sun light affecting the process of photosynthesis which ultimately imbalances the food chain in that corresponding ecosystem. Highly turbid water can act as a catastrophe in free fish movements leading to collisions and injuries.

The transparency of Bhavthana reservoir ranged from 57-130 cm during the entire study period with average values of 94.58, 93.25 and 92.79 and 92.79, 95.1 and 95.91 at site I, II and III during 2012-2013 and 2013-14 respectively.

Water transparency variation followed the seasonal pattern of change being less transparent during monsoon as compared to winter and summer. High values of transparency were noted during summer. Similar views were also expressed by Sakhare (2007) and Singh *et.al.* (1993).

pH is one of the expression of production and growth of algae and macrophytes, and depends upon ionic composition of water and buffering capacity of lake (Shardendu and Ambsht, 1990). The variation of pH is often linked with the species composition and life processes of animal and plant communities inhabiting them. According to Hutchinson (1967) pH is dependent on the concentration of hydrogen ions and an array of dissolved organic compounds which form carbo-amino carboxylic acid complexes.

Klein (1973) have pointed out that the pH values below 5.0 and above 8.8 are detrimental. In the present investigation the pH varied between 7.6 and 8.7.Thus, the reservoir water was alkaline throughout the investigation period.

Many workers have reported that most of the small confined waters are alkaline in nature, particularly from India (Sahi and Sinha 1969; Verma 1969; Sharma and Jain 2000 and Sakhare 2007, 2012).According to Swingle (1967) the pH value range of 6 to 9 is appropriate for pond fish culture while more than 9 are unsuitable. Thus, the pH of Bhavthana reservoir is appropriate for fish culture.

According to Tyagi and Mehra (1990), high TDS are one of the major sources of sediments which reduce the penetration of light in to water and decrease the rate of photosynthesis and finally reduces the dissolved oxygen level of waste water which results in decreased purification of waste water by micro-organisms. Further, Rajkumar (1984) and Balakrista Reddy (1989) are of the opinion that the polluted water bodies contain more of total dissolved solids when compared to unpolluted water.

Total dissolved solids in Bhavthana reservoir ranged from 120-260 mg/l with average values 174.23, 178.49 and 188.6 during 2012-2013 at site I, II and III respectively and 192.65 (site I), 195.98 (site II) and 193.46 (site III) during 2013-2014.

The lowest value (120) at site I was found in the months of June, July April and September. At site II the lowest values were found in the months of September (120.2) while at site III it was observed in the month of June (150), during the first year of study. The highest values of TDS were found to be 260, 210.5 and 250 at site I, II and III in the months of March, July and March respectively, during first year of study.

In case of second year of study the lowest values were recorded in the month of June (160), July (170) and November (168.8) at site I, II and III respectively. The highest value of TDS was found to be 250, 260 and 250 at site I, II and III in the month of February at all the three sites.

Total dissolved solids recorded during the present investigation fall under the range between 120 and 260 mg/l. Total dissolved solids reached its maximum in summer season and the minimum value during monsoon season. Kiran and Puttaiah (2010) recorded higher amounts of total dissolved solids in summer season. In the present investigation maximum value of total dissolved solids was during summer season. Therefore, the present observation are an essential agreement with that of the above researchers.

Dissolved oxygen finds a place of paramount importance in the study of aquatic environment in view of its important participation in many chemical and biological reactions. At normal atmospheric pressure water contains about 12.7 mg/l of oxygen at 5°C but 9.14 mg/l at 20°C (Mukherjee, 1996). However, the concentration is considerably modified by the biota. The concentration of oxygen present at various depths determines the type of organisms that can live.

The main sources of dissolved oxygen in water are the atmosphere, and by photosynthetic activity of aquatic plants. Atmospheric oxygen enters the aquatic system by direct diffusion at the surface, and through the various forms of surface water agitations, viz. wave action, waterfalls and turbulences due to obstructions. Aquatic chlorophyll bearing plants release oxygen as a byproduct of photosynthesis, which gets distributed into the different layers of lake water by movements. In most lakes the phytoplankton contributes to bulk of oxygen supply because of the huge amounts of chlorophyll of algae in epilimnion zone. In shallow waters like ponds and swamps the limnetic phototrophs may be overshadowed by littoral macrophytes, attached algae, and the benthic algal mass. In the rivulets and brooks the periphyton algae amount for most of the production of oxygen (Munshi and Munshi, 1995).

The concentration of oxygen, in an aquatic ecosystem is a function of biological processes such as photosynthesis and respiration and physical processes such as water movement and temperature (Munshi and Munshi, 1995).

The amount of oxygen in a lake or pond depends on the extent of contact between water and air, on the circulation of water and on the amounts produced and consumed by the lake community (Mukherjee, 1996). The oxygen available in standing waters at a given point of time depends on the balance between the two processes, production and consumption, and ideally these processes should be in dynamic equilibrium. However, in aquatic ecosystems having an abundant quantity of phytoplankton and submerged weeds, there may be a marked diurnal fluctuation in the oxygen concentration, and severe oxygen deficiency may result at night.

Oxygen is an unavoidable element to all forms of life and declined values can be a cause of mortality or physical weakness of some sensitive organisms. The production of dissolved oxygen in an ecosystem should not be less than its consumption. Amount of dissolved oxygen in a stagnant water body is always less than in a running water channel or a river; as the flowing water dissolves more atmospheric oxygen. Cold-blooded animals like fishes utilize more oxygen at higher temperatures as their metabolic rates are increased. Adequate amount of dissolved oxygen is necessary to maintain quality of water. If dissolved oxygen levels in water drop below 5.0 mg/l, aquatic life is put under stress and further decrease in this value for a longer period can be a cause of death of fishes.

Dissolved oxygen in Bhavthana reservoir ranged from 5-12.2 mg/l during entire period of study and low values were observed during premonsoon months which corroborate with the findings of Madhu *et.al.,* (2007).

Navatha *et.al.* (2013) observed dissolved oxygen in the range of 5.2-8 mg/l and the highest value was observed during winter which supports the present findings. High values of dissolved oxygen during all the seasons are the indication of unstressed aquatic environment.

Only 0.035% volume of free CO_2 is present in atmosphere which is very meager. Chief sources of free CO_2 in atmosphere are the combustion of coal, respiration of living organisms and decomposition of living matter. It is an elementary requirement of process of photosynthesis for green plants. The atmospheric carbon dioxide mixes with the water when it comes in contact with the water surface, as it is readily soluble in water. As the partial pressure of carbon dioxide in air is low, the amount which remains in solution in water at a given temperature is also low. Carbon dioxide is added in water as a byproduct of decomposing organic matter which is a common phenomenon in natural waters. Respiratory processes produce and release large quantities of carbon dioxide into the water. The quantities so found are governed by the magnitude of aquatic flora and fauna, the relative size of the individual organism and those factors which determine the rate of respiration (Munshi and Munshi, 1995).

In case of aquatic animals its concentration must be kept in check to avoid stressful conditions. Increased concentration of CO_2 for a longer period can be a cause of fish mortality. In aquatic ecosystem as the rate of photosynthesis increases there is decrease in concentration of CO_2.

The concentration of CO_2 was observed to be 0.2 and 0.3 mg/l at site II and III during 2012-2013 and 2013-14 respectively. The free CO_2 was absent at all sites in all months during the entire study period.

The phenolphthalein alkalinity of Bhavthana reservoir ranged from 25.4 to 42 mg/l during the entire study period with average values of 32.6, 32.66 and 33.41 and 33, 33.18 and 33.52 at site I, II and III during 2012-2013 and 2013-14 respectively.

During 2012-2013 the lowest value of phenolphthalein alkalinity was recorded in the month of February (28.4 mg/l), February and March (28 mg/l) and March (27.9 mg/l) at site I, II and III respectively. The highest value was found during the month of October (40mg/l), September (40.1mg/l) and September (41.5mg/l) at site I, II and III respectively.

During 2013-2014 the lowest value of Phenolphthalein Alkalinity was recorded in the month of February (25.4 mg/l), February (25.6 mg/l) and January (26.6 mg/l) at site I, II and III respectively. The highest value was found during the month of October (42 mg/l), September (41.5 mg/l) and September (42 mg/l) at site I, II and III respectively.

Alkalinity values in natural waters depend upon the location, season, plankton population and nature of bottom deposits. Water in heavy-rainfall areas, and infested with submerged weeds usually have low total alkalinity values. However, stagnant waters in tropical plains, in low-rainfall areas are likely to have a high total alkalinity during the summer season.

Many workers (Krishnaram *et.al.* 2012; Vasanthkumar and Vijaykumar 2012, Sakhare and Jetithor 2009) have discussed the seasonal fluctuations in the total alkalinity of various water bodies.

The total alkalinity in Bhavthana reservoir ranged from 162 to 383 mg/l. Waters having 40 mg/l or more total alkalinities are considered to be more productive than waters of low alkalinities (Moyle,1945).During the present investigation the total alkalinity was more than 40 mg/l, indicating that the reservoir water is productive.

The role of alkalinity in the determination of productivity of aquatic environment has been described by Phillipose (1959). According to some authors waters with low alkalinity are comparatively low in production. According to Northcote and Larkin (1956), the total alkalinity of 50 mg/l is an indication of high productivity.

Highest concentration of total alkalinity was observed in winter months which is in accordance with the findings of Sakhare (2007, 2010, 2012) and Sakhare and Jetithor (2009). Vaishnav and Dewanagan (2013) observed the total alkalinity in the range of 241 to 847 mg/l.

Hardness is the total amount of soluble calcium and magnesium salts present in the water and is expressed as its calcium carbonate equivalent. Total hardness also includes the sulphates and chlorides of calcium and magnesium. Bicarbonates form temporary hardness, while sulphates and chlorides cause permanent hardness (Mukherjee,1996).

As reported by Alderice (1988) aquatic animals can survive in a variable range of total hardness but lower hardness especially low concentration of calcium has unfavorable effects on aquatic life; as environmental calcium is necessary for calcification of larval skeletal structures, embryonic development and for membrane permeability.

Most inland surface waters have total hardness values in the range from less than 5 to 200 mg/l as $CaCO_3$ but values more than 200mg/l are also found frequently in arid regions with high deposits of relatively soluble chloride and sulfate salts of calcium and magnesium (Boyd and Tucker 2009).

Total hardness of Bhavthana reservoir ranged from 98.5-249 mg/l. If the two yearly averages are taken into consideration, maximum hardness was observed in summer season. A similar observation has also been made by Navatha *et.al.* (2013), Kiran and Puttaiah (2010).

Chloride contents in the reservoir water was found highest during summer and lowest during monsoon season. The higher values of chloride during summer months may be due to the low level of reservoir water. Mishra and Yadav (1978), Tripathi and Pandey 1990 and Pandy *et.al.* (1995) also reported increased values of chloride in summer and have correlated this gradual decrease in the amount of water. Moreover, the increase in amount of excreta laid by the different aquatic fauna may also account for the increased value of chloride during summer.

The chloride concentration of Bhavthana reservoir ranged from 14.18 to 46.50 mg/l. Trivedy (1993) observed the chlorides in Dhom reservoir of Maharashtra in the range of 3.52 to 71 mg/l.

The Salinity of inland surface waters range from less than 0.01ppt to over 200 ppt (Boyd and Tucker 2009). The salinity of Bhavthana reservoir ranged from 25.62 to 83.96 mg/l in year 2012-13 and 25.62 to 83.96 mg/l in year 2013-14.

5

Plankton Diversity of Bhavthana Reservoir

INTRODUCTION

The term 'plankton' has been variously defined by many authors. Hensen (1887) originally defined the term as denoting all that floats in water. Kolkwitz (1912) defined the term as the natural community of those organisms that are normally living in water and are passively carried along by water currents. Rylov (1922) used the terms 'obligoplankton', referring to true planktons only, and 'facultative planktons', referring to those forms found in both limnetic and littoral zones. A common definition includes those forms with little or no resistance to currents, living a free-floating or suspended existence in open or pelagic waters, Wesenberg-Lund (1908), Smith (1920) and Krieger (1927) all have attempted to classify plankton in terms of plankton constituents and relations to the habitats.Griffith (1923) classified plankton algae in terms of the ecological features prevalent in the habitat. Such attempts have arisen some terms as "rheoplankton" (river), "benthoplankton" (shallow pond), "limnoplankton" (deep pond), "heleoplankton" (pond), and many others, all describing the plankton on the basis of habitats.

Plankton includes very small organisms which float on the water surface and drift at the mercy of water currents. Those of plant origin are called phytoplankton, the producers belonging to first trophic level while those of animal origin are the zooplankton which are the primary consumers belonging to second trophic level. Phytoplanktons are economically significant as they trap radient energy of sunlight and convert into chemical energy. Many herbivores, mostly zooplanktons graze upon the phytoplankton; thus passing the stored energy to its subsequent trophic levels. The role of phytoplankton in energy budgets of aquatic ecosystems and their importance in establishing their steps is well known.

The density of plankton in a water body determines the stocking rate of fishes because they are the chief source of food of many economically important fishes. Plankton, due to its key role in ecosystem of the environment, is directly related to the fish catch potential of a reservoir.

An insight into the distribution, composition and succession of plankton gives valuable clue for determining the fishing grounds selection of suitable species for stocking and determining the level of utilization of the available food by the existing fish stock (Sakhare, 2009)

Phytoplankton constitutes the basis of nutrient cycle of an aquatic ecosystem. They play a key role in maintaining proper equilibrium between abiotic and biotic component of aquatic ecosystem. Phytoplanktons have been regarded as the chief primary producers of the aquatic ecosystem. The density of Phytoplanktons is affected by the water quality (Bilgrami and Dutta Munshi 1985). Rainfall and high turbidity produced by high wind velocity during rainy season has a direct bearing on phytoplankton population redicing them to minimum numbers (Pandey *et.al.* 1995).

The phytoplankton is consisting of micro and macroscopic suspended or free floating non-motile or weekly motile unicellular, colonial or filamentous algae. The majorities of phytoplanktons are non-motile and are therefore at the mercy of water turbulence within the upper water mass. However, few motile phytoplanktons are unable to swim against water current.

The phytoplankton drift in a medium which is either a dilute or concentrated solution of inorganic and organic particulate, colloidal and dissolved matter derived either from drainage or from secretion, excretion and death of organisms in the water (Agarwal, 1999).

Generally, the morphology of freshwater phytoplankton is more or less similar to that of marine phytoplankton; no species is common to the two habitats, except that same oceanic species may occur in same inland saline lakes. Phytoplanktons fix solar energy and convert it into chemical energy which is transferred from one level to another level of the food chain. By photosynthetic activity phytoplankton re-oxygenate the water in which they are growing (Venkateswarlu, 2006).

Phytoplanktons respond actively to environmental changes and are considered good indicators of water quality and trophic conditions because of their short generation time and fast population renewal (Thakur *et.al.* 2013). They have a short life span and responds quickly to environmental changes (Zebek, 2004).

Phytoplanktons gain their importance as native potential source of protein and also the means of controlling pollution in aquatic ecosystems. Phytoplanktons of the freshwater habitats such as green algae, blue green algae, diatoms, euglenoids, desmids etc. are the important among the aquatic flora. They are ecologically important as they occupy the most important position in aquatic food chain and a prominent role in the environment dynamics of aquatic system.

Few lakes have low diversity of phytoplankton due to nutrient concentration, while some explanations for high diversity are based on the fact that interaction in the planktonic environment is highly complex. Diversity can be measured by recording the number of species by describing their relative abundance or by using a measure which combines the two components. Diversity measures are very useful in lake ecosystems where large number of phytoplankton appear.

The dominant planktons and their seasonality are highly variable in different water bodies depending on their nutrient status, age, morphometry, and other locational factors. Hence planktons have been used as an indicator of a lake's trophic state (Sampaio *et.al.* 2002).

The density of phytoplankton determines the stocking rate of fishes because they are the chief source of food of many economically important culturable fishes.

Chlorophyceae, also known as 'green algae' have mostly three categories of organization i.e; unicellular, colonial and filamentous. They exhibit motile and non-motile representatives exhibiting a great range in cell size and morphology. The planktonic members of chlorophyceae exhibit a widespread distribution in terms of latitudes, but different ecotypes may occur in different geographical regions. Green algae are characteristic component of phytoplanktons in lakes or ponds of relatively high nutrient status during periods of stable thermal stratification. Amylase and amyloprotein is the major food reserve. Flagella, when present; are two (rarely four), equal, smooth and apically inserted. Only male gamets flagellated.

Cyanophyceae, also known as 'blue green algae' exist either in the form of single coccoid cells or as filaments. The planktonic members of cyanophyceae resemble the bacteria in lacking organized nuclei, mitochondria, chloroplast etc and in manner of cell division by constriction. They undergo rapid rate of vegetative reproduction either by cell division, homogonia or a kinete formation and have no sexual reproduction and flagella. Some members of cynophyaceae have the habit of floating high in the water column and can withstand extensive exposure to high photosynthetically active radiation accompanying ultraviolet radiation striking the surface they inhabit.

The members of cyanophyceae are often sole inhabitants of extremely nitrogen-deficient waters. It is because of the ability of certain members of biologically fix atmospheric nitrogen into ammonium by means of an oxygen sensitive enzyme complex nitrogenose.

Some members also revealed a high degree of tolerance or a favourable growth response to excessive nutrient or pollutants loading. A large number of blue-green algae shows a negative growth response to acidic conditions and have a distinct preference for neutral to alkaline conditions and are rapidly replaced by chrysophytes and chlorophytes under acidic conditions. Some blue-green algae like *Microcystis aeruginosa* and *Nodularia spumigena* produce metabolites or decay products which are toxic and can cause painful gastro-intestinal upset, vomiting or fever in animals that drink water from lakes containing their dense algal bloom.

Bacillariophyceae members commonly known as 'diatoms' are a popular tool for monitoring environmental conditions of aquatic ecosystem. They are represented by 200 genera (Bold and Wynne, 1978) and 6000 species (Chapman and Chapman, 1973). Diatoms reproduce vegetatively by cell-division and sexually by producing auxospores. Some of the common freshwater planktonic diatoms are *Fragilaria, Cyclotella, Tabellaria, Melosira* etc. Most of the diatoms prefer eutrophic waters (Agarwal, 1999). The diatom blooms in temperate waters during spring and autumn season are mainly due to availability of more silicon at that time due to water over turn. The major pigments of diatoms are chlorophyll a, chlorophyll c, β-carotene, fucoxanthin, diatoxanthin and diadinoxanthin. They are uninucleate and possess heavily silicified walls with ornamentation. The male gametes are flagellated and each possesses a single hairy flagellum.

An appreciable research work has been done in India on qualitative and quantitative analysis of phytoplankton diversity (Singh 1960; Goel *et.al.*, 1968, Hosmani and Bharti 1980; Goel *et.al.* 1986, Singh and Sahai 1986, Singh *et.al.* 1987, Singh and Mahajan 1987; Khatri 1987a, Khatri 1987b, Doddagoudar 1989, Kulshreshta *et.al.* 1989, Shukla *et.al.* 1989; Singh and Ahmed 1990; Anjana *et.al.*1998; Bahura 2001, Somani and Pejaver 2003, Pulla Reddy 2004, Mahajan and Nandan 2004, Bankar *et.al.* 2005; Nandan and Jain 2005, Kavitha *et.al.* 2005; Nafeesa Begum and Narayana 2006, Tiwari and Chauhan 2006, Balasingh and Shamal 2007, Anitha Devi and Singara Charya 2007; Chaudary and Lakhpat 2007, Sivakumar and Karuppasamy 2008; Murugan 2008; Hafsa and Gupta 2009, Laskar and Gupta 2009; Hulyal and Kaliwal 2009, Leela *et.al.* 2010; Shanker 2010, Siddamallayya and Pratima Mathad 2010, Ajayan and Naik 2011, Nafeesa *et.al.* 2011a, Nafeesa *et.al.* 2011b, Sayeswara *et.al.* 2011, Verma *et.al.* 2012; Patil and Sahu 2012, Karennawar and Khabade 2013; Shrirame *et.al.* 2014, Motlagh *et.al.* 2014a, Motlagh *et.al.* 2014b).

Zooplanktons play a significant role in determining the productivity of aquatic ecosystem and form food for many aquatic organisms which in turn are good sources of food for water birds. Zooplanktons are ecologically and economically important heterogeneous group of tiny aquatic organisms that can move at the mercy of water currents, as they have weak power of locomotion. They are either herbivores, feeding on phytoplankton or carnivores feeding on other zooplankton. Zooplankton is the intermediate link between phytoplankton and fish. Zooplankton assume a great ecological significance in aquatic ecosystem as they play vital role in food web, nutrient recycling, and in transfer of organic matter from primary producers to secondary consumers like fishes. The zooplanktons determine the quantum of fish stock. The failure of fishery resources is mainly attributed mostly to the reduced zooplankton population. Hence zooplankton communities, based on their quality and species diversity, are used for assessing the productivity, fishery resource, fertility and health status of the ecosystem. The productivity of aquatic environment is directly correlated with the density of zooplankton.

The diversity of zooplankton of country is considerably rich as compared to world fauna (Khan, 2003). As per a rough estimate, the rotifera (330 species),cladocera (110 species) and copepoda (88 species) of the country, comprise nearly 13.20%, 25.88% and 17.60% respectively of the world fauna.

The zooplankton study has been a fascinating subject for a long time. Enough literature exists on the zooplankton diversity of various water bodies in India (Singh 1986, Bhati and Rana 1987, Khan 1987, Verma and Dutta Munshi 1987, Chauhan 1988, Saha and Pandit 1988, Birasal *et.al.* 1989, Ghosh and George 1989, Mishra and Saksena 1990, Chauhan 1993, Siddiqui and Chandrasekhar 1993, Sinha and Sinha 1993, Kaushik and Sharma 1994, Pandey *et.al.* 1994, Bais and Agarwal 1995, Singh and Sinha 1995, Chandrasekhar 1996, Chandrasekhar and Kodarkar 1997, Selvaraj *et.al.* 1997, Choudhary and Singh 1999, Choudhary and Singh 2000, Sarma 2000, Singh 2000, Mishra and Saxena 2002, Prakash *et.al.* 2002, Sinha and Islam 2002, Das and Srivastava 2003, Maruthanayagam *et.al.* 2003, Pathak and Mudgal 2004, Sheeba *et.al.* 2004, Sukand and Patil 2004, Angedi *et.al.* 2005, Khare 2005, Mishra 2005, Sharma 2005, Chandrasekhar 2006, Bhagat and Meshram 2007, Kiran *et.al.* 2007, Bhandarkar and Gaupale 2008, Kudari and Kanamadi 2008, Sing and Saxena 2008, Chattopadhyay and Barik 2009, Majagi, and Vijaykumar 2009, Rajashekar *et.al.* 2009, Bennamma and Yamakanamardi 2010, Rajasekhar *et.al.* 2010 Rawat and Sharma 2010, Deenadayalamoorthy and Sultana 2011, Purushothama *et.al.* 2011, Jalizadeh and Yamakanamardi 2012, Sharma and Singh 2012, Chouhan and Kanhere 2013, Sharma and Pachuau 2013, Srivastava 2013, Lata *et.al.* 2014, Sayeswara *et.al.* 2014 *etc*). Such studies from Maharashtra have been very recently initiated and the only contributions on this aspect are those of CIFRI 1997, Charjan *et.al.* 2001, Deshmukh 2001, Sakhare and Joshi (2002, 2006), Pawar *et.al.* 2003, Pulle and Khan 2003, Lendhe and Yeragi 2004, Somani and Pejavar 2004, Pawar and Pulle 2005, Bhagat and Meshram 2007, Sakhare 2007, Bhandarkar and Gaupale 2008, Sakhare 2008, Mohite 2010, Dhembare 2011, Joshi 2011, Bhadane 2012a, Goswami and Mankodi 2012, Manjare and Muley 2012 Manjare *et.al.* 2012, Sakhare 2012 a, 2012b, Patil 2013, Malthane 2013, Khabade *et.al.* 2014, Shrirame *et.al.* 2014 etc).

The cladocerans, commonly known as "waterfleas" form a primitive group of microcrustaceans. They play an important role in the aquatic food chain and also contribute to zooplankton dynamics and secondary productivity in freshwater ecosystems.

The order cladocera belongs to the subclass Branchiopoda and includes minute crustaceans generally in the size range of 0.02 to 5.0mm. This order has 11 families and is known to contain about 400 species distributed throughout the world. Cladocerans are mostly to be found in freshwater habitats, although eight species belonging to the three genera i.e; Penilia, Evadne and Podon are known to be truly marine. These microcrustaceans usually inhabit every type of habitat in the littoral, limnetic or benthic zones of freshwater ecosystems. However, they are known to be generally intolerant to high salt concentrations in the medium, though there are species that frequently occur in brackish water habitat. Most species are transparent especially those which inhabit the open waters, while others found among the weed beds of the littoral and benthic zones are darkly pigmented with shades of yellow, brown or red.

The order cladocera belongs to subclass branchiopoda of class crustacea and constitutes substantially the planktonic composition of any freshwater body. They occur in almost all types of fresh waters. They are characterized by a distinct head and body covered by a fold of cuticle, which extends backwards and downwards from the dorsal side of the head and constitutes the carapace, which has a general bivalve appearance but is actually a single folded piece that gaps ventrally. The shape of the shell differs considerably from species to species. In lateral view it may be oval, circular, elongated or angular. The body generally has surface reticulations, striations and other types of markings.

Cladocerans form a primitive group of microcrustaceans. They play an important role in the aquatic food chain and also contribute to zooplankton dynamics and secondary productivity in freshwater ecosystems.

Cladocera are a crucial group among zooplankton and form the most useful and nutritive group of crustaceans for higher members of fishes in the foodchain. Cladocerans are highly sensitive against even low concentration of pollutants. The two large second antinae are responsible for giving the cladoceran their common name.

Of the 11 families listed under the order Cladocera, nine are known from Indian waters (Michael and Sharma, 1988). The order Cladocera belongs to subclass Branchiopoda of class Crustacea and constitutes substantially the planktonic composition of any freshwater body. They occur in almost all types of fresh waters. They are characterized by a distinct head and body covered by a fold of cuticle, which extends backwards and downwards from the dorsal side of the head and constitutes the carapace, which has a general, bivalve appearance but is actually a single folded piece that gaps ventrally. The shape of the shell differs considerably from species to species. In lateral view it may be oval, circular, elongated or angular. The body generally has surface reticulations, striations and other types of markings.

A review of the literature revealed a good amount of work on cladocera in different parts of India (Biswas, 1966, 1971, Nayer, 1971, Murugan 1975, Patil 1976, Sharma, 1978, Battish, 1981, 1983, 1992, Rane 1983, Raghunathan 1983, Sharma and Michael 1983, Sharma *et.al.* 1984, Michael and Sharma, 1988, Murugan, 1989, Raghunathan 1989, Singh *et.al.* 1993, Kumar and Dutta 1994, Rao and Choubay 1993, Chandrasekhar, 1995, 1996, 2006, Murugan *et.al.* 1998, Venkataraman, 1999, Khan 2003, Shivakumar and Altaff 2004, Mishra, 2005, Sharma *et.al.* 2005, Sharma and Sharma 2008, Jalizadeh and Yamakana 2012, Sharma *et.al.* 2012, Shinde, 2012., Shinde *et.al.* 2014 etc).

Rotifers are called as "rotatoria" or "wheel animalcules". They constitute an important component in the aquatic food chain and are also regarded as valuable indicators of trophic status of their environments. These organisms have specialized organ systems. They are more important in freshwater ecosystems because of their occurrence in practically all biotopes, but they are not homely in marine or brackish waters. Rotifers also occur in decomposing vegetable debris, inn mosses and in soil. A few species are reported to be parasitic on some colonial or filamentous algae and aquatic worms. A few species are known to be commensels or having synoecious association with freshwater cladocerans, prawns and insect larvae. The phylum rotifera consists of approximately 2030 described species (Segers, 2007).

Indian rotifer fauna attracted good attention during the latter half of the 20th century. Though the number of species reported is 300 and more, some genera and species requires further investigations (Dhanapathi, 2000).

Rotifers are morphologically well adapted to the aquatic habitats and acquired different characteristics suitable to different biotopes they inhabit. The body of a typical rotifer consists of head, trunk and foot. The head bears the rotator organ or the wheel organ called 'carona', mouth and sense organs. In some species the bodies are covered by tough structure called lorica. Such forms are generally known as loricate forms. Other forms which do not have lorica, but soft, thin and transparent skin are known as illoricate froms.

Ostracods are shrimp-like crustaceans that are sensitive to changes in the water quality and are regarded as valuable bio-indicators therefore they are used in investigation of water quality. Their community structure not only allows estimating of the level of pollution, but also indicates the trend of general conditions over time. If changes in species diversity and population abundances result from either direct or indirect environmental stressors, then the changes in biota may be used to elucidate changes in the environment. Ostracods may be excellent organisms to use as indicators of water quality, but such an idea requires detailed knowledge about their ecology, distribution, biology and habitat requirements.

The ostracods shells are also used for geochemical analysis such as ostracod chemistry that reveals trace elements of Mg and Sr uptake. Oxygen and carbon isotope analysis is done on ostracods shells in lacustrine settings which provide a carbonate shell in an environment where other carbonate fossils are largely absent. In temperate deep lakes benthic ostracod shell chemistry is related to the isotopic water composition. In marginal marine settings ostracod shell chemistry is related to salinities. In the deep ocean, Mg in the benthic ostracod shells is related to ocean bottom water temperatures (Holmes and Chivas, 2002). Ostracod shells are being used in DNA evolutionary genetic studies (De Dekker, 2002).

Copepods are minute (0.3 to 2.5 mm) crustaceans. They lack a distinct shell fold and having a simple median eye. The body is elongated and segmented, divided into a broad appendage bearing part called the metasoma and posterior urosoma separated by a major articulation. The urosome ends in a caudal furca of the antennae, the first are often longer and uniramous. The maxillipeds are the first thoracic appendages, followed by four biramous swimming legs with the fifth leg reduced and uniramous. Gravid females carry their eggs in one or two egg sacs. Copepods pass through a series of naupliar and copepodid stages during their development (Battish, 1992).

Copepods are the most important planktonic constituent. They form an essential link in the aquatic food chain and constitute more than 50% of the planktonic diversity in majority of freshwater lakes of the world (Khan, 2003). Out of 6 orders of the subclass copepoda, the free living planktonic forms belong to the orders calanoida and cyclopoida. These are minute crustaceans, having elongated and segmented body, divisible into a broad appendage bearing anterior part, the metasome has a narrower posterior part, the urosome, separated by a major articulation. The first antennae are generally longer and uniramous. The first thoracic segment is fused with head and bears a pair of maxillipeds and each of five subsequent thoracic segments bears one pair of biramous swimming legs, with fifth leg reduced or modified. Egg sacs are attached to body, near the articulation of urosome and metasome (Khan, 2003). Up till now nearly 50 valid species of calanoida and 32 species of cyclopoida have been reported from India (Khan, 2003).

There are 7500 known species belonging to seven orders, of which calanoida, cyclopoida and harpacticoida are free living. In the free living copepods there are 10 trunk segments (fewer in female because of fusion), followed by a telson bearing a furca.

In calanoida the major articulation lies between thorax and abdomen (legs 5 and genital segment) anterior to the gonopore-bearing segment.

In cyclopoida the major articulation lies anterior to the last thoracic somite (between legs 4 and 5). The body region anterior to the major articulation is called the prosoma. The urosoma is the posterior part. The proximal region distinguished into anterior cephalosoma (cephalothorax) consisting of head with which one or two thoracic segmenta bearing maxillipeds are fused. The posterior prosomal part is called the metasoma including most Copepods of the order Cyclopoida are the most important food items in freshwater aquaculture, and their nauplii are especially valuable for feeding fry (Szalauer and Szlauer, 1980). Copepoda can also be cultured to supply food for fish. Culture methods for marine copepods are well advanced (Ogle 1979, Ohno and Okamura 1988, Payne and Rippingale 2001), but relatively few attempts have been made to culture freshwater copepods.

There are 7500 known species belonging to seven orders, of which calanoida, cyclopoida and harpacticoida are free living. In the free living copepods there are 10 trunk segments (fewer in female because of fusion), followed by a telson bearing a furca.

MATERIALS AND METHODS

Phytoplankton collection was made towing a net made-up of bolting silk Net No. 25 for five minutes. Sedimentation of phytoplankton was made in 5% formaldehyde. Algal monographs of Hustedt (1976), Prescott (1982) and Tripathi and Pandey (1990) were followed to identify the phytoplankton. Drop count method of Trivedy and Goel (1984) was followed for enumeration of phytoplankton and expressed as organisms per liter.

The studies on the zooplankton diversity and density were carried out for a period of two years (2012-13 to 2013-14) in Bhavthana reservoir. Qualitative zooplankton samples were collected with the help of plankton net made of bolting cloth No. 25 (mesh size approximately 56µ) from three different zones of the reservoir. For the collections from littoral zones, sweeps were made in all directions with the help of a long pole. For the collection from pond waters, net was thrown to maximum possible distance from the shore and towed gradually avoiding littoral macrophytes. Net was also towed from the boat for some distance in open water as and when feasible. Similarly, vertical hauls were made from open water by dropping the net with anchor from the boat to the bottom and pulling rapidly.

For the quantitative samples, 50 litres of water was filtered through the net, both from littoral and open water zones. Samples were transferred to a small enamel tray. The inside of the net was washed so as to collect any sticking plankter. Few drops of formalin were put to nacrotize the animals and when they became motionless and settled down, the supernatant water was discarded slowly and concentrated samples were collected. All samples were preserved in 5% formaldehyde solution. Preserved zooplankton samples were examined under a binocular microscope with different magnifications. Detailed taxonomic identification was carried out following Needham and Needham (1962), Edmondson (1959), Mellan by (1963), Pennak (1978), Tonapi (1980), Sehgal (1983), Michael and Sharma (1988), Battish (1992), Ahmad (1996), Shiel (1995), Murugan *et.al.* (1998), Roy (1999), Sharma (1999), Dhanapathi (2000), Khan (2003)3, Lynne (2004).

RESULTS

Phytoplankton Diversity

The study of the phytoplankton sampled in Bhavthana reservoir showed 16 species (Table 5.1). The phytoplankton assemblage was represented by three classes viz. Bacillariophyceae, Cynophyceae and Chlorophyceae.

The class Bacillariophyceae was represented by maximum genera. It was reported by 7 species. The class was represented by species of genera *Fragilaria sp, Synedra sp, Cymbella sp, Nitzschia sp, Navicula sp, Melosira sp* and *Pinnularia sp.*

The class Cynophyceae was represented by 5 species. It was represented by *Merismopedia sp, Oscillatoria sp, Nostoc sp, Anabaena sp* and *Calothrix sp.*

The class Chlorophyceae was represented by 4 genera i.e; *Pediastratum, Chlorella, Spirogyra* and *Scenedesmus.*

During first year of study (2012-2013), the phytoplankton consisted of 51% of Bacillariophyceae, 26.30% of Cynophyceae and 22.75% of Chlorophyceae. Bacillariophyceae members were the dominant forms, followed by Cynophyceae and Chlorophyceae. It was revealed that the class Bacillariophyceae was dominant with annual average of 920 (1140 units/liter), followed by Cyanophyceae 484 (5808 units/liter) and Chlorophyceae 395 (4748 units/liter).

Merismopedia sp and *Anabaena sp* were recorded in nine months. These species were absent in three months of monsoon season (Table 5.2). *Calothrix sp* was observed in summer and two months of winter season. The density of *Merismopedia sp* ranged from nil to 100 units/liter, *Oscillatoria sp.* 100 to 352 units/liter, *Anabaena orientalis* nil to 128 units/liter and *Calothrix sp* nil to 128 units/liter.

Table 5.2: Species Composition of Phytoplankton (Units/Liter) during Year 2012-13

	June	July	Aug.	Sept.	Oct.	Nov.	Dec.	Jan.	Feb.	Mar.	Apr.	May
Chlorophyceae												
Pediastrum sp.	120	100	112	80	100	140	140	128	140	120	180	160
Chlorella sp.	00	00	00	00	00	80	100	120	80	60	80	60
Spirogyra sp.	60	40	80	100	140	120	80	100	160	100	120	140
Scenedesmus sp.	48	100	80	120	140	120	160	120	120	120	160	120
Cyanophyceae												
Merismopedia sp.	00	00	60	00	80	80	60	80	88	100	80	100
Oscillatoria sp.	120	100	100	100	152	128	140	168	180	352	208	300
Nostoc sp.	80	88	120	112	120	128	140	120	140	148	160	140
Anabaena sp.	60	00	00	00	60	80	80	88	100	120	128	120
Calothrix sp.	00	00	00	00	00	60	00	80	100	80	112	128
Bacillariophyceae												
Fragilaria sp.	128	168	152	200	108	240	140	272	240	272	288	328
Synedra sp.	00	00	00	00	80	72	152	140	128	160	148	180
Cymbelca sp.	00	00	00	00	00	00	00	00	120	140	80	100
Nitzschia sp	160	168	100	208	220	220	240	248	240	260	272	240
Navicula sp.	120	140	140	192	240	220	220	230	248	230	288	280
Melosira sp.	00	00	00	00	72	80	72	100	140	128	140	120
Pinnularia sp.	60	00	00	80	88	80	60	120	140	168	120	112
Total	468	476	392	680	808	912	884	1112	1256	1360	1336	1360

The green algae were represented by *Pediastrum sp*, *Chlorella sp*, *Spirogyra sp.* and *Scenedesmus sp.* This group did not exhibit any characteristic seasonal pattern. The population density of green algae was between 228 to 540 units/liter and contributed to 22.7% of the phytoplankton (Fig.5.1) and 16.6% of the total plankton population (Fig.5.2). It was recorded maximum (540 units/liter) in April and minimum (228 units/liter) in June. Among the green algae, *Pediastrum sp*, *Spirogyra sp.* and *Scenedesums sp.* were observed throughout the study period, while *Chlorella sp* was present only in seven months (Table 5.2). Higher population density of *Pediastrum sp* was recorded in April and minimum in September. The population density of this species varied from 80 to 180 units/liter. Similarly, population density of *Spirogyra sp.* and *Scenedesmus sp.* was in the range of 40 to 160 units/liter and 48 to 160 units/liter respectively. The population density of *Chlorella sp* varied from nil to 120 units/liter.

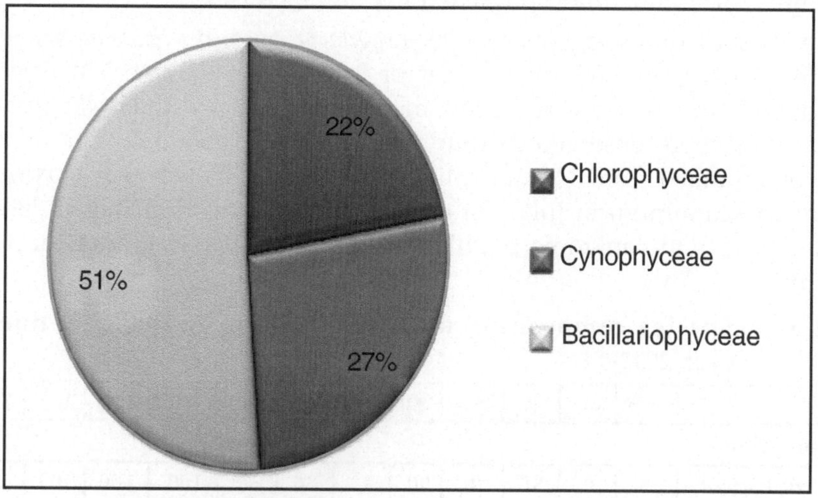

Fig. 5.1: Quantitative Occurance of Phytoplankton (Year 2012-2013)

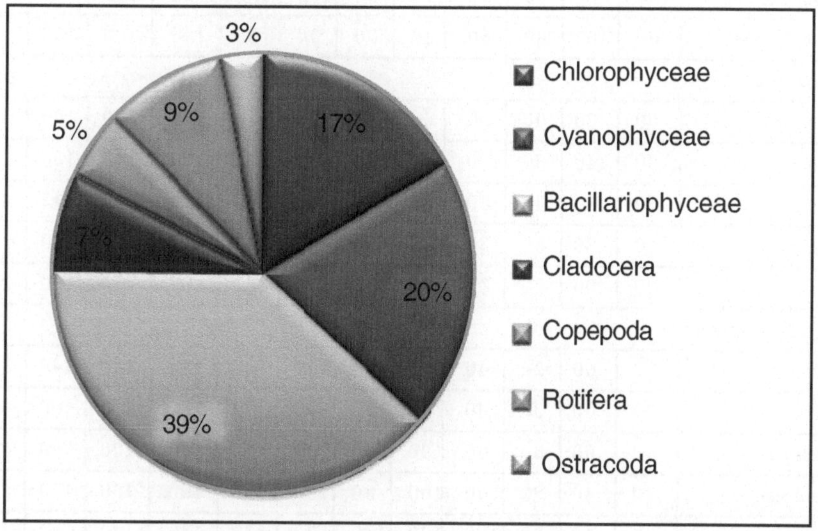

Fig. 5.2: Quantitative Occurance of Phyto and Zooplankton (Year 2012-2013)

During second year (2013-2014) of investigation, a total number of 16 species (7 species of Bacillariophyceae, 5 species of Cyanophyceae and 4 species of Chlorophyceae) of phytoplanktons were recorded in Bhavthana reservoir. The phytoplankton consisted of 38.38% of Bacillariophyceae,

33.41% of Cyanophyceae and 28.20% of Chlorophyceae (Fig. 5.3). Bacillariophyceae members were the dominating forms, followed by Cyanophyceae and Chlorophyceae. The class Bacillariophyceae was dominant with annual average of 442 units/liter, followed by Cyanophyceae (385 units/liter) and Chlorophyceae (325 units/liter).

In case of diatoms, *Navicula sp*, *Fragilaria sp.* and *Nitzschia sp.* were recorded throughout the second year of investigation (Table 5.3). *Synedra sp* and *Melosira sp.* were recorded in summer season. *Cymbella sp.* and *Pinnularia sp* were observed in four months only (Table 5.3). The density of diatoms ranged from 140 units/liter to 940 units/liter. It was maximum in May and minimum in July. On an average, diatoms contributed 38.38% of the total phytoplanktonic population (Fig. 5.3) and 25.46% of the total plankton (Fig. 5.4).

Table 5.3: Species composition of phytoplankton (units/liter) during year 2013-14

	June	July	Aug.	Sept.	Oct.	Nov.	Dec.	Jan.	Feb.	Mar.	Apr.	May
Chlorophyceae												
Pediastrum sp.	120	100	80	80	00	00	80	100	100	160	200	160
Chlorella sp.	00	00	00	00	00	00	00	00	100	120	140	200
Spirogyra sp.	60	60	60	40	120	80	100	120	140	120	180	200
Scenedesmus sp.	60	100	80	60	40	00	00	80	100	100	160	120
Cyanophyceae												
Merismopedia sp.	00	00	00	00	60	60	72	80	100	80	100	112
Oscillatoria sp.	80	140	80	100	128	120	120	140	100	140	180	160
Nostoc sp.	60	60	40	60	80	80	80	100	120	88	112	120
Anabaena sp.	60	80	60	80	120	80	88	80	152	120	140	128
Calothrix sp.	00	00	00	00	00	20	40	72	80	60	80	100
Bacillariophyceae												
Fragilaria sp.	20	60	20	40	60	80	100	120	140	140	140	180
Synedra sp.	00	00	00	00	00	00	00	00	100	120	60	140
Cymbelca sp.	40	00	00	00	00	00	00	00	00	100	80	100
Nitzschia sp.	40	40	80	60	100	80	100	88	100	140	120	140
Navicula sp.	60	40	80	100	120	140	100	120	140	120	160	140
Melosira sp.	00	00	00	00	00	00	00	00	120	140	200	80
Pinnularia sp.	00	00	00	00	00	00	00	00	140	160	60	160
Total	160	140	180	200	280	300	300	328	740	920	820	940

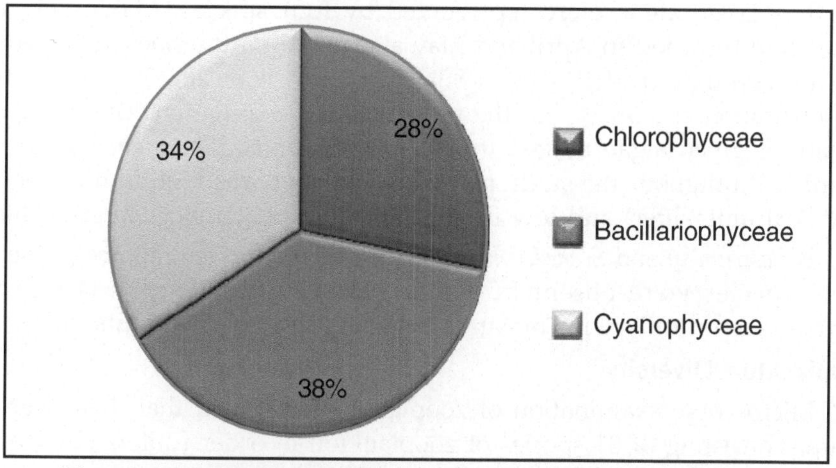

Fig. 5.3: Quantitative Occurance of Phytoplankton (Year 2013-14)

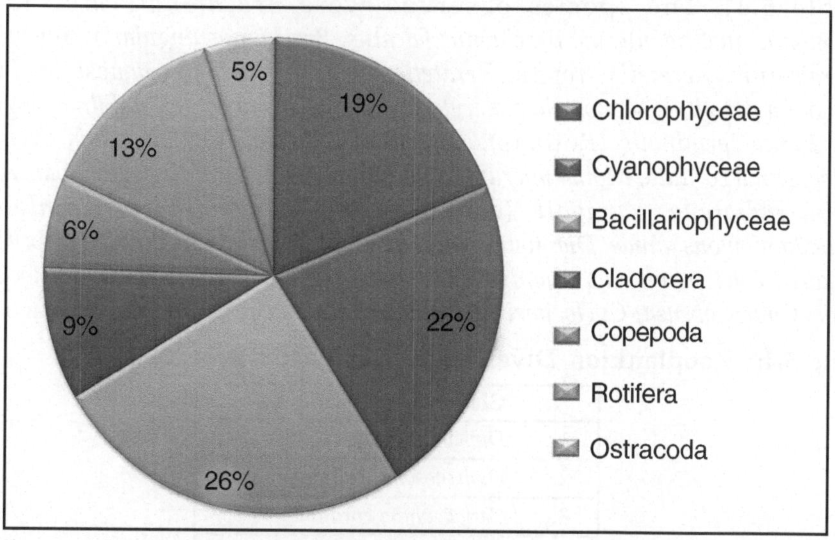

Fig. 5.4: The Percentage of Composition of Plankton in Bhavthana Reservoir (Year 2013-2014)

The blue green algae were represented by five species. *Anabaena sp*, *Nostoc sp.* and *Oscillatoria sp.* were observed throughout the year. *Merismopedia sp* appeared only in summer and winter season and *Calothrix sp* in seven months of the study period. The variation in the population density of blue green algae ranged from 180 to 620 units/liter and contributed to about 33.41% of the total phytoplankton population and 22.16% of the total planktonic population of second year. The density of *Merismopedia sp* ranged from nil to 112 units/liter, *Oscillatoria sp.* from 80 to 180 units/liter, *Nostoc sp.* from 60 to 120 units/liter, *Anabaena sp* from 60 to 152 units/liter and *Calothrix sp* from nil to 100 units/liter (Table 5.3).

The green algae were represented by four species. Maximum green algae were recorded in April and May and minimum number in November. The percentage contribution of green algae was 28.20% of the total phytoplankton and 18.71% of the total plankton population. The population density of green algae ranged from 80 to 680 units/liter. *Spirogyra sp.* was recorded throughout the study period. Its number was high in the month of May (200 units/liter) and low in the months of September (40 units/liter).

Pediastrum sp and *Scenedesmus sp.* were observed in ten months (Table 5.3). These species were absent in winter season. *Chlorella sp* was found in summer season only with maximum density in May (200 units/liter).

Zooplankton Diversity

Microscopic examination of zooplanktons revealed that there were for groups consisting of 31 species of zooplankton in order rotifers (13 species), cladocerans (8 species), copepods (6 species) and ostracods (4 species) (Table 5.4). The species observed were *Brachionus calyciflorus, Brachionus quadridentatus, Brachionus falcatus, Brachionus angularis, Brachionus diversicornis, Keratella tropica, Keratella quadrata, Lecane (monostyla) bulla, Trichocera porcellus, Monostyla quadridenta, Asplanchna intermedia, Filina longiseta* and *Filina terminalis* (Rotifers); *Diphanosoma sarsi, Diphanosoma excisum, Ceriodaphnia cornuta, Moina micrura, Macrothrix spinosa, Alona rectangular, Alona nana, Indialana ganapati* (cladocerans); *Heliodiaptomus contortus, Phyllodiaptomous annae, Diaptomous orientalis, Mesocyclops hyalinus, Mesocyclops leuckarti, Cyclops vicinus uljanin, Mesocyclops leuckarti (Copepoda); Stenocypris major, Cypris obensa, Cyclocypris globosa* and *Candocypria osborni* (Ostracoda).

Table 5.4: Zooplankton Diversity of Bhavthana Reservoir

	Cladocera
1.	*Diphanosoma sarsi*
2.	*Diphanosoma excisum*
3.	*Ceriodaphnia cornuta*
4.	*Moina micrura*
5.	*Macrothrix spinosa*
6.	*Alonella nana*
7.	*Alona rectangular*
8.	*Indialona ganapati*
	Rotifera
1.	*Brachionus calyciflorus*
2.	*Brachionus quadridentatus*
3.	*Brachionus falcatus*
4.	*Brachionus angularis*

(Table Contd...)

5.	*Brachionus diversicornis*
6.	*Keratella quadrata*
7.	*Keratella tropica*
8.	*Monostyla quadridentata*
9.	*Lecane(Monostyla) bulla*
10.	*Trichocera porcellus*
11.	*Asplanchna intermedia*
12.	*Filinia longiseta*
13.	*Filinia terminalis*
	Copepoda
1.	*Heliodiaptomus contortus*
2.	*Phyllodiaptomus annae*
3.	*Diaptomus orientalis*
4.	*Mesocyclops hyalinus*
5.	*Mesocyclops leuckarti*
6.	*Cyclops vicinus uljanin*
	Ostracoda
1.	*Stenocypris major*
2.	*Cypris obensa*
3.	*Cyclocypris globosa*
4.	*Candocypria osborni*

Plate 5.2: Phytoplankton Diversity of Bhavthana Reservoir

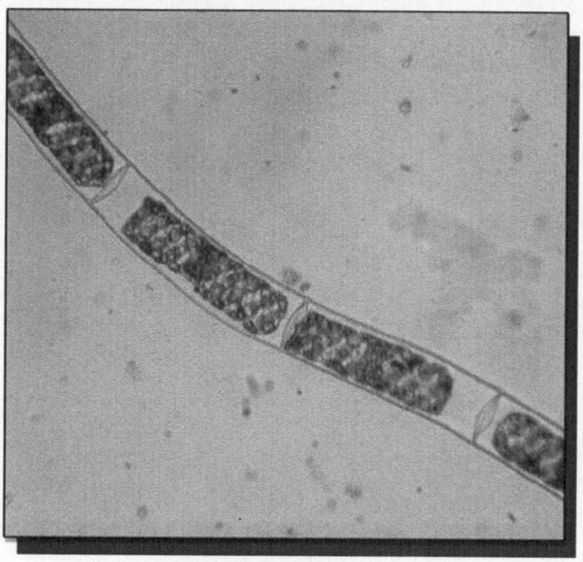

Spirogyra spp.

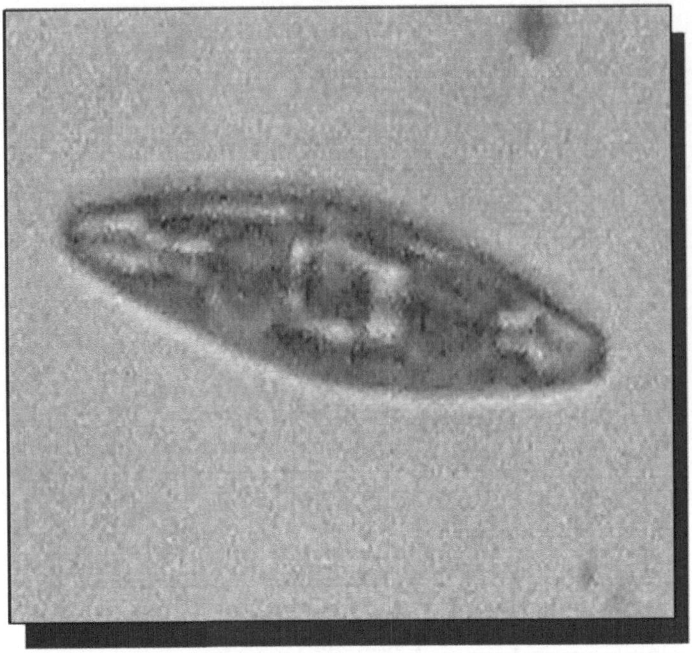

Navicula spp.

Plate 5.3: Zooplankton Diversity of Bhavthana Reservoir

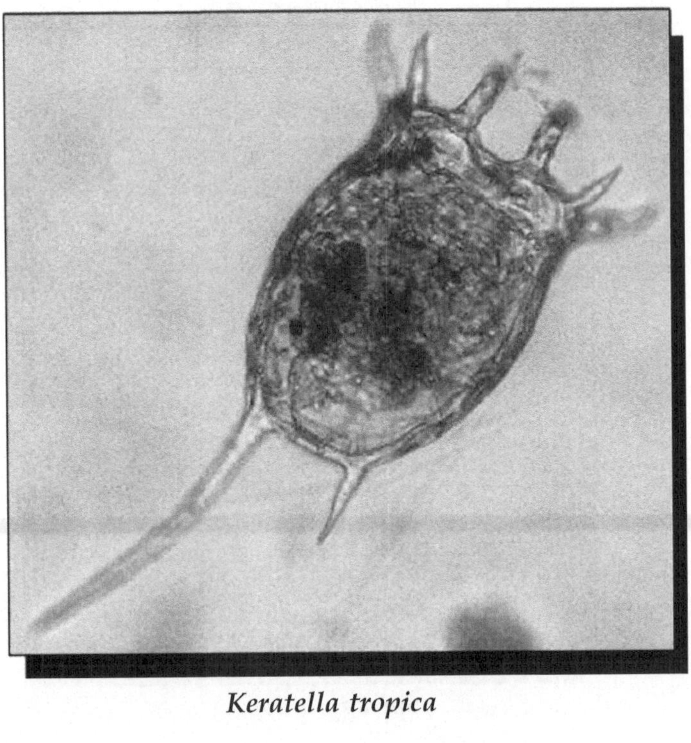

Keratella tropica

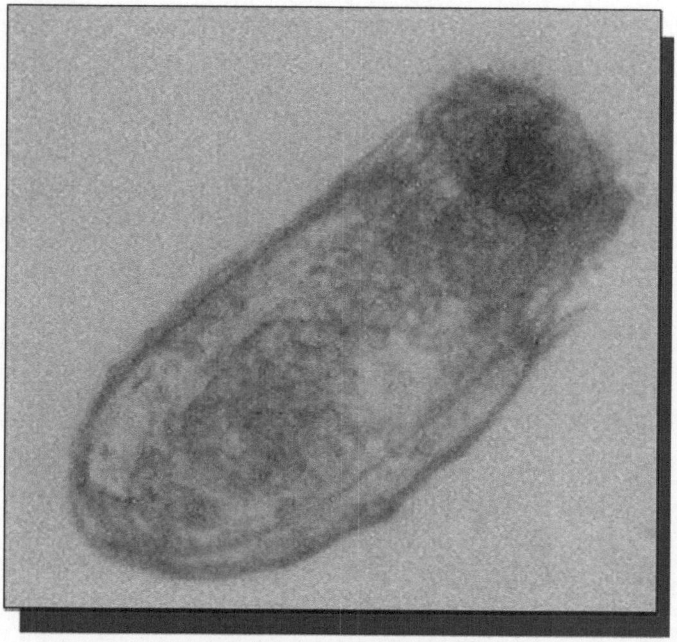

Asplanchna intermedia

Plate 5.4: Zooplankton Diversity of Bhavthana Reservoir

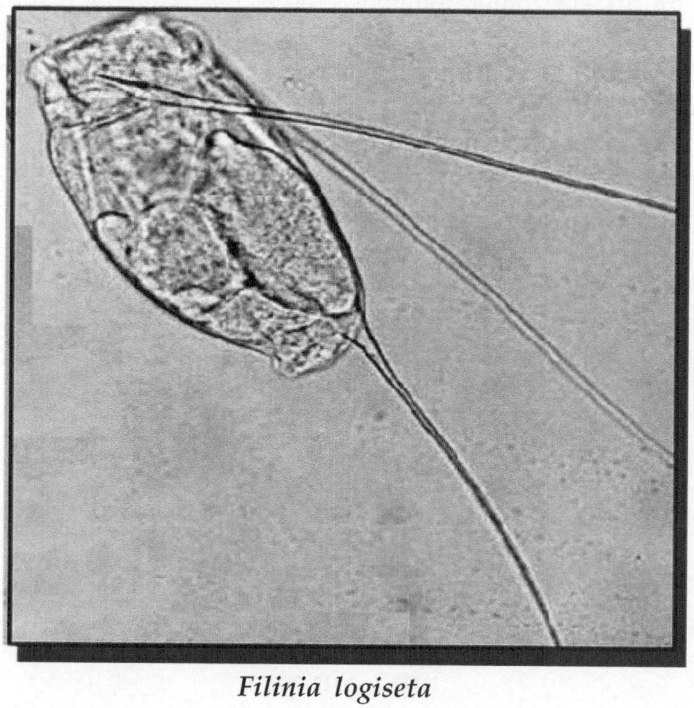

Filinia logiseta

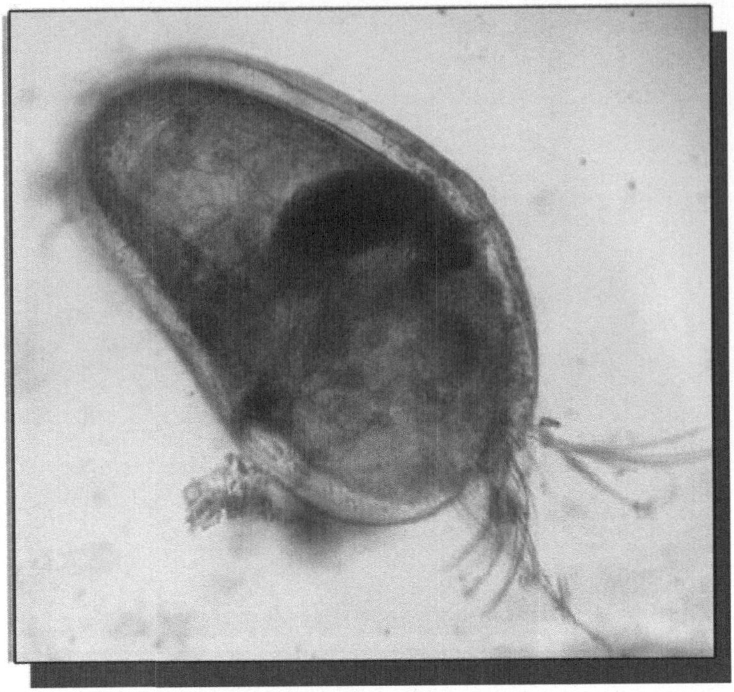

Stenocypris major

During 2012-13, rotifer dominated the zooplankton population (39.38%), followed by cladocera (26.84%), copepoda (20.94%) and ostracoda (12.76%) are presented in fig. 5.5. Summer months exhibited higher population of zooplankton. Cladocerans, rotifers, copepods as well as ostracods showed the summer maxima and minima in monsoon season.

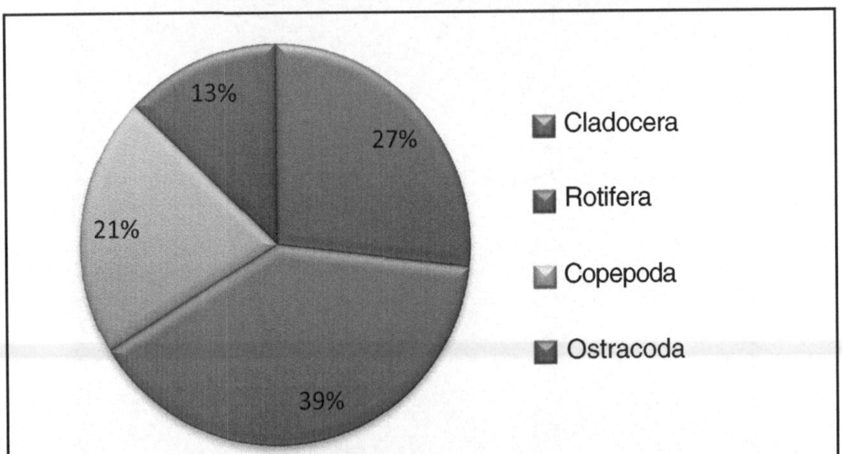

Fig. 5.5: The Percentage of Composition of Zooplankton in Bhavthana Reservoir (Year 2012-2013)

Rotifers were represented by 13 species. During present investigation, 5 species of *Brachionus* were recorded which contributed highest amount of rotifer population (Table 5.5). The species *Brachionus falcatus, Brachionus diversicornis, Keratella tropica, Monostyla quadridenta* and *Filinia terminalis* were absent in September 2012, June 2012, September 2012, July 2012 and September 2012 respectively. The maximum rotifer population was recorded in February 2013 (340 organisms/liter) and minimum population in September 2012 (110 organisms/liter).

Cladocerans were represented by 8 species (Table 5.5), and species *Diphanosoma excisum, Ceriodaphnia cornuta* and *Macrothrix spinosa* were absent in January 2013, June 2012, and July 2012 respectively. The peak period of cladocerans was observed in the month of April 2013 (255 organisms/liter) and it was minimum in the month of July 2012 (95 organisms/liter) (Table 5.6).

Copepods were represented by 6 species (Table 5.7). The maxima was 180 organisms/liter in the month of February and May and minima was 55 organisms/liter in the month of August 2012.

Ostracods were represented by 4 species (Table 5.8). *Cypris obensa* was not recorded in July 2012. The highest density of ostracods was observed in March 2013 (125 organisms/liter), while lowest density was recorded in July 2012 (30 organisms/liter).

During second year of investigation (2013-14), zooplanktons were represented by rotifer, cladocera, copepod and ostracoda. The percentage composition of zooplankton in Bhavthana reservoir is shown in fig. 5.6. Among zooplankton, rotifers dominated (37.70%), followed by cladocerans (27.85%), copepod (19.33%) and ostracods (15.2%).

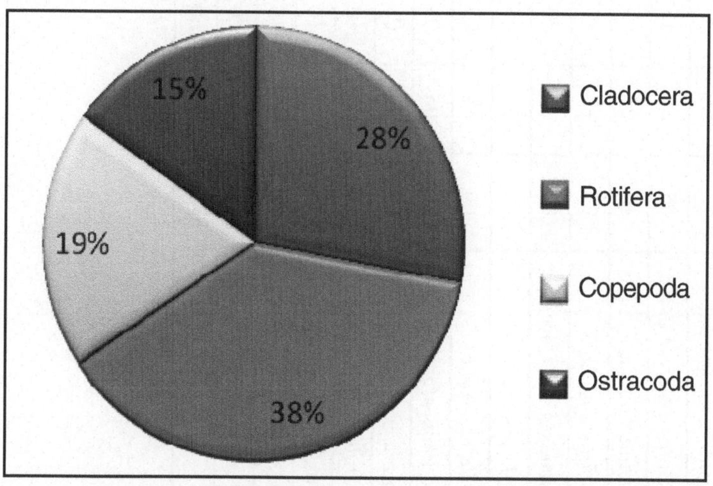

Fig. 5.6: Quantitative Occurance of Zooplankton (Year 2013-2014)

Table 5.5: Species Composition of Rotifera (Density: Organisms/Liter) during year 2012-13

Species/Month	June	July	Aug.	Sept.	Oct.	Nov.	Dec.	Jan.	Feb.	Mar.	Apr.	May
Brachionus calyciflorus	15	5	20	10	15	20	15	10	30	25	45	35
Brachionus quadridentatus	05	20	15	20	25	20	25	15	25	15	35	15
Brachionus falcatus	10	05	05	00	15	20	05	20	25	30	10	40
Brachionus angularis	25	10	15	05	25	05	35	25	20	10	05	30
Brachionus diversicornis	00	05	20	10	20	30	15	30	15	25	10	05
Keratella tropica	10	25	05	00	20	25	25	15	40	30	15	10
Keratella quadrata	05	05	15	10	30	25	15	10	35	25	35	30
Lecane (monostyla) bulla	20	05	05	05	15	15	05	20	10	20	20	15
Trichocera porcellus	05	05	05	05	10	10	10	05	15	05	05	10
Monostyla quadridenta	20	00	10	10	20	15	20	20	20	40	10	30
Asplanchna intermedia	15	20	10	25	25	15	15	20	35	30	25	05
Filina longiseta	15	05	15	10	15	20	25	15	40	35	30	20
Filina terminalis	05	10	20	00	30	15	10	30	30	25	05	25
Total	150	12	160	110	265	235	220	235	340	315	250	270

Table 5.6: Species Composition of Cladocera (Density: Organisms/Liter) during year 2012-13

Species/Month	June	July	Aug.	Sept.	Oct.	Nov.	Dec.	Jan.	Feb.	Mar.	Apr.	May
Diphanosoma sarsi	15	20	15	10	30	25	10	10	40	30	55	40
Diphanosoma excisum	20	05	20	20	15	20	05	00	15	25	35	10
Ceriodaphnia cornuta	00	20	05	15	15	20	25	30	40	20	20	25
Moina microra	15	20	05	15	15	20	15	25	00	00	00	00
Macrothrix spinosa	20	00	10	15	30	10	25	35	20	35	35	15
Alona rectangular	20	15	25	15	15	20	25	25	25	45	25	35
Alonella nana	15	05	20	20	25	15	30	10	15	10	50	15
Indialona ganapati	05	10	10	10	20	30	20	35	30	25	40	35
Total	110	95	110	120	165	145	155	170	185	190	255	175

Table 5.7: Species composition of Copepoda (density:organisms/liter) during year 2012-13

Species/Month	June	July	Aug.	Sept.	Oct.	Nov.	Dec.	Jan.	Feb.	Mar.	Apr.	May
Heliodiaptomus contortus	10	25	10	25	25	15	20	15	35	25	25	40
Phyllodiaptomous annae	10	05	15	10	10	20	25	15	20	25	25	25
Diaptomous orientalis	20	10	05	05	05	15	15	20	25	20	20	25
Mesocyclops hyalinus	15	05	00	20	25	25	20	20	30	35	20	15
Mesocyclops leuckarti	20	30	05	05	25	20	15	15	35	25	30	35
Cyclops vicinus uljanin	10	15	20	15	20	15	20	20	35	30	25	40
Total	85	90	55	80	110	110	120	105	180	160	145	180

Table 5.8: Species Composition of Ostracoda (Density: Organisms/Liter) during year 2012-13

Species/Month	June	July	Aug.	Sept.	Oct.	Nov.	Dec.	Jan.	Feb.	Mar.	Apr.	May
Stenocypris major	10	05	10	15	20	30	15	20	35	30	35	00
Cypris obensa	05	00	15	25	20	25	15	25	20	45	25	00
Cyclocypris globosa	10	15	20	30	10	15	30	20	25	30	25	00
Candocypria osborni	20	10	05	05	15	10	25	20	40	20	20	00
Total	45	30	50	75	65	80	85	85	120	125	105	00

Rotifers accounted for about 37.70% during year 2013-14, and were represented by 13 species (Table 5.9). The highest density of rotifers was observed in the month of March 2014 (300 organisms/liter) and lowest in July and September 2013 (140 organisms/liter). Throughout the summer months, rotifer population was maximum. However, during rainy season, the rotifer population was less. The species *Brachionus quadridentus, Brachionus diversicornis, Monostyla quadridenta* and *Lecane bulla* were absent in July 2013, September 2013, August 2013 and July 2013 respectively.

Cladocerans were represented by 8 species and accounted for about 27.85%. The peak period of Cladocerans was observed in the month of February 2014 (240 organisms/liter) and it was minimum in the month of July 2013 (95 organisms/liter). All Cladocerans species were observed in second year of investigation (Table 5.10).

Copepods accounted for about 19.33% and were represented by 6 species (Table 5.11). The population was more during summer and least during rainy season. The maximum density was 175 organisms/liter in February 2014. *Phyllodiaptomus annae* was not observed in July 2013, while *Mesocyclops hyalinus* was not observed in two months (June and August 2013) of monsoon season.

Ostracoda come 4th in the order of occurrences, and were represented by 4 species. The population was more during summer and least during rainy season. The maximum density was 135 organisms/liter in March 2014 and minimum was 35 organisms/liter in July 2013.During second year of investigation all 4 species were observed (Table 5.12).

DISCUSSION

Thakur *et.al.* (2013) studied limnobiotic status of three lakes of Himachal Pradesh using physico-chemical and biological parameters and reported 148 species belonging to nine groups of phytoplankton. They revealed that the distribution of plankton species depended upon the physico-chemical parameters of the environment.

Table 5.12: Species Composition of Ostracoda (Density: Organisms/Liter) during year 2013-14

Species/Month	June	July	Aug.	Sept.	Oct.	Nov.	Dec.	Jan.	Feb.	Mar.	Apr.	May
Stenocypris major	20	15	15	20	25	30	20	25	15	30	25	40
Cypris obensa	25	05	10	20	35	15	25	30	30	55	25	30
Cyclocypris globosa	10	10	35	10	15	15	20	20	30	15	35	25
Candocypria osborni	15	05	05	15	10	20	20	25	30	35	10	20
Total	70	35	65	65	85	80	85	100	105	135	95	115

Jana (1973) carried out limnoplanktonic study of a freshwater pond in West Bengal and discussed the role of physico-chemical factors in determining different planktonic population. He also reported three peaks of phytoplankton with predominant over zooplankton.

Giripunde *et.al.* (2013) reviewed phytoplankton ecology of freshwater Indian lakes for the better understanding of the phytoplankton distribution. They also discussed the relations between phytoplankton and physico-chemical parameters and concluded that each lake habitat is different from other lake habitat.

Singh (2011) reported sixteen genera of phytoplankton from freshwater fish pond at Malawan where phytoplankton populations were always dominant over zooplankton population. He also reported percentage composition of phytoplankton at 72.16%. Dabgar (2012) reported 31 species of phytoplankton belonging to 17 families from Wadhvana Wetland of Gujarat. Out of 17 families, oscillatoriaceae, nostocaceae, coelastrceae, volvocaceae, chroococcaceae, zygenemaceae were dominant.

Kaparpu and Rao (2013) studied seasonal distribution, correlation coefficient and biodiversity indices of phytoplankton in Riwada reservoir of Visakhapatnam (Andhra Pradesh) and reported 57 genera belonging to four groups i.e; chlorophyceae (27 genera), bacillariophyceae (14 genera).Cyanophyceae (13 genera) and euglenophyceae (3 genera). Maximum and minimum total phytoplankton population and percentage were recorded in pre-monsoon and monsoon respectively.

Lata *et.al.* (2014) reported 18 species belonging to three algal groups i.e. chlorophyceae (6 species), cyanophyceae (4 species) and bacillariophyceae (8 species) from human interfered temple pond at Kodamdesar in Bikaner district of Rajasthan.

Mishra *et.al.* (2010) documented plankton diversity in Dhaura and Baigul reservoirs of Uttarakhand and reported 30 species of phytoplankton belonging to chlorophyceae (10 species), cyanophyceae (06 species) and bacillariophyceae (11 species) and dinophyceae (3 species). The values of diversity indices indicate less disturbance level and medium productivity.

Study of physico-chemical and biological parameters revealed that these reservoirs have medium productivity and if managed properly, production at all the trophic levels can be enhanced.

Gurkar and Mahesh (2011) recorded 28 species of bacillariophyceae, 7 species of cyanophyceae, 6 species of desmids, 3 species of chlorococcales, 2 species of euglenaceae and 5 species of chlorophyceae from Varuna Lake of Mysore. The percentage distribution of the plankton indicates that the bacillariophyceae was the highest with 57% followed by cyanophyceae with 13% and the others fluctuated between 4 and 18%.

Sourba and Sangeetha (2011) reported 40 species of phytoplankton belonging to 4 classes. Of the total 40 species, 11 species belonged to class cynophyceae, 18 species belonged to the class chlorophyceae, 9 species comes under the class bacillariophyceae and 2 species under class Euglenophyceae.

Senthilkumar and Sivakumar (2008) noted that the phytoplankton population of the reservoir is closely related with seasonal variations in hydrography.They observed maximum phytoplankton diversity during post-monsoon season and minimum diversity in pre-monsoon season. The population density trend showed gradual increase during post-monsoon and summer season and attained the peak during the month of April which was due to nutrient richness and the moderate temperature.

Mahadik and Jadhav (2014) worked on algal biodiversity of Ujani reservoir (Maharashtra) and reported 75 species belonging to chlorophyceae, charophyceae, bacillariophyceae and cyanophyceae. Chlorophyceae was dominant followed by cyanophyceae, bacillariophyceae and charophyceae.

Nasare *et.al.* (2009) reported 10 members of chlorophyceae, 7 members of cyanophyceae, 4 members of bacillariophyceae, 2 members of Charophyceae and 2 members of Euglenophyceae from Vinjasan Lake of Bhadrawati town of Chandrapur district (Maharashtra). Similarly Meshram and Nasare (2011) identified 44 genera of phytoplankton belonging to cynophyceae, chlorophyceae and bacillariophyceae from Futala Lake in Nagpur.

Sakhare (2012) studied the ecology along with ichthyofauna of Ekruk reservoir near Solapur and observed higher density of plankton during the summer season.

Such type of studies on phytoplankton diversity in India were also carried out by Anjana *et.al.*, (1998), Banakar *et.al.* (2005), Begum and Narayana (2006), Laskar and Gupta (2009), Leela *et.al.* (2010), Nafeesa *et.al.* (2011 a), Nafeesa *et.al.* (2011b), Sayeswara *et.al.* (2011), Shanker (2010), Tiwari and Chauhan (2006), Kavitha *et.al.* (2006), Murugan (2008), Hosmani and Bharathi (1980), Hosmani (2010), Sivakumar and Karuppasamy, (2008), Goel *et.al.* (1986) and Mohite and Joshi (2011).

Venkateshwaru (1969a, 1969b) investigated the algal ecology in relation to water pollution of Moosi river, Hyderabad. By using biological community, Rama Rao *et.al.* (1978) assessed the water pollution of Khan river (Indore). The appearance of blue green algae in relation to industrial pollution in Gomti river of Lucknow was recorded by Prasad and Saxena (1980).

Motlagh *et.al.* (2014) reported 109 species of phytoplankton from Mir Alam Lake in Hyderabad and revealed that the Mir Alam Lake is polluted with deteriorated water quality and is a eutrophic lake. The species belonged to four groups viz., chlorophyceae, cyanophyceae, bacillariophycee and euglenophyceae. Among these four groups bacillariophyceae constituted the highest percentage and followed by chlorophyceae.

In the present investigation the peak of zooplankton was found during summer season. Summer peak of zooplankton has been also reported by George, (1966), Selot, (1977), Sukhija, (2010), Alone *et.al.*, (2012) and Pandey *et.al.* (2013). Presence of maximum zooplankton in summer might be due to presence of higher population of bacteria. According to Singh (1991) and Pandey *et.al.*, (1995) optimal thermal and nutritional condition and higher concentration of oxygen might be responsible for higher zooplankton population.

The lower density of zooplankton during rainy season might be due to flood and fast water current. Normally, the monsoon is associated with lower population densities due to its dilution effect and decrease in photosynthetic activity by primary producers. Similar results have been shown by Baker (1979) and Ude *et.al.*, (2011).

Sayeswara *et.al.* (2012) reported 38 species of phytoplankton representing four main taxonomic groups such as chlorophyceae, cyanophyceae, euglenophyceae and bacillariophyceae were recorded. Relative abundance of phytoplankton in Purle pond showed maximum of chlorophyceae (33.3%), followed by bacillariophyceae (23%), cyanophyceae (23%) and euglenophyceae (17.9%). *Microcystis aeroginosa, Merismopedia glauca, Euglena gracilis* and *Scenedesmus quadricauda* were the common pollution indicators.

According to Sharma (2010) the rotifer communities exhibit higher species diversity, higher evenness, lower dominance and lack of quantitative dominance of any individual species. The rotifers comprise the dominant qualitative component of zooplankton (171 species) of Deeper Beel of Aasam. Vanjare and Pai (2010) reported 13 rotifer species from a pond in Pune (Maharashtra).Of the 11 families listed under the order cladocera, nine are known from Indian waters (Michael and Sharma, 1988).Uma *et.al.* (2014) reported eight varieties of ostracods from Ambattur Lake of Tamil Nadu.

A total of 31 species of zooplankton belonging to rotifers (13 species, cladocerans (8 species), copepods (6 species) and ostracods (4 species) were recorded from Bhavthana reservoir. The zooplankton density in different season was in order of summer> winter > monsoon. Increase in temperature and high evaporation during summer season enhances the rate of decomposition due to which the water becomes nutrient rich resulting in increase in population density of zooplankton. Low population density during monsoon may be due to the dilution effect by rain water and high water level (Akbulut, 2004 and Mulani *et.al.* 2009).

Rotifers were the dominant group among zooplankton community constituting 39.38% and 37.70% of the total zooplankton population during year 2012-13 and 2013-14 respectively. In the present study, 5 species of *Brachionus* were recorded which contributed highest among rotifer population. The population density of rotifers was maximum in summer and minimum in monsoon season. The study shows similarities with Sakhare (2007) and Balakrishna *et.al.* (2013) in occurrence of highest density in summer and lowest in monsoon.

Kanagasabapathi and Rajan (2010) recorded 12 genera of rotifers from Irrukkangudi reservoir of Tamil Nadu.

Khan (2003) reported 43 species of rotifers belonging to 12 families which constituted nearly 29% of the species reported from West Bengal and 13% of the India's rotifer fauna.

Ingole (2013) reported 11 genera of rotifers from Majalgaon reservoir and observed *Brachionus angularis, B. longiseta, F. opoliensis, Kelliocottia sp, Notholocaocum minota* and *Rotaria sp.* as dominant species.

Karuthapandi *et.al.* (2013) reported 114 species of freshwater rotifers from Andhra Pradesh.

The cladocerans are micro-crustaceans usually inhabit every type of habitat in the littoral, limnetic or benthic zones of freshwater ecosystems. Cladocerans occupy the second trophic level i.e; primary consumer level in an aquatic ecosystem. Besides this, cladocerans also serve as diet for fishes. There are many published reports on seasonal occurrences of different cladoceran species (Michael and Sharma 1988; Sharma and Kotwal 2011; Gupta 2002; Raghunathan 1989; Raghunathan and Kumar 2003; Sharma and Chanderkiran 2011; Sharma *et.al.* 2005; Thakur *et.al.* 2013; Shah and Pandit 2014; Siraj *et.al.* 2007).

Sharma and Kotwal (2011) accounted diversity and dynamics of cladocera in a subtropical pond at Sungal (J & K) in which cladocera was represented by eight species. The population of cladoceran passed through two minimas and maximas.

Sakhare (2007) reported plankton population dynamics of Yeldari reservoir (Maharashtra) in which cladocera was represented by 7 species.

The group showed maxima in summer and minima in winter. In Bhavthana reservoir, the cladoceran occurred more during summer months and least during monsoon months.

Jalizadeh and Yamakanamardi (2012) studied the seasonal fluctuation of cladocera abundance with special reference to seasonal changes in physico-chemical parameters in lentic ecosystem of Mysore. The physico-chemical variables influencing the abundance of cladocera were dissolved oxygen, NO_3, BOD and conductivity in Bannur Lake; COD, turbidity and water temperature in Lingambudi Lake. No physico-chemical variables revealed correlation with the abundance of cladocera in Hebbal Lake.

Hutchinson (1967) pointed out that water temperature increases the development of cladocera while Patalas (1972) stated that temperature is the primary factor influencing the zooplankton abundance. Quadri and Yousuf (1980) also recorded the significance of temperature in occurrence and the distribution of cladocera in Kashmir Lake. The present investigation corroborate with the findings of Hutchinson (1967).

Copepods are the most important food items in freshwater aquaculture, and their nauplii are especially valuable for fish fry (Szlauer and Szlauer, 1980). In Central Europe, efforts have been made to use copepods and other components of zooplankton for feeding fish in aquaculture (Szlauer and Szlauer, 1980; 1982).

Copepods prefer a more stable environment and are generally considered as water pollution-sensitive taxa as they disappear in severely contaminated waters (Das *et.al.* 1996). On the contrary, a change in the number of copepods with seasonal occurance in the different Indian lakes and reservoirs has been reported (Thakur *et.al.* 2013; Jadhav *et.al.* 2013; Tijare and Thosar 2010; Sakhare 2002, 2007, 2008; Alfred and Thapa 1995).

Ostracods look like seed, hence calles 'seed shrimps'. Patil and Talmale (2005) stated that in freshwaters of Maharashtra there are 38 species of ostracods under 15 genera. Patil (2002) reported 7 ostracod species from Ujani wetland. Shinde *et.al.* (2014) revealed the presence of 17 species of ostracods from different localities of Northern Western Ghats. Of the 17 species of ostracods, 13 were recorded in the pools on the basaltic mesa.

Ostracods are small bivalve crustaceans. They are very common in the most inland waters, where they abound in the benthic and periphytic animal communities, but they also occur in marine interstitial and even semi-terrestrial environments. They are of great interest as a model group in various ecological and evolutionary studies. This is because the calcified valves of non-marine ostracod can be very common in lake sediments and this adds a real-time frame to the evolution of ostracod lineages as well as of their biological traits (Jalizadeh and Yamakanamardi, 2012).

Sakhare (2012) studied seasonal variation of zooplankton community in Udyan sarovar tank of Ambajogai and reported 4 species of ostracods viz. *Stenocypris spp, Cypris obensa, Cyclocypris globosa* and *Candocypria osborni.* In Bhavthana reservoir also same species were recorded. In the present study, higher density of ostracods was recorded during summer season. This is in confirmation with the findings of Deshmukh (2001) and Sakhare (2007).

6

Conclusion and Recommendations

Systematic ecology based fisheries investigations on Bhavthana reservoir in Beed district of Maharashtra were carried out for the period of two years (2012-13 and 2013-14). The conclusions of this study have been summarized under different aspects and are as follows:

1. It is a typical example of 'put and take' system of culture-based fisheries. In Bhavthana reservoir there is a direct relationship between stocking and yield rates. On an average reservoir produced fish yield of 238.29 kg/ha/yr which is quite more than the average fish production from small Indian reservoirs. Constant good landings of Indian major carps and the catfishes suggest that they are well adapted to the lentic condition of the reservoir.
2. Reservoir is regularly stocked by the fry stage of Indian major carps (*Catla catla, Labeo rohita, Cirrhinus mrigala*) along with few exotic like *Cyprinus carpio, Hypophthalmichthys molitrix* and *Ctenopharyngodon idella*.The size of the fry stocked was usually so small that they fall an easy prey to the predatory fishes.
3. During the present investigation a total of 33 species of fishes belonging to 5 orders, 11 families and 20 genera have been recorded from Bhavthana reservoir.Order cypriniformes (45.45%) was dominated by 15 species which was followed by perciformes (27.27%) with 9 species, order siluriformes (18.18%) was represented by 6 species, order osteoglossiformes (6.06%) by 2 species and order cyprinodontiformes (3.03%) was represented by a single species
4. The average income per fisherman per day varied from Rs. 30 to Rs. 170. The average annual earning per family was computed to be Rs. 20,000.Majority of the fishermen are part time and illiterate. Their children hardly get higher education. Fisherwomen were found to be engaged in household works and mending and making fishing nets. Many of them were indebted to money-lending fish merchants. Lack of transport facilities and preservation facilities prevented the fishermen undertaking their own fish sale business.

5. Analysis of physico-chemical parameters of reservoir revealed that reservoir water is suitable for fish culture and free from pollution.
6. The study of the phytoplankton sampled in Bhavthana reservoir showed 16 species. The phytoplankton assemblage was represented by three classes viz. bacillariophyceae, cyanophyceae and chlorophyceae.
7. Microscopic examination of zooplanktons revealed that there were for groups consisting of 31 species of zooplankton and were represented by rotifers (13 species), cladocerans (8 species), copepods (6 species) and ostracods (4 species)

These conclusions lead to the following recommendations for improvement of fish and fisheries of Bhavthana reservoir:

1. During summer season, the water level in reservoir goes down; hence it is recommended to maintain certain minimum level of water level for the survival of fish.
2. Fishermen are illiterate and poor. Co-operative should provide more incentives for purchase of nets and crafts.
3. Co-operative society should avoid the role of intermediaries and should undertake the transport and marketing of fish itself and eliminate the intermediaries. This will help to provide proper return to fishermen for their fish catch. Short term loans may be provided to the fishermen co-operative on priority basis and progress made in this regard be reviewed every year at district level by the fisheries department.
4. Cage culture could promote yield from this reservoir.
5. Seed stocked is in the form of fry stage. The size of the seed may also be raised to 100 mm or above as is practiced in some of the CIFRI managed small reservoirs. To achieve more fish production, it is recommended that the fishermen's co-operative society should contact NFDB for stocking of the seed of quality carp seed.
6. Since this reservoir is almost free from pollutants and weed infestation, this can be taken up as a model reservoir to achieve a set target yield. The high population of catfishes calls for a selective fishing for them so that the reservoir harbours chiefly the fishes nearer to the base of the food chain.
7. There is need to improve gears, crafts and mode of their operation. Strict regulations should be enacted to restrict the mesh size of nets. Indiscriminate fishing practice needs to be stopped to allow the proper fish growth.

References

Adak, M.D., Adak, S. and Purohit, K.M. 2002. Studies on Water Quality of Village Timjore, Orissa: Part-I. Physico-chemical Parameters, *Ind. J.Environ. Prot.*, 22 (9): 1040-1046.

Agrawal, A.K. and Rajwar, G.S. 2010. Physico-chemical and Microbiological Study of Tehri Dam Reservoir, Garhwal Himalaya, India. *Journal of American Science*.6 (6): 65-71.

Agarwal, S.C. 1990. Fishery Management, Ashish Publishing House, New Delhi, pp. 462. Agarwal, S.C. 1999. Limnology, APH Publishing Corporation, New Delhi.

Ahirrao, K.D. 2014. Fish Diversity of the Bori Dam at Tamaswadi, Parola, District Jalgaon, Maharashtra State. Golden Research Thoughts, 3(12): 1-5.

Ahirrao, S.D. and Mane, A.S. 2000. The Diversity of ichthyofauna, Taxonomy and Fisheries from Freshwaters of Parbhani District, Maharashtra State. *J. Aqua.Biol.* 15(1&2): 40-43.

Ahmad, M.S. 1996. Ecological Survey of some Algal Flora of Polluted Habitats of Dharbhanga. *J. Environ. Pollut.* 3: 147-151.

Ahmad Manzoor, M.,1980. Dal Lake: A Rich Fishery Resources of Kashmir. *India Today and Tomorrow.* 8(4): 184-186.

Ajayan, K.V. and Parameswara, Naik, T. 2011. Seasonal Temperature and Pollution Indicator of Phytoplankton in Lentic Water Bodies of Bhadrawati Taluka, Shimoga District Karnataka. *Ecology and Fisheries*, 4(1): 71-76.

Akbulut, E.N. 2004. The Determination of Relationship between Zooplankton and Abiotic Factors using Canonical Correspondence Analysis (CCA) in the Ova Stream (Ankara/Turkey), *Acta Hydrochimica Hydrobiologica*, 32(6): 434-441.

Alam, M.1980. Limological Studies of Sambhar Lake and its Reservoir. Ph.D. Thesis. University of Jodhpur, India: 158pp.

Alderice, D.F. 1988. Osmotic and Ionic Regulation in Teleost Eggs and Larvae. Fish Physiology, Volume XIA, Hoar, W.S. and D.J. Randall, eds. New York: Academic Press.

Alfred, J.R.B. ad Thapa, M.P., 1996. Limnological Investigation on Ward's Lake-A Wetland in Shillong, Meghalaya, N.E. India. Rec. Zool. Surv. India. Occ. Paper No. 169: 1-125 (Published by the Director, Zool.surv.India, Kolkata).

Ali, S., 1996. The Book of Indian Birds. Bombay Natural History Society and Oxford University Press.

Alone, M., Alone, A. and Bhagel, A.2012. Water Quality of Man River in Relation to Physico-chemical Characteristics of Zooplanktons. *Flora and Fauna*, 18(1): 81-84.

Amore, D.L. 1955. "Powai" Hindu Kitab Ltd. Publisher, Mumbai.

Angadi, S.B., Shidda Mallaiah, N. and Patil, P.C. 2005. Limnological Studies of Papnash Pond, Bidar, Karnataka. *J. Environ. Biol.* 26: 213-216.

Anitha, Devi, U. and Singara, Charya, 2007. Phytoplankton in Lower Manair Dam Kakatiya Canal, Karim Nagar, Andhra Pradesh, *Nature, Environment and Pollution Technology*. 6(4): 643-648.

Anitha, G., Chandrasekhar, S.V.A. and Kodarkar, M.S. 2005. Limnological Studies on Mir Alam Lake, Hyderabad. *Poll. Res.* 3: 681-687.

Anitha, G., Kodarkar, M.S. and Chandrasekhar, S.V.A., 2006. Studies on Macro-zoobenthos in Mir-Alam lake, Hyderabad, Andhra Pardesh. In: Ecology of Lakes and Reservoirs (Ed. V.B. Sakhare), Daya Publishing House, Delhi, pp. 1-15.

Anjana, S; Gujarathi, S; and Kanhere, R.R. 1998. Seasonal Dyanamics of Phytoplankton Population in Relation to Abiotic Factors of a Fresh Water Pond at Barwani (M.P.). *Poll. Res.* 17: 133-136.

Anna Mercy, T.V; Thomas Raju and Jacob Eapen. 2002. Potential Ornamental Fishes of the Western Ghats (Boopendranath, M.R; Meenakumari, B; Joseph, J; Sankar, T.V; Pravin, P. and Edwin, L. Eds.), p 151-161, Society of Fisheries Technologists (India), Cochin.

Anon, 1984. Studies on Energy Flow and Productivity of Lake Jaisamand in Relation to Fisheries Potential. Dept. Limn. Fish., RCA, Udaipur., Final Report of the ICAR Project: 24p.

Anon, 1999. Handbook of Statistics, Department of Animal Husbandry and Dairying, Ministry of Agriculture, Government of India, New Delhi.

Arshaduddin, M.D. and Khan, M.A. 1991. Rotifer Fauna of some Seasonal Ponds of Osmania University Campus, Hyderabad (AP). India. *Indian J. Microbiol.Ecol.* 2: 29-40.

Ashashree, H.M; Venkateshwarlu, M. and H.M. Renuka Swamy 2008. Diversity of Fish Fauna in Nagathibelagulu Pond, Shimoga, Karnataka. In: Advances in Aquatic Ecology (Vol. 2), Ed. V.B. Sakhare, pp. 95-97, Daya Publishing House, New Delhi.

Awasthi, U. and Tiwari, S. 2004. Seasonal Trends in Abiotic Factors of a Lentic Habitat (Govindgarh Lake), Rewa, M.P., India. *Eco. Env. and Cons.*, 10(2): 165-170.

Ayyappan, S. and Krishnan, M. 2004, Indian Fisheries: dimensions of development, *Indian Journal of Agricultural Economics*, July-Sept. 2004, 59(3); 391-412 (Annual Conference of Indian Society of Agricultural Economics, TNAU, Coimbatore – Lead paper).

Bade, B.B., Kulkarni, D.A. and Kumbhar, A.C. 2009. Physico-chemical Limnology of Sai Reservoir in Latur District, Maharashtra. *Ecology and Fisheries*. 2(2): 83-90.

Bagde, U.S. and Varma, A.K. 1985. Physico-chemical Characteristics of Water of J.N.U. Lake at New Delhi. Indian *J.Ecol.* 12 (1): 151-156.

Bahura, C.K. 2001a. Phytoplanktonic Community of a Highly Eutrophicated Temple Tank, Bikaner, Rajasthan, India. *J. Aqua.Biol.* 13(172): 47-51.

Bahura, C.K. 2001b. Diurnal Cycle of Certain Abiotic Parameters of a Fresh Water Lake the Ganjer Lake (Bikaner) in the Thar Desert of India. *J. Aqua. Biol.*,16 (12): 45-48.

Baiju, M. and Haridayanathan, C. 2002. Fishing Gears of Muvattupuzha River System of Kerala, In: Riverine and Reservoir Fisheries of India (Boopendranath, M.R; Meenakumari, B; Joseph, J; Sankar, T.V; Pravin, P. and Edwin, L. Eds.) p. 256-263; Society of Fisheries Technologists (India), Cochin.

Bais, V.S. and Agarwal, N.C. 1995. Comparative Study of the Zooplanktonic Spectrum in the Sagar Lake and Military Engineering Lake. *J. Environ.Biol.* 16(1): 27-32.

Baker, R.L.1979. Specific Status of *Keratella cochlearis* (Goose) and *K. eurlinare ahlao* from (Rotifera and Brachionidae) Morphological and Ecological Consideration. *Canadian Journal of Zoology*, 57: 1719-1722.

Balakrista Reddy, G. 1989. Ecological Studies in the River Kagna near Tandor (Andhra Pradesh) with Special Reference to Water Quality and Pollution. Ph.D. Thesis, Osmania University, Hyderabad.

Balasubramaniam, S. and Bankey Bihari. 2002. Socio-economic Variables of Fishermen in Hirakud Reservoir and the Technology Adoption, p. 426-432. In: Boopendranath, M.R.; Meenakumari, B; Joseph, J; Sankar, T.V; Pravin, P. and Edwin, L. (Eds.). Riverine and Reservoir Fisheries of India. Society of Fisheries Technologists (India), Cochin.

Balasubramaniam, S; Bankey Bihari and Brajmohan. 2001. Socio-economic Status of Marine Fishermen in Two Fishing Villages of Orissa. *Fish. Technol.* 38(1): 51-55.

Balkhi, M.H. and Yousuf, A.R. 1990. Distributional Pattern of Copepod in the Freshwaters of Kashmir. In: Contributions to the Fisheries of Inland Open Water Systems in India (Part I) (Eds. A.G. Jhingran, V.K. Unnithan and Amitabha Ghosh), pp. 47-51, Inland Fisheries Society of India, Barrackpore.

Banakar, A.B; Manjappa, S; Kiran, B.R; Puttaiah, E.T. and Ravikumar, M. 2005. Phytoplankton Diversity in Relation to Abiotic Factors in Chandravalli Lake at Chitradurga, Karnataka. *J. Aqua. Biol.* 20: 25-30.

Banerjea, S.M. 1967. Water Quality and Soil Condition of Fish Ponds in some States of India in Relation to Fish Production. *Indian J. Fish.*,14(1&2): 115-144.

Baruah, D; Dutta, A. and Pravin, P. 2013. Traditional Fish Trapping Devices and methods in the Brahmaputra Village of Assam. *Indian J. Traditional Knowledge*, 12(1): 123-129.

Basavakumar, K.V; Devendrappa, S. and Sreevivas, S.T. 2011. A Study on Profile of Fishing Community of a Village in Karnataka. Karnataka. *J. Agric. Sci*; 24(5): 684-687.

Battish, S.K. 1981. Studies on some Chydorid and Macrothricid (Crustacea: Cladocera) from Punjab with the Description of Three New species Researches on Crustacean. 11: 17-25.

Battish, S.K. 1983. Ecology and Systematic of Cladocera (Daphnia: Branchiopoda) inhibiting Punjab, India. *Researches on Crustacea*, 12: 63-76.

Battish, S.K. 1992. Freshwater Zooplankton of India, Oxford Publishing Co. Pvt. Ltd., New Delhi; pp. 233.

Battul, P.N; Rao, K.P; Navale, R.A; Begale, M.B. and Shah, N.V. 2007. Fish Diversity from Ekrukh Lake near Solapur, Maharashtra. *J. Aqua.Biol.* 22(2): 68-72.

Beegum, S. 2006. Socio-economic Condition of Inland Fishermen – A Case Study of Kerala, Ph.D. Thesis, Mahatma Gandhi University, Kerala.

Begum, N.B. and Narayana, J. 2006. Phytoplankton Diversity of Floor Lentic Water Bodies in and around Davangarere City, Karnataka. *J. Aqua. Biol.* 21(2): 13-18.

Bennamma, Joseph and Yamakanamardi, S.M. 2010. Winter, Summer and Rainy Seasonal Changes in the Abundance and Biomass of Zooplankton in Relation to Environmental Variables in Kukkarahalli Lake of Mysore, Karnataka State, India.

Bhadane, R.S. 2012a. Zooplankton Dynamics of Gangapur Dam at Nashik, *Ecology and Fisheries*. 5(2): 51-56.

Bhadane, R.S. 2012b. Studies of Monthly Variations in DO, BOD and COD Parameters of Gangapur Dam Water at Nashik, Maharashtra. *Ecology and Fisheries*, 5(1): 47-54.

Bhagat, M.J. 1977. Ecology and Sport Fishery of Freshwater Lake, M.Sc. Thesis, University of Mumbai.

Bhagat, V.B. and Meshram, C.B. 2007. Zooplankton Dynamics of Ambadi Dam Ear Akot, Ankola, Maharashtra. *J.Aqua. Biol*. 22(1): 19-20.

Bhalerao, S.N., 2012. Study of Fish Diversity and Water Quality at Kasar Sai dam, Hinjewadi, Pune, MS, India, *International Research Journal of Biological Sciences. 1(4): 51-55,* Paper available online at www.isca.in.

Bhandarkar, S.V. and Gaupale, D.T. 2008. Correlation Coefficient of Physico-chemical Properties with Zooplankton Population in Sagar Lake, Bhandara, Maharashtra. *J.Curr. Sci.* 17: 547-550.

Bhati, D.P.S. and Rana, K.S. 1987. Zooplankton in Relation to Abiotic Components in the Fort Moat of Bharatpur. *Proc. Nat. Acad. Sci. India,* 57 (13): 237-242.

Bhatta, Ramchandra. 2003. Socio-economic Issues in Fisheries Sector in India, p. 17-42. In: A Profile of People, Technologies and Policies in Fisheries Sector in India (eds). Anjani Kumar, P.K. Katiha and P.K. Joshi, National Centre for Agriculture Economics and Policy Research, New Delhi.

Bhattacharya, B.K; Manna, R.K. and Choudhary, M. 2005. Fishing Crafts and Gear of Northeast India. Bull. No. 142, CIFRI.

Bhaumik, Utpal; Singh, U.P.; Paria, T. 2009. Ecology and Management of the Dhaura Reservoir, Uttaranchal for Enhancing Fish Production. *Indian Journal of Fisheries*. 56(3): 189-193.

Bilgrami, K.S. and Dutta Munshi, J.S. 1985. Ecology of River Ganges. Impact of Human Activities and Conservation of Aquatic Biota (Patna to Farakka) Allied Press, Bhagalpur, India.

Birasal, N.R; Nadkarni, V.B. and Gouder, B.Y.M. 1989. Ecology of Zooplankton of Sepa Reservoir of Kali River during the Filling Phase Western Ghats, Karnataka. *J. Freshwater Biol.* 1(1): 15-23.

Biswas, S. 1966. Five Species of Daphnidae (Crustacea: Cladocera) from Shimla Hills in India with a New record of *Alona costata sars* from Kameng Division; NEFA.*J. Zool. Soc. India,* 16(1-2): 92-98.

Biswas, S. 1971. Fauna of Rajasthan, Part II (Crustacea: Cladocera). Rec. 2001. Surv. India, 63: 95-141.

Bold H.C. and Wynne, M.J. 1978. Introduction to the Algal Structure and Reproduction, Prentice Hall of India, New Delhi.

Boyd, C.E. and Tucker, C.S. 2009. Pond Aquaculture Water Quality Management.

Bradka, J. and Rehackova, V., 1964. Mass Destruction of Fish in the Slapy Reservoirs in Winter 1962-63, In: Vodni, 1-10 spodarstvi, 14: 451-452.

Braj Mohan, 2002. Economic Status of the Fishermen of Malampuzha Reservoir. In: Riverine and Reservoir Fisheries of India (Proc. of the Nat. Seminar on Riverine and Reservoir Fisheries-Challenges and Strategies). Editors: Boopendranath, M.R., Meenakumari, B., Joseph, J., Sanakr, T.V., Pravin, P. and Edwin, L.), p. 421-425. Society of Fisheries Technologists (India), Cochin.

Chandanshive, N.E; Kamble, S.M. and Yadav, B.E. 2006. Fish Fauna of Pavana River of Pune, Maharashtra. *J. Aqua.Biol.* 21(3): 7-9.

Chandra, Ravish, 1989. Riverine Fisheries Resources of the Ganga and the Brahmputra. In: Conservation and Management of Inland Capture Fisheries Resources of India (Ed. Jhingran, A.G. and Sugunana, V.V.). Inland Fisheries Society of India, Barrackpore, pp. 33-39.

Chandrasekhar, S.V.A. 1995. Cladocera (Crustacea: Branchiopoda) Inhabiting Osmansagar, Hyderabad. *Geobios New Reports.* 14: 56-60.

Chandrasekhar, S.V.A. 1996. Ecological Studies on Saroornagar Lake, Hyderabad, Ph.D. Thesis, Osmania University, Hyderabad, pp. 80.

Chandrasekhar, S.V.A. 2006. Limnological Studies on Kondakarla Lake Vishakha District, Andhra Pradesh. In: Ecology of Lakes and Reservoirs (Ed. V.B.Sakhare), pp. 63-104, Daya Publishing House, Delhi.

Chandrasekhar, S.V.A. 2011. Rotifer Diversity in a Few Lakes of Andhra Pradesh. Rec. Adv. in Bio. of India, 121-124.

Chandrasekhar, S.V.A. and M.S. Kodarkar 1997. Diurnal Variation of Zooplankton in Saroornagar Lake, Hyderabad. *Indian J. Environ. Hlth.* Vol. 39 No. 2: 155-159.

Chapman, V.J. and Chapman, D.J. 1973. The Algae, Macmillan Book Company, London. Charak, K.S. and Fayaz, F.A. 2006. Ecological Status of Salal Reservoir. *Fishing Chimes*, 26(9): 38-40.

Charak, K.S. and Fayaz, F.A., 2006. Strategies for the Development of Fisheries in Jammu & Kashmir. *Fishing Chimes.* 26 (1): 204-206.

Charak, K.S. and Fayaz, F.A., 2007. Preliminary Study on Status of Fisheries in Salal Reservoir and Suggestive measures for Development. In: Advances in Aquatic Ecology (Ed. V.B. Sakhare), pp. 124-131, Daya Publishing House, Delhi.

Charjan, A.P; Dabhade, D.S. and Malu R.A. 2001. Population Trends of Rotifers in Washim Dist. (M.S.). Souvenir of Nat. Conf. on Fish and Fisheries: Challenges in the Millennium, at P.G. College of Science, Osmania University Hyderabad, 14-15 March 2001. Abstract No. 66.

Chatterjee, P.R. and Raziuddin, M. 2003. Analysis of Physico-chemical Parameters of Loco Tank - A Reservoir in Asansol Town, West Bengal.*Nat. Environ. Pollt. Tech.*, 2: 171-172.

Chattopadhyay, C. and Barik, A. 2009. The Composition and Diversity of Net Zooplankton species in a Tropical Freshwater Lake. *International Journal of Lakes and Rivers*, 2(1): 21-30.

Chaudhary Ruchira and Pillai, R.S. 2008. Studies on the Physico-chemical Parameters of Sathamcotta Lake (India) with Reference to Suitability for Aquaculture. *Journal of Environmental Research and Development*. 2(3): 402-405.

Chauhan, R. 1988. Seasonal Abundance of Zooplankton in Rawalsar Lake. *Geobios New Reports*. 7: 117-121.

Chauhan, R. 1993. Seasonal Fluctuation of Zooplankton in Renuka Lake, Himachal Pradesh. *Uttar Pradesh J. Zool.*, 111(1): 17-20.

Chauhan, Ramesh. 1993. Zooplankton Species and their Dominance in Rewalsar Lake, Himachal Pradesh, *Uttar Pradesh Jr. of Zoology*. 13(2): 143-147.

Choudhary, M. 1989. An Economic Study on the Socio-economic Status of the Fishermen Community in Lower Assam. *J. Assam. Sci. Soc.* 21(1): 40-41.

Choudhary, S. and Singh, D.K. 1999. Zooplankton Populations of Boosra Lake at Muzaffarpur, Bihar, *Environment and Ecology*, 17(2): 444-448.

Chouhan, Pushpa and Kanhere, R.R. 2013. Diversity of Zooplankton in Barwani Tank of West Nimar, M.P., India. *Res.J. Animal, Veterinary and Fishery Science*. 1(3): 7-13, Available online at www.isca.in.

Chouhan, R. 1988. Seasonal Abundance of Zooplankton in Rewalsar Lake, M.P. *Geobios New Report*, 7(2): 117-121.

CIFRI. 1997. Ecology and Fisheries of Bhatghar Reservoir, Central Inland Capture Fisheries Research Institute, Barrackpore, West Bengal, pp. 27-28.

CIFRI. 1998. Ecological and Fisheries Status of Reservoirs in India - A Recent Survey. In: Das, Manas Kr. (ed.). *The Inland Fisheries News*, Newsletter of CIFRI. 3 (1): 1-2.

Clay, C.H.,1961. Desigh of Fish Ways and Other Fish Facilities, Development of Fisheries of Canada, Ottawa.

CMFRI. 2008. Annual Report 2007-2008, Cochin, India.

CMFRI. 2008. CMFRI Research Highlights 2007-2008, Cochin, India.

Dabgar, P.J. 2012. Phytoplankton Diversity on Wadhvana Wetland at Dabjoi Taluka (Gujrat), India. *Plant Sciences Feed*. 2(5): 85-87.

Das, A.K. and Srivastava, N.P. 2003. Ecology of Sarni Reservoir (M.P.) in the Context of Fisheries. *Poll. Res.* 22(1): 533-539.

Das, A.K., Ch. Gopalkrishnayya and Ramakrishniah, M. 2001. Guidelines for Management of Andhra Pradesh Reservoirs. *Fishing Chimes*, 21(5): 25-28.

Das, P., 1989. Exotic Fish Germplasm Resources in India and their Conservation. In: Exotic Aquatic Species in India (Joseph, M.M.Ed.), Asian Fisheries Society, Indian Branch, Special Publication Number 1, Mangalore, pp. 49-50.

Das, P. 2008. Challenging Experiences of Exotic Fish Introductions: An Overview, pp. 35-44, In: Fish Introductions in India: Status, Potential and Challenges (Eds.W.S. Lakra, A.K. Singh and S.Ayyapan), Narendra Publishing House, Delhi.

David, A., Ray, P., Govind, B.V., Rajagopal, K.V. and Banerjee, R.K., 1969. Limnology and Fisheries of the Tungabhadra Reservoir. Bull. No. 13, Central Inland Fisheries Research Institute, Barrackpore.

Dawson, Percy. 2002. Trawling in Indian Reservoirs. In: Riverine ad Reservoir Fisheries of India (Boopendraath, M.R. Meeakumari, B., Joseph, J., Sankar, T.V., Pravin, P., and Edwin, L. Eds.), P. 264-267, Society of Fisheries Technologists (India), Cochin.

Day, F., 1967. *The Fishes of India,* Vols. 1 and 2. Jagamander Book Agency, New Delhi.

De Dekker, P. 2002. Ostracode Paleoecology, in Ostracode Applications in Quanternary Research, Geophysical Monograph 131, American Geophysical Union, pp. 125-132.

Deenadayalamoorthy, G. and Mazher Sultana. 2011. Identification of Zooplakton Species Collected from Different Ponds of Arakkonam Town,Vellore District, Tamil Nadu. *J.Biosci.Res.* 2(2): 72-75.

Dehadrai, P.V. 2002. Reservoir Fisheries in India, in : Riverine and Reservoir Fisheries of India (Boopendranath, M.R; Meenakumari, B; Joseph, J; Sankar T. V; Pravin, P. and Edwin, L; Eds.), p. 97-103, Society of Fisheries Technologists (India), Cochin.

Deorari, B.P., 1993. Productive Potential of a Manmade Reservoir of Tarai of Uttar Pradesh with Particular Reference to Fish Fauna. Ph.D. Thesis, Rohilkhand University, Bareiliy, 291 pp.

Desai, S.S. 1980. Fisheries of Nathsagar Reservoir, *India Today & Tomorrow,* 8 (4): 181 & 161.

Desai, V.R. 2008. Reservoirs can Boost Inland Fish Production. *Fishing Chimes.* 28(1): 39-46.

Desai, V.R. 2013. On Increased Capture and Culture Fish Production from Indian Reservoirs. *Fishing Chimes,* 32(10): 81-84.

Desai, V.R., Shrivastava, N.P. and Kumar, D., 2007. Constraints in Reservoir Fishery Development: A Case Study of Ravishankar Sagar Reservoir. *Fishing Chimes.* 27 (4): 19-22.

Deshmukh, U.S., 2001. Ecological Studies of Chhatri Lake, Amravati; with Special Reference to Planktons and Productivity. Ph.D. Thesis, Amravathi University, Amravathi.

Devaraj, K.V., Basavaraju, Y. and Seenappa, D., 2008. Introduced Food Fishes of Karnataka: An Overview, pp. 235-241, In: Fish Introductions in India: Status, Potential and Challenges (Eds. W.S. Lakra, A.K. Singh and S.Ayyapan), Narendra Publishing House, Delhi.

Devaraj, K.V. and Mahadeva, H.S. 1990. Socio-economic Status of Fishermen Operating Around Hemavathi Reservoir, Karnataka, p 102-105. In: Jhingran A.G. and Unnithan (eds.). Reservoir Fisheries in India. Proceedings of the National Workshop on Reservoir Fisheries, 3-4 January, 1990. Special Publication 3, Asian Fisheries Society, Indian Branch, Mangalore, India.

Devaraj, M., Prabhavathy G., and Goswami, P.K., 1990. Assessment of Optimum Fish yields from Reservoirs in Tamil Nadu. p. 118-130. In: Jhingran, Arun G. and Unnithan, V.K. (eds.). Reservoir Fisheries in India. Proceedings of the National Workshop on Reservoir Fisheries, 3-4 January, 1990. Special Publication 3, Asian Fisheries Society, Indian Branch, Mangalore, India.

Devaraj, M. and Smita, P. 1988. Economic Performance of Mechanical Trawlers in the State of Kerala, India. *Fish. Res.* 6(3): 271-286.

Devi, Sarala B. 1997. Present Status, Potentialities, Management and Economics of Fisheries of Two Minor Reservoirs of Hyderabad. Ph.D. Thesis, Osmania University, Hyderabad.

Dhanalakshmi, B. and Priyatharsini, P. 2015. An Assessment of Freshwater Piscine Diversity in Selected Wetlands in Coimbatore District, Tamil Nadu, India - A Preliminary Study. Open Access Library Journal. z:e2236. http://dx.doi.org/10.4236/oalib. 1102236.

Dhanapathi, M.V.S.S.S. 1973. On the Occurrence of the Rare Rotifer *Rotatria neptunia Eherenberg* in India. *Curr. Sci.* 42(21): 770.

Dhanapathi, M.V.S.S.S. 2000. Taxonomic Notes on the Rotifers from India (from 1889-2000) IAAB, Hyderabad Publ.10, 1-178.

Dhanapathi, M.V.S.S.S. and Rama Sarma, D.V. 2000. Further Studies on the Rotifers from Andhra Pradesh, India, including a New species. *J. Aqua.Biol.* 15(1&2): 6-15.

Dhawan, Asha, 2010. Punjab to go Ahead in Aquaculture. *Fishing Chimes*.30 (1): 166-168. Dhembare, A.J. 2011. Statistical Approaches for Computing Diversity and Density of Zooplankton with Water Factors in Mula Dam, Rahuri, M.S; India. *Euro. J. Expt. Biol.* 1(2): 68-76, Available online at www.pelagiaresearch library.com.

Dixitulu, J.V.H. 1999. Render Indian Reservoirs Sustainably Fishful. *Fishing Chimes*. 19 (2): 5-7.

Dixitulu, J.V.H. 2010. Why is the Giant Sleeping still? *Fishing Chimes*, 29(10): 5-6.

Doddagoudar, S.F. 1989. An Ecological Study of Phytoplankton of Four Fresh Water Bodies of Dharwad. Ph.D Thesis, Karnatak University, Dharwad.

Doddamani, P.L; Panda Kamalesh, S. Benkakappa, M.A. Rather and B.T. Naveen Kumar. 2011. Indian Reservoirs: An Untapped Inland Fisheries Resource, *Fishing Chimes*, 30(12): 42-45.

Dua, Anish and Chander Prakash, 2009. Distribution and Abundance of Fish Populations in Harike wetland-a Ramsar site in India. *J.Environ.Biol.*30 (2): 247-251.

Dubey, Ashwani Kumar, Shukla Sandeep Kumar and Verma Hemlata. 2012. Ichthyo-diversity of Banisagar Dam at Chhatarpur, Madhya Pradesh, India. *International Journal of Fisheries and Aquaculture Sciences*. 2(3): 157-161.

Dubey, G.P. 2008. 50 Years of Fisheries Development in Gandhisagar. *Fishing Chimes*, 28(2): 8-16.

Edmondson, W.T. 1959. Rotifera, pp. 420-497. In: Freshwater Biology (Eds. H.B. Ward and G.C. Whipple) (2nd Edition, W.T. Edmondson) John Wiley and Sons Inc; New York: 1-1248.

Ekka, A; Katiha, P.K; Pandit Arun; Barik, N; Salim Shyam and Ganesh Kumar, B. 2012. Socio-economic Status of Fishers of Reservoirs in India. *J. Inland Fish. Soc. India*. 44(2): 79-87.

Fish Base, 2004. CD-Rom World Fish Centre: 205 Bloomingdak Bldg. Salceds St. Legapse Village, Makati City, Metro Manilla, 1200, Philippines.

Garg, R.K., Rao, R.J. and Saksena, D.N. 2008. Water Quality and Conservation Management of Ramasagar Reservoir, Datia, Madhya Pradesh. *J.Environ. Biol.* 30(5): 909-916.

Goel, P.K; Kulkarni, A.Y. and Khatavkar, S.D. 1968. Species Diversity in Phytoplankton Communities in a Few Freshwater Bodies in Southern Maharashtra. *Geobios*, 15: 150-156.

George, M.G.1966. Diurnal Variations in Physico-chemical Factors and Zooplankton in Surface Layer of three Fresh Water Ponds. *Indian Journal of Fisheries*, 13: 48-82.

George, V.C. 2002. Fishing Techniques of Riverine and Reservoir Systems - Present Status and Future Challenges. In: Riverine and Reservoir Fisheries of India (Boopendranath, M.R; Meenakumari, B; Joseph, J; Sankar, T.V; Pravin, P. and Edwin, L. Eds.), p. 196, Society of Fisheries Technologists (India), Cochin.

Ghosh, A. and George, J.P. 1989. Studies on the Aboitic Factors and Zooplankton in a Polluted Urban Reservoir- Hussainsagar, Hyderabad: Impact on Water Quality and Embryonic Development of Fishes, *Indian J. Environ. Hlth*; 31(1): 49-59.

Gill, A.S., 1984. Effect of Dams and Water-ways on Fish Fauna in Rivers of Punjab, pp. 125-126. In: Status of Wildlife in Punjab. Indian Ecological Society, Ludhiana, India.

Gireesha, O.; Basavaraja, N.Tyagi Avinash C., and Shanmukha, S.N., 2003. Tungabhadra Reservoir: Rearing of Rohu Spawn and Common Carp Fingerlings in Pens. *Fishing Chimes*.23 (9): 21-24.

Girijakumari, S. 2007. Resource Potential of Sasthamkotta Lake with Special Reference to Fish Fauna and their Sustainability, Ph.D. Thesis Mahatma Gandhi University, Kottayam.

Giripunde, M.D; Fulke, A.B; Khairnar, Krishna; Meshram, P.U. and Paunikar, W.N. 2013. A Review of Phytoplankton Ecology in Freshwater Lakes of India, Lakes, Reservoirs and Ponds (*Romanian Journal of Limnology*). 7(2): 1-4.

Goel, P.K; Khatavkar, S.D; Kulkarni, A.Y. and Trivedi, R.K. 1986. Limnological Studies of Few Freshwater Bodies in Southwestern Maharashtra with Special Reference to their Chemistry and Phytoplankton. *Poll. Res.* 5(2): 79-84.

Goswami, A.P. and Mankodi, P.C. 2012. Study on Zooplankton of Fresh Water Reservoir Nyari-II Rajkot District, Gujarat, India, *ISCA J. Biological Sci.*1(1): 30-34.

Griffith, B.M. 1923. The Phytoplankton of Bodies of Fresh Water and the Factors Determining its Occurrence and Composition. *Jour. Ecol.*, 11:184-213.

Gupta, G.P. 1975. Sediment Production Status Report on Data Collection Land Utilization. Soil. Cons. Digest. 3(2): 10-21.

Gupta, S. 2002. Studies on the Diversity of Cladocerans in the Lake Mansar, Jammu. M. Phil. Dissertation, University of Jammu, Jammu.

Gupta, S.C. and Mathur, G.C.D. 2001. Hydrochemistry of Udaipur Lakes. *Indian Journal of Environmental Health*, 43(1): 3844.

Gurumayum, S.D. and Choudhary, M. 2009. Fishing methods in the Rivers of Northeast India. *Indian J. of Traditional Knowledge*, 8(2): 237-241.

Hafsa, S.L. and Gupta, S. 2009. Phytoplankton Diversity and Dynamics of Chatla Floodplain Lake, Barak Valley, Assam, North East India-A Seasonal Study. *J. Environ. Biol.*, 30(6): 1007-1012.

Hazarika, Arup, K. and Datta, A. 1998. Interrelationship of Certain Physicochemical Parameters and Plankton Community of Tasek Lake (Meghalaya). *Environ. and Ecol.*, 16 (3): 561-567.

Hensen, V.1887. Uber Die Bestimmung des Planktons oder des im Meere treibende Materials an Pflanzen und Thieren. 5. Bericht der Kommission zur Wissenschaftlichen Untersuchung der deutschen Meere, 1882-1886, Bd.12-16: 1-107.

Hilborn, R. and Walters, C.J. 1992. *Quantitative Fisheries Stock Assessment:* Choice, Dynamics and Uncertainty. Chapman and Hall. 570 pp.

Hiware, C.J. 2006. Ichthyofauna from Four Districts of Marathwada Region, Maharashtra, India. *Zoos' Print Journal*, 21 (1): 2137-2139.

Holden, P.B. and Stalnaker, C.B., 1975. Distribution and Abundance of Mainstream Fishes of the Middle and Upper Colorado River Basins,1967-1973, In: Transcations of the American Fisheries Society, 104: 217-231.

Holmes, J.A. and Chivas, A.R. 2012. The Ostracoda, Applications in Quanternary Research, Geophysical Monograph 131, American Geophysical Union, Washington D.C.

Hosmani, S.P. 2010. Phytoplankton Diversity in Lakes of Mysore District, Karnataka State, India. *The Ecoscan.* 4(1): 53-57.

Hosmani, S.P. and Bharathi, S.G. 1980. Limnological Studies in Ponds and Lakes of Dharwad- Comparative Phytoplankton Ecology of Four Water Bodies. *Phykos.* 19(1): 27-43.

Hubbs, C. and Pigg, J.1976. The Effects of Impoundments on Threatened Fishes of Oklahoma Annals of the Oklahoma Academy of Scienc, 5: 133-177.

Huet, M. 1960. General Principles of Pond Construction and Management Productivity and Stocking. ETAP, FAO Lecture at the IIIrd International Training Centre, Boger, Indonesia, 1955, 2.

Hulyal, S.B. and Kaliwal, B.B. 2009. Dynamics of Phytoplankton in Relation to Physico-chemical Factors of Almatti Reservoir of Bijapur District, Karnataka State. *Environ. Monit. Assess.*, 153: 45-59.

Hutchinson, G.E. 1967. A Treatise on Limnology. Introduction to Lake Biology and the Limnoplankton. John Wiley and Sons, New York London, pp. 115.

Ingole, S.B. 2013. Correlation of Rotifers with Physico-chemical Factors at Majalgaon Reservoir, Maharashtra. In: Emerging Trends in Fisheries and Aquaculture (Eds. V.B. Sakhare and B.Vasanthkumar), pp. 225-231, Astral International Pvt. Ltd. New Delhi.

Ingole, S.B; Kadam, G.A; Naik, S.R. and Kulkarni G.K. 2011. Water Quality of Majalgaon Dam with Special Reference to Zooplankton, In: *Limnology: Current Perspectives* (Ed. V.B. Sakhare) Daya Publishing House, Delhi.

Isaiarasu, L; Murugavel, P. and Murugan, N. 2001. Biodiversity of Zooplankton Observed in a Seasonal, Tropical Pond Near Sivakasi, Tamil Nadu, India. *Ecol. Env. and Cons.* 7(3): 257-261.

Iwama, G.K., M.M. Vijayan, and J.D. Morgan.2000. The Stress Response in Fish. Icthyology, Recent Research Advances 453 pp. Oxford and IBH Publishing Co., Pvt. Ltd., N. Delhi.

Jadhav, R.N; Pimpliskar Mukesh and Handa Shruti. 2013. Zooplankton Diversity of Nirmal Lake, Vasai, Dist. Thane (M.S.) India. *J. Aqua. Biol.* 27(1): 1-6.

Jain, S.M., Sharma, M. and Thakur, R. 1996. Seasonal Variations in Physico-chemical Parameters of Halali Reservoir of Vidisha District, India. *J.Ecobiol.*, 8: 181-188.

Jalizadeh, Koorosh and Yamaknamardi, S.M. 2012. Abundance of Ostracod in Three Contrasting Lentic Ecosystems of Mysore, Karnataka. In: Perspectives in Ecology (Eds. V.B. Sakhare and J.S. Mohite) pp. 127-134, Oxford Book Company, Jaipur.

Jalilzadeh, Koorosh and Yamakanamard, S.M. 2012. Abundance of Cladocera in three Contrasting Lentic Ecosystems of Mysore, Karnataka In: Perspectives in Ecology (Eds. V.B. Sakhare and J.S. Mohite), Oxford Book Company, Jaipur, pp. 134-143.

Jalilzadeh, Koorosh and Yamakanamard, S.M. 2012. Total Zooplankton Abundance and Biomass in Three Contrasting Lentic Ecosystems of Mysore, Karnataka State, In: Advances in Aquatic Ecology (Vol. 6) (Eds. V.B. Sakhare. and Patricio Rene De los Rios Escalante), pp. 34-49. Daya Publishing House, New Delhi.

Jameela Beevi K.S. and Ramacharan, A. 2002. Potential Ornamental Fishes of Muvattupuzha River, in Ernahulum District, Kerala (Boopendranath, M.R; Meenakumari, B; Joseph, J; Sankar, T.V; Pravin, P. and Edwin, L. Eds.), p. 400-414, Society of Fisheries Technologists (India), Cochin.

Jana, B.B. 1973. Seasonal Periodicity of Plankton in a Freshwater Pond in West Bengal, India. *International Review of Hydrobiology*. 58(1): 127-143.

Jaybhaye, U.M. and Khedkar, G.D. 2008. Fish Diversity of Sawana Dam in Hingoli District of Maharashtra. *J. Aqua.Biol.* 23(1): 26-28.

Jesu Arockia Raj. A., Seetharaman, S., Haniffa, M.A. and Singh, S.P., 2004. Food and Feeding Habits of a Threatened Featherback, *Notopterus Notopterus. J, Aqua.Biol.* 19 (1):115-118.

Jetithor, S.G. 2010. Studies on some Aspects of Ecology and Fisheries of Harni (Katgaon) Reservoir in Osmanabad District, Maharashtra, Ph.D. Thesis, Dr. B.A.M.U. Aurangabad.

Jha, P., Mandel, A. and Barat, S. 2004. Mahananda Reservoir, West Bengal. Its ichthyofauna, Fishery and Socio-economic Profile of Fish Production. *Fishing Chimes*, 24(6): 14-17.

Jhingran, A.G. 1986. Artificial Recruitment and Fisheries of Indian Reservoirs. Bull. No. 45, Central Inland Fisheries Research Institute, Barrackpore, West Bengal, 60p.

Jhingran, A.G. 1988. Reservoir Fisheries in India. *Journal of the Indian Fisheries Association*, 18: 261-273.

Jhingran, A.G. 1990. Recent Advances in Inland Fisheries Development in India. Technologies for Inland Fisheries Development, Central Inland Fisheries Research Institute, Barrackpore, West Bengal, 1-11.

Jhingran, A.G; Natarajan, A.V; Banerjea, S.M; and David, A. 1969. Methodology on Reservoir Fisheries Investigations in India. CIFRI, Bulletin No. 12.

Jhingran, A.G. and Sugunan, V.V., 1990. General Guidelines and Planning Criteria for Small Reservoir Fisheries Management. In Reservoir Fisheries in India (Jhingran, A.G. and V.K. Unnithan Eds.) pp. 1-8. Asian Fisheries Society, Indian Branch, Mangalore, India.

Joseph, K.M. and Narayanan, K.P. 1965. Fishing Gear and methods of the River Brahmaputra in Assam. *Fish. Tech.* 2: 205.

Joshi, H.C. 1990. Water Pollution Problems in Indian Reservoirs, p. 21-28. In: Jhingran, A.G. and Unnithan, V.K. (eds.). Reservoir Fisheries in India. Proceedings of the National Workshop on Reservoir Fisheries, 3-4 January, 1990. Special Punlication 3, Asian Fisheries Society, Indian Branch, Mangalore, India.

Joshi K.D., Singh B.K., Mishra S.S. Srivastava R.S., Jha D.N., Alam M.A. and Das S.C.S. (2013). Impact Assessment of Multiple Habitat Alterations on Ecosystem Functions and Fisheries in Rivers. CIFRI Annual Report 2013.

Joshi, P.K. and Sakhare, V.B. 2012. Ecology and Ichthyofauna of Bori Reservoir in Maharashtra. *Fishing Chimes*, 22(4): 40-41.

Joshi, P.S. 2011. Studies on Zooplanktons of Rajura Lake of Buldhana District, Maharashtra, India. *Science Research Reporter*. 1(3): 132-137.

Joshi, S.N. and Khanna, S.S. 1980. Relative Fecundity of *Labeo gonius* (Ham.) from Nanaksagar Reservoir. *Proceedings: Animal Sciences*. 89(5): 493-503.

Kalavathy, M.H. 1985. Ethical and Socio-cultural Background of Marine Fishing Communities in Orissa. In Tietz; U.(G.) Artisanal Marine Fisher Folk of Orissa, pp. 59-67.

Kalbande, Subhangi, Telkhade, Pravin and Zade, Suresh, 2012. Fish Diversity of Rawanwadi Lake of Bhandara District, Maharashtra, India. *Abhinav Journal*. 2(2): 30-33, Paper Available on wwww.abhinavjournal.com.

Kalpana Ojha, Ravi Kumar Goel, Subhashini Sharma, Shweta Sharma, Archana Yadav, Nivedita Yadav and K.P. Sharma.2013. Impact of Colourful Textile Prints on Ground Water Quality of Sanganer Jaipur, Rajasthan, India. *Poll. Res.*32 (3): 595-598.

Kamalkannan, K. and Namasivayam, N. 2005. Economic Impowerment of Women through Entrepreneership Development. *Kisan World*, 32(9): 26-28.

Kamble, A.T. and Mudkhede, L.M. 2013. Study of Fish Fauna and Productivity of Loni Reservoir, Tq. Kinwat (Maharashtra). *International Journal of Biomedical and Advance Research*. 4(3): 155-159.

Kamble, S.M; Mohekar, A.D. and Bhagwan, H.K. 2006. Biodiversity of Fishes of River Manjara Near Kallam, District Osmanabad (M.S.), India. *J. Aqua. Biol.* 21(3): 3-4.

Kanagasabapathi, V. and Rajan, M.K. 2010. A Preliminary Survey of Plankton in Irrukkangudi Reservoir, Virudhunagar District, Tamil Nadu, India. *J. Phytol.* 2(3): 63-72.

Kaparapu, J. and Rao, M.N.G. 2013. Seasonal Fluctuation of Phytoplankton in Riwada Reservoir, Visakhapatnam, Andhra Pradesh, India. *Not. Sci. Biol.* 5(3): 290-295.

Karamchandani, S.J. and Mishra, D.N.,1980. Prelininary Observations on the Status of Silver Carp in Relation to Catla in the Culture Fishery of Kulgarhi Reservoir. *J.Bombay Nat.Hist.Soc;* 77: 261-269.

Karennawar, M.H. and Khabade, S.A. 2013. Planktonic Diversity Study of some Freshwater Lakes of Jath Tehsil of Sangli District (Maharashtra): *Ecology and Fisheries*. 6(1): 91-94.

Karmarkar, A.K. and Datta, A.K. 1988. On a Collection of Fish from Bastar District, Madhya Pradesh. Records of the Zoological Survey of India, Occasional Paper No. 98, Zoological Survey of India, Calcatta, pp. 50.

Karuthapandi, M; Rao, D.V. and Xavier Innocent. 2013. Freshwater Rotifers of Andhra Pradesh- checklist, *International Journal of Life Science and Educational Research* 1(1): 1-13. Paper available online at http://www.ijlser.com.

Kataria, H.C. and Jain, O.P. 1995. Physico-chemical Analysis of River Ajhar. *Indian J. Environ. Protec.*, 5: 569-571.

Kathia, P.K., Vass, K.K., Das, A.K. and Shrivastava, N.P., 2009. Improved Productivity of Reservoir Fisheries in India, Central Inland Fisheries Research Institute, Barrackpore.

Kaul, V. and Handoo, J.K. and Raina, R. 1980. Physico-chemical Characteristics of Nilnag – A High Altitude Forest Lake in Kashmir and its Comparison with the Valley Lakes. *Proceedings of Indian National Sci.Acad.*, B. 46 (4): 528-541.

Kaur Kamaldeep and Dhawan, Asha. 1997. Introduction to Inland Fisheries. Nat. Agri. Techl. Infor. Center, Ludhiana, India.

Kaushik, S. and Sharma, N. 1994. Physico-chemical Characteristics and Zooplankton Population of a Perennial Tank, Matsya Sarowar, Gwaliar. *Environment and Ecology*, 12(2): 429-434.

Kavitha, A; Ragini Bala, Singh G.S. and Raj, A.D.S. 2005. Freshwater Phytoplankton Assemblages of Two Temple Ponds of South Tamil Nadu. *Indian Hydrobiol.* 8(1): 61-65.

Khabade, S.A. and Mule, M.B. 2009. Studies on Aquatic Insects in Relation to Physico-chemical Parameters of Anjani Reservoir from Tasgaon Tahsil of Sangli District, Maharashtra. *Ecology and Fisheries.* 2(1): 57-68.

Khabade, S.A., Muley, M.B. and Sathe, S.S. 2002. Studies on Physico-chemical Parameters of Iodhe Water Reservoir from Tasgaon Tehsil (Maharashtra), India *J. Environ. & Ecoplan.* 6(2): 301-304.

Khabade, S.A., Patil Archana and Murgunde, Rekha. 2014. Plankton Diversity in Panchganga River Water near Ichakaranji City, Maharashtra. In: Advaces in Aquatic Ecology (Vol. 8), (Eds. V.B. Sakhare and B.Vasanthkumar), Astral International Pvt. Ltd., pp. 230-234.

Khalid, M.A., Siddiqui, M.S.,1990. Reservoir Fishery Potential of Nasik District in Maharashtra with Special Reference to Girna Dam Reservoir Fisheries, pp. 97-101. In: In Reservoir Fisheries in India (Jhingran A.G. and V.K. Unnithan Eds.) pp.1-8. Asian Fisheries Society, Indian Branch, Mangalore, India.

Khan, A.A., Dawson, P., Rao, J.S.R., and Varghese, M.D., 1992. Fishing in Impounded Waters — A Case Study in Hirakud Reservoir, Orissa, CIFT, Cochin.

Khan, A.A; Kartha, K.N; Percy Dawson and V.C. George. 1991. Fish Harvesting Systems in Indian Reservoirs. Proc. of Nat. Workshop on Low Energy Fishing, 8-9th August, 1991, pp. 152-154.

Khan, M.A.1987. Observations on Zooplankton Composition, Abundance and Periodicity in Two Floodplain Lakes of the Kashmir Himalayan Valley. *Acta Hydrochemica Hydrobiologia.* 15: 167-174.

Khan, M.A., Dwivedi, R.K., Mehrotra, S.N., Srivastava, K.P., Tyagi, R.K. and Katiha, P.K., 1990. Stocking as a Management Tool in Optimising Fish yield from a Small Reservoir (Bacchra) in Ganga Basin. In: Jhingran, Arun G. and V.K. Unnithan (eds.). Reservoir Fisheries in India. Proceedings of the National Workshop on Reservoir Fisheries, 3-4 January, 1990. Special Publication 3, Asian Fisheries Society, Indian Bracnch, Mangalore, India, p. 71-76.

Khan, M.A. and Nagma. 2013. Studies on Freshwater Fish Fauna of District Bijnor in Western Uttar Pradesh, India. *Int. J. Lifesc. Bt. & Pharm. Res.* 2(3): 410-417.

Khan, R.A. 2003. Faunal Diversity of Zooplankton in Freshwater Wetlands of Southeastern West Bengal, Zoological Survey of India, Kolkata, Occasional Paper No. 204, pp. 107.

Khan, Sirajuddin. 1990. Present Status of Fisheries of Hirakud Reservoir in Orissa and Strategy for Enhancing yield and Betterment of the Fishermen Communities. pp. 150-154. In: Jhingran, Arun G. and V.K. Unnithan (eds.) Reservoir Fisheries in India. Proceedings of the National Workshop on Reservoir Fisheries, 3-4 January, 1990. Special Publication 3, Asian Fisheries Society, Indian Branch, Mangalore, India.

Khanna, D.R; Seth, T.R; Malik, D.S. and Sing, R.K. 1999. Fishes and the Ecology of the River Suswa at Raiwala Dehradun. In: Sustainable Ecosystems and Environment, (Eds. D.R. Khanna, Ashutosh Gautam and Aditya Gautam), p. 105-110.

Kharat, S.S; Paingankar, M; and Dahanukar, N. 2012. Freshwater Fish Fauna of Krishna River at Wai, Northern Western Ghats, India. *Journal of Threatened Taxa*. 4(6): 2644-2652.

Khare, P.K. 2005. Physico-chemical Characteristics in Relation to Abundance of Plankton of Jagat Sagar Pond, Chhatarpur, India. In: Advances in Limnology (Ed. S.R. Mishra), pp. 162-174. Daya Publishing House, Delhi.

Khatri, T.C. 1984. Seasonal Variations in the Ecosystem of the Lakhotia Lake in Rajasthan. *Indian Jr. of Fisheries* 31(1): 122-129.

Khatri, T.C. 1985. Diurnal Fluctuations in Physico-chemical Parameters during Summer Season in Lakhotia Lake of Pali (Rajasthan). *Env.Ecology* 2(2): 95-97.

Khatri, T.C. 1987a. Seasonal Distribution of Phytoplankton in Idukki Reservoir of Kerala, India. *Environment and Ecology*, 5(1): 71-74.

Khatri, T.C. 1987b. Nutrient Level and its Influence on Phytoplankton Population in Lokhotia Lake of Pali (Rajasthan). *J. Inland Fish. Soc. India*, 19(2): 37-46.

Kiran, B.R. and Puttaiah, E.T. 2010. Water Quality Assessment of Bhadra Reservoir of Karnataka with Reference to Physico-chemical Characteristics. In: Aquatic Ecosystem and its Management (Eds. K. Vijaykumar and B. Vasanthkumar), pp. 71-101, Daya Publishing House, Delhi.

Kiran, B.R. and Puttaiah E.T. and Devidas Kamath. 2007. Diversity and Seasonal Fluctuation of Zooplankton in Fish Pond of Bhadra Fish Farm, Karnataka. *Zoo's Print Journal*, 22(2): 2935-2936.

Klein, L. 1973. River Pollution. II. Causes and Effects (5th imp.), Butterworth and Co. Ltd. Kodarkar, M.S. 2008. Conservation of Lakes (Applied Limnology for Global Perception and Local Action), Indian Association of Aquatic Biologists, Hyderabad, pp. 101. Kokate, K. and Upare, S. 2005. Role of Fisheries in Rural Development. *Kurushetra*, 53(8): 33-37.

Koli, K.B. and Muley, D.V., 2012. Study of Zooplankton Parameters in Tulshi Reservoir of Kolhapur District (M.S.) India. *E-International Scientfic Research Journal*, 4(1): 38-46.

Koliyar, J.G. and Rokade, N.S. 2008. Water Quality in Powai Lake, Mumbai, Maharashtra. In: Proceedings of TAAL-2007: The 12th World Lake Conference (Eds. Sengupta, M. and Dalwani, R.), 1655-1659.

Kolkwitz, R. 1912. Plankton und Seston. Berichte d. Deutschen Bot. Gesellschaft., 30: 334-346.

Kottelat, M. and Whitten, T. 1996. Freshwater Biodiversity of Asia with Special Reference to Fish. World Bank Technical Paper No. 343, The World Bank, Washington, D.C; USA; 59p.

Krieger, W.1927. Zur Biologic des Flussplanktons. Pflanzenforschung, 10: 1-66.

Krishna Rao, D.S., Katre, Shakuntala, Jayaraj, E.G. and Reddy, S.R. 1999. Limnology and Status of the Fishery of Nelligudda Reservoir (Bangalore: India). *Indian J.Fish.* 46(3): 251-264.

Krishnaram, H., Ramchandra, M.M., Shivabasavaiah and Rmanjnath. 2012. Assessment of Water Quality of Byramangla Lake in Bangalore City, pp. 234-243. In: Advances in Aquatic Ecology, Edited by V.B. Sakhare and Patricio Rene De los Rios Escalante (Vol. 6), Daya Publishing House, Delhi.

Kudari, V.A. and Kanamadi, R.D. 2008. Impact of Hanged Trophic Status on Zooplankton Composition in Six Waterbodies of Dharwad District, Karnataka State. *Environmental Monitoring and Assessment*, 144(1-3): 301-313.

Kulkarni, C.V. 1947. Note on Freshwater Fishes of Bombay and Salsette Islads, *J.Bombay Natural History Society*, 47 (2): 319-326.

Kulshrestha, S.K., George, M.P., Saxena Rashmi, Malini Johri and Manish Shrivastava. 1992. Seasonal Variations in the Limnochemical Characteristics of Mansarovar Reservoir of Bhopal. In S.R. Mishra and D.N. Saksena (eds), Aquatic Ecology, Ashish Publishing House, New Delhi, pp. 275- 292.

Kulshreshta, S.K; Saxena, R; George, M.P; Shrivastava, M. and Tiwari, A. 1989. Phytoplankton of Eutrophic Mansarovar Reservoir of Bhopal. *Ind. J. Ecol. Environ. Sci.* 15: 205-215.

Kumar, K. 1990. Management and Development of Gobindsagar Reservoir. A Case Study. *Proc. Nat. Workshop on Reservoir Fisheries.* 13: 13-20.

Kumar Naik A.S. Benakappa S., Somashekara S.R., Anjaneyappa H.N., Jitendra Kumar., Mahesh V., Srinivas H. Hulkoti and Rajanna K.B., 2013. Studies on Ichthyofaunal Diversity of Karanja Reservoir, Karnataka, India. *Int. Res. J. Environment Sci.*. 2(2), 38-43, Paper available online at www.isca.in.

Kumar, S. and Dutta, D.P.S. 1994. Population Dynamics of Cladocera in a Subtropical Pond, Jammu. *Indian J. Environ.* 36(1): 19-23.

Kumar, Varun and Kumar, Kamal. 2013. A Preliminary Study on Fishing Craft and Gears in Dhaura Reservoir, Uttarakhand, India. *Int. Res. J. Biological Sci.* 2(8): 76-78. K.

Kurup, Madhusoodana, B. 2002. Rivers and Streams of Kerala Part of Western Ghats – Hotspots of Exceptional Fish Biodiversity and Endemism, (Boopendranath, M.R; Meenakumari, B; Joseph, J; Sankar, T.V; Pravin, P. and Edwin, L. Eds.), p. 204-217, Society of Fisheries Technologists (India), Cochin.

Lalrinsanga, P.L; Asha, Landge and Umashankar Prasad. 2006. Stocking as a Tool for Inland Fisheries Management: Principles and Strategies. *Fishing Chimes*, 26(2): 25-29.

Lakra, W.S. and Singh, A.K. 2007. Exotic Fish Introduction in Indian Waters: Past Experience and Lesson for the Future. *Fishing Chimes*. 27 (1): 30-34.

Lanka, L.P. and Khabade, S.A. 2012. Socio-economic Study of Fishermen Community with Special Reference to Jawahar Reservoir Nipani from Chikodi Tahsil of Belgaon District, Karnataka. *Ecology and Fisheries*, 5(2): 83-90.

Laskar, H.S. and Gupta, S. 2009. Phytoplankton Diversity and Dynamics of Chatla Foodplain Lake, Barak Valley, Assam, Northeast, India.

Lata, Poonam, Sharma Ankush, Kaur Harbhajan and Rathore, N.S. 2014. Plankton Diversity in Highly Human Inerfed Temple Pond. In: Advaces in Aquatic Ecology (Vol. 8), Astal International Pvt. Ltd. (Eds.V.B. Sakhare and B.Vasanthkumar), pp. 215-219.

Laxmappa, B., Jithender Kumar Naik, S. and Vamshi, S. 2014. Ichthyofaunal Diversity of Koilsagar Reservoir in Mahbubnagar District, Telangana, India. *International Journal of Fisheries and Aquatic Studies*, 2(3): 23-30.

Laxmappa, B; Satya Parameshwar, B. and Sreenivas Reddy, 2013. Status of Freshwater Prawn Farming in Ramanpad Reservoir in Mahabubnagar District of Andhra Pradesh, India, *Fishing Chimes*, 33(7): 29-31.

Laxmappa, B. and Vijay Babu, G. 2014. Opportunities in Mahabubnagar District, A.P. for Improving the Livelihood of Fishers through Reservoir Fisheries. *Fishing Chimes*, 33(12): 26-28.

Leela, J.B; Patil, S.M; Suresh, N.D. and Sathe, S.S. 2010. Occurance of Phytoplankton in the Water Bodies of Miraj Tehsil of Maharashtra. *The Ecoscan*, 4(1): 73-76.

Lendhe, R.S. and Yeragi, S.G. 2004. Physico-chemical Parameters and Zooplankton Diversity of Phirange Kharbav Lake, Dist. Thane, Maharashtra. J. Aqua.Biol. 19(1): 49-52.

Liu, J.K. and Yu, Z.T., 1992. Water Quality Changes and Effects on Fish Populations in the Hanjiang River, China, following Hydroelectric Dam Construction, Regulated Rivers: Research and Management, 7(4): 359-368.

Lohar, P.S. and Borse, S.K. 2003. Diversity of Fish Fauna in River Tapti, Maharashtra. *J. Aqua.Biol.* 18(1): 47-48.

Lorenzen, K. 1994. Dynamics and Management of Asian Culture based Reservoir Fisheries. Aquaculture News, October 20.

Lynne, M.W. 2004. Practical Guide to Identify Freshwater Crustacean Zooplankton, Cooperative Freshwater Ecology Unit, Dept. of Biology, Laurentian University, Sudburg, Ontario, Canada, Available on http://coopunit./aurentian.ca.

Madhu, N.V., Jyotibabu, R., Balachandran, K.K., Honey, U.K., Martin, G.D., Vijay, J.G., Shiyas, C.A., Guptha, G.V.M. and Achuthankutty, C.T. 2007. Monsoonal Impact on Planktonic Standing Stock and Abundance in a Tropical Estuary. (Cochin backwaters-India), *Estuarine, Coastal and Shelf Science* 73: 54-64.

Madhyastha, M.N. and Murugan, S. 1993. Socio-economic Status of Fisherfolk in Relation to Fish and Fisheries of Hemavathy Reservoir. *Indian Journal of Fisheries*. 40(4): 267-269.

Mahadik, B.B. and Jadhav, M.J. 2014. A Preliminary Study on Algal Biodiversity of Ujani Reservoir (M.S.) India. *Bioscience Discovery*, 5(1): 123-125.

Mahajan, S.R. and Nandan, S.R. 2004. Blue Green Algae of Hartala Lake, Jalgaon, Maharashtra. *J. Aqua.Biol.* 19(1): 11-12.

Mahapatra, Dipti Kumar. 2003. Present Status of Fisheries of Hirakud Reservoir Orrisa. *Fishing Chimes*, 22 (10 & 11): 76-79.

Mahor, R.K. 2011. A Survey of Fish and Fisheries of the Fresh Water Reservoir Tighra, Gwalior, Madhya Pradesh. *Shod Samiksha aur Mulyanka*. 2(25): 49-50.

Majagi, S. and Vijaykumar, K. 2009. Ecology and Abundance of Zoolplankton in Karanja Reservoir. *Environ. Monit. Assess.*, 152: 451-458.

Malhotra, Y.R., Gupta K, Khajuria, Anil. 1991. On the Diel Activity of Benthic Macro Invertebrates in Relation to some Physico-chemical Parameters of Lake Mansar, Jammu. *J. Hydrobiol.*, 7 (1): 11-15.

Mali, R.P. and Bondhare, S.O. 2012. Fishing Crafts and Gear in River Godavari at Nanded, Maharashtra. *Ecology and Fisheries*, 5: 37-40.

Mali, R.P. and Shaikh, Afsar. 2012. Fish Diversity of Lake Hussain Sagar, Hyderabad. In: Perspectives of Ecology (Eds. V.B. Sakhare and J.S. Mohite), pp. 109-112, Oxford Book Company, Jaipur.

Mallen-Cooper, M. and Harris, J. 1990. Fishways in Mainland South-Eastern Australia. In: Proceedings of the International Symposium on Fishways' 90, pp. 221-230.

Malthane, G.A. 2013. Diversity of Zooplanktons of Nalganga Reservoir Nalgangapur, Buldhana District, Maharashtra. *Ecology and Fisheries*. 6(2): 113-116.

Mani Bharat and S.A. Gaikwad. 1998. Physico-chemical Characteristics of Lake Pokharn. *Indian J. Environ. & Toxicol.*, 8(2): 56-58.

Manjare, S.A. 2015. Comparative Study of Ichthyofauna and Fishery Potential of Perennial Tanks of Kolhapur District (Maharashtra). Research Journal of Life Sciences, Bioinformatics, Pharmaceutical and Chemical Sciences, 1(1): 26-32. Paper Available on www.rjlbpcs.com.

Manjare, S.A; Vhanalkar, S.A. and Muley, D.V. 2012. Physico-chemical Condition and Occurrence of some Zooplankton in a Laxmiwadi Tank, Maharashtra. *Ecology and Fisheries*; 5(2): 45-50.

Manjare, S.A. and Muley, D.V. 2012. Physico-chemical Parameters and Zooplankton Population in a Tamdalge Tank, Maharashtra. *Ecology and Fisheries*. 5(2): 77-82.

Manna, R.K; Das, A.K; Krishna Rao, D.S; Karthikeyam, M. and Sing, D.N. 2011. Fishing Crafts and Gear in River Krishna. *Indian J. Traditional Knowledge*. 10(3): 491-197.

Manoharan, D. and Isaiarasu, L. 2012. Zooplankton Diversity in Three Temple Ponds in Tiruparankundram, Madurai, Tamil Nadu. In: Perspectives in Ecology (Eds. V.B. Sakhare and J.S. Mohite) pp. 159-168, Oxford Book Company, Jaipur.

Manojkumar, T.G. and Madhusoodana Kurup, B. 2002. Fish Habitat Diversity and Species Assemblage Structure with Reference to Five Major River Systems of Kerala (Boopendranath M.R; Meenakumari, B; Joseph, J; Sankar, T.V; Pravin, P. and Edwin, L. Eds.), p. 141-150, Society of Fisheries Technologists (India), Cochin.

Maruthanayagam, C; Sasikumar, M. and Senthilkumar, C. 2003. Studies on Zooplankton Population in Thirukulam Pond during Summer and Rainy Seasons. *Nature, Environ. Pollut. Technol.* 2: 13-19.

Mathew, P.M., 1985. Seasonal Trends in the Fluctuation of Plankton and Physico-chemical Factors in a Tropical Lake (Govundgarh Lake, M.P.) and their Interrelationships. *J. Inland Fish. Soc. India*, 17(1 & 2): 11-24.

Mathew, P.M. and Mohan, M.V. 1990. Reservoir Fisheries in Kerala – Status and Scope for Development. National Workshop on Reservoir Fisheries, Asian Fisheries Society, Indian Branch, CIFRI, Barrackpore, West Bengal.

Mathur, Nalini and Summarwar, Sudha, 2007. Survey of the Status of Fisheries in Bisalpur Reservoir, Rajasthan, India. *Eco. Env. & Cons.*13 (2): 279-282.

Medudhula Thirupathaiah, Ch.Samatha and Chintha Sammaiah. 2012. Analysis of Water Quality using Physico-chemical Parameters in Lower Manair Reservoir of Karimnagar District, Andhra Pradesh. *International Journal of Environmental Sciecnes.* 3(1): 172-180.

Mellanby, H. 1963. Animal Life in Freshwater, 6th Edition, Chapman and Hall Ltd; London.

Menon, A.G.K. 1999. Checklist of Freshwater Fishes of India. Zoological Survey of India. Occ. Pop. No. 175, p. 366.

Meshram, Manisha and Nasare, P.N. 2011. Phytoplankton Diversity of Futala Lake in Nagpur, Maharashtra. *Ecology and Fisheries*, 4(1): 67-70.

Michael, R.G. and Sharma, B.K. 1988. Fauna of India and Adjacent Countries, Indian Cladocera (Crustacea: Branchiopoda: Cladocera), Zoological Survey of India, Calcutta, pp. 262.

Minimol, K.C. 2001. Fishery Management in Periyar Lake, Ph.D. Thesis, Mahatma Gandhi University.

Mishra, Ashutosh, Chakraborthy, S.K., Jaiswar, A.K., Sharma, A.P., Deshmukhe, Geetanjali and Mohan Madan, 2010. Plankton Diversity in Dhaura and Baigul Reservoirs of Uttarakhand. *Indian J.Fish.* 57(3): 19-27.

Mishra, B.B., Chaturvedi, G.B. and Tiwari, D.D., 2008. Water Quality Index and Suitability of Water of Kohargaddi Dam at District Balrampur, India. *Poll. Res.* 27 (3): 497-500.

Mishra, G.P. and Yadav, A.K. 1978. A Comparative Study of Physico-chemical Characteristics of River and Lake Water in Central India, *Hydrobiol.* 59 (3): 275-278.

Mishra, S.R. 2005. Zooplankton and their Seasonal Variations in a Sewage Collecting River at Gwalier, Madhya Pradesh, In: Advances in Limnology (Ed.S.R. Mishra), pp. 1-44, Daya Publishing House, Delhi.

Mishra, S.R and Saxena, D.N. 1990. Seasonal Abundance of the Zooplankton of Waste Water from the Industrial Complex at Birla Nagar (Gwaliar) India. *Acta. Hydrochim. Hydrobiol;* 18: 215-220.

Mitchell, C.,1995. Fish Passage Problems in New Zealand. In: Proceedings of the International Symposium on Fishways' 95, Gifu, Japan.

Mohite, J.S. 2006. Ichthyofauna of Reservoirs from Solapur District, Maharashtra. In: Ecology of Lakes and Reservoirs (Eds. V.B. Sakhare) p. 181-185, Daya Publishing House, New Delhi.

Mohite, J.S. 2010. Studies on some Aspects of Ecology of Ramdara Reservoir, Tuljapur (District Osmanabad, Maharashtra), Ph.D. Thesis, Swami Ramanand Teerth Marathwada University, Nanded.

Mohite, J.S. and Joshi, P.K. 2011. Phytoplankton Diversity in Ramdara Reservoir near Tuljapur, Maharashtra. In: Advances in Aquatic Ecology (Vol. 5), (Eds.V.B. Sakhare), pp. 22-23, Daya Publishing House, New Delhi.

Mohite, S.A. and Mohite, A.S. 2009. Scope of Women Self-help Group (SHG's) and Cooperative Societies in Fishery Sector of India. *Fishing Chimes*, 29(1): 177-185.

Molur, S. and Walker, S. (Eds.) 1998. Report of the Workshop on Conservation Assessment and Management Plan for Freshwater Fishes of India. Zoo Outreach Organization Conservation Breeding Specialist Group, India, Coimbatore, India, 156p.

Motlagh, Amin Hossaini, Navatha, K. and Manikya Reddy, P. 2014. Assessment of Pollution in Mir Alam Lake, Hyderabad, A.P., India. *Asian Jr.of Microbiol. Biotech. Env. Sc.* 16(1): 103-106.

Moyle, J.B. 1945. Some Chemical Factors Influencing the Distribution of Aquatic Plants in Minnesota. *Amer. Midl. Natur.*, 34: 402-420.

Moyle, J.B. 1949. Some Indices of Lake Productivity. Trans. Amer. Fish. Soc. 76: 322-334.

Moza, Usha and Mishra, D.N., 2008. Current Status of Harike Wetland vis a vis its Ecology and Fishery. In Proceedings of TAAL - 2007: The 12th World Lake Conference (Sengupta M. and Dalwani, R. Eds.), pp. 1470-1476.

Mukherjee, Biswarup. 1996. Environmental Biology, Tata McGrow-Hill Publishing Company Limited, New Delhi, pp. 691.

Mukharjee, Madhumita and Praharaj Aloknath. 2009. Kangsbati Reservoir Fisheries Development: New Policy Approaches through Multidisciplinary Field Demonstrations to Rural People. *Fishing Chimes.* 29(1): 112-121.

Mulani, S.K; Mule, M.B. and Patil, S.U. 2009. Studies on Water Quality and Zooplankton Community of the Panchganga River in Kolhapur City, *J. Environ. Biol*; 30: 455-459.

Mule, D.V. and Patil, I.M., 2006. A Study of Water Quality and Fish Diversity of Pauna River, Maharashtra. *J. Aqua. Biol.* 21(1): 68-75.

Munna, R.K., Bhaumik, U., Satpathy, B.B., Das, S.K., Sahoo, A.K. and Roy, A. 2013. Studies for Hilsa Fisheries in Different River Systems of India for Sustainable Management. CIFRI Annual Report, 2013.

Munshi, J.D. and Munshi, J.S.D. 1995. Fundamentals of Freshwater Biology, Narendra Publishing House, Delhi, p. 222.

Murugan, J. 2008. An Inventory of the Algal Flora of Temple Tanks of Kanchipuram. *Indian J. Hydrobiol.* 11(1): 99-102.

Murugan, N. 1975. The Biology of *Ceriodaphnia cornuta Sars. J. Inland Fish. Soc. India*; 7: 80-87.

Murugan, N. 1989. Dynamics of a Population of Ceriodaphnia Cornuta Sars (Crustacea: Cladocera) from a Seasonal Pond in Madras. *Proc. Indian Acad. Sci. (Anm.Sci.).* 99(2): 151-161.

Murugan, N., Murugavel, R. and Kodarkar, M.S. 1998. Cladocera: The Biology, Classification, Identification and Ecology, Indian Association of Aquatic Biologists, Hyderabad.

Mushtaa Ahmad Ganie, Mohammad Iqbal Khan and M. Parveem. 2012. Seasonal Variations in Physico-chemical Characteristics of Pahuj Reservoir, District Jhansi, Bundelkhand Region, Central India. *Int. Jr. of Current Research*. 4(12): 115-118.

Nafeesa, Begum and Narayana, J. 2006. Phytoplankton Diversity of Four Lentic Waterbodies in and Around Devangarere City, Karnataka. *J. Aqua. Biol*. 21(2): 13-18.

Nafeesa, B; Sayeswara, H.A; and Mahesh, A.G. 2011A. Physico-chemical Profile and Phytoplankton Density and Diversity in Hadadi Lake, Karnataka, India. *The Ecoscan*. 5(3 & 4): 159-164.

Nafeesa, B; Sayeswara, H.A; and Naik, K.L. 2011B. Seasonal Variations of Phytoplankton Diversity of Bethur Pond near Davangere, Karnataka. *Environment and Ecology*. 29(3A): 1355-1359.

Nair, N.B. 1989. Report of the Expert Committee on Marine Fishery Resource Management in Kerala. 116 p.

Nakhwa, D. 2003. Role of Fisherwomen in Development of Fisheries in Orissa. Report of the National Workshop on Best Practices in Microfinance Progrmmes for Women in Coastal Fishing Communities in India, Panji, Goa, 1-4 July 2003, pp. 31: 1-12.

Nandan, S.N. and Jain, D.S. 2005. Study of Algae Tolerating Organic Pollution of Sonvad Dam and Devbhane Dam of Maharashtra. Advances in Limnology (Ed. S.R. Mishra), Daya Publishing House, New Delhi, pp. 214-222.

Nandeesha, M.C; Murthy, C.K; Ramchandra Bhat and Devaraj, K.V. 1984. An Evaluation of the Socio-economic Status of the Fishermen Community of Mugad Village of Dharwad District, Karnataka. *Coop. Perspective*, 19(3): 62-68.

Nasare, P.N; Wadhane, N.S; Harrey N.V. and Sitre, S.R. 2009. Studies on Phytoplankton Diversity of Vinjasan Lake in Bhadrawati Town of Chandrapur District, Maharashtra. *Ecology and Fisheries*, 2(1): 95-100.

Natarajan, A.V. 1976. Ecology and the State of Fishery Development in some of the man-made Reservoirs in India. Symp. on the Development and Utilization of Inland Fishery Resources, IPFC/76/Sym/25. Colombo, Sri Lanka.

Natarajan, A.V; Ramakrishaiab, M. and Khan, M.A. 1976. *J.Inland Fisheries Society of India,* 1, 65.

Navatha, K., K. Nirmala and P. Manikya Reddy. 2013. Trophic Status of Ibrahimpantnam Lake, with Reference to Physico-chemical and Phycological Characteristics. *Poll. Res.* 32 (3): 473-476.

Nayar, C.K.G. 1971. Cladocera of Rajasthan. *Hydrobiologia.* 37: 509-519.

Needham, J.G. and Needham, R.R. 1962. A Guide to Study of Freshwater Biology. Holden Day Inc; San Francisco, USA.

Nimisha P. and Sheeba S.2013. Physico-chemical Characteristics of Water in Lower Stream Reaches of Periyar River in Kerala, India. *Eco. Env. & Cons. 19 (2): 2013; pp. (369-374).*

Niture, S.D. and Chavan, S.P. 2009. Crafts and Gears used in Yeldari Reservoir, Maharashtra. *Ecology and Fisheries.* 2: 113-120.

Niture, S.D. and Chavan, S.P. 2014. Ichthyofaunal Diversity of Siddheshwar Reservoir, Hingoli District, Maharashtra. In: Advances in Aquatic Ecology (Vol. 8) (Eds.V.B. Sakhare and B. Vasanthkumar), pp. 208-214, Astral International Pvt. Ltd. New Delhi.

Northcote, T.G. and Larkin, P.A. 1956. Indices of Productivity in British Columbia. J. Fish. Res. Bd. Canada, 13: 515-540.

Ogle, J. 1979. Adaptation of a Brown Water Culture Technique to the Mass Culture of the Copepod Acartia Tonsa. *Gulf Res. Rep.* 6: 291-292.

Ohno, A. and Okamura, Y. 1988. Propagation of the Calanoid Copepod, *Acartia tsuensis* in Outdoor Tanks. *Aquaculture* 70: 39-51.

OMCAR. 2013. Socio-economic Status of Keezhathottam. Publication of OMCAR, Pattukkottai, Tamil Nadu, India.

Panayotou, T. (Ed.). 1985. Small-scale Fisheries in Asia: Socio-economic Analysis and Policy. IDRC–229c. Ottawa, Ontario. 283p.

Pandey, B.N., Jha, A.K., Das, P.K.I. and Pandey, K. 1994. Zooplankton Community in Relation to Certain Physico-chemical Factors of Kosi Swamp, Purnia, Bihar. *Environ. Ecol.,* 12: 563-569.

Pandey, B.N., Mishra, A.K., Das, P.K.L. and Jha, A.K. 1995. Studies on Hydrological Condition of River saura in Relation to its Impact on Biological Health. In: Recent Researches in Aquatic Envirnment (Eds. Ashutosh Gautam and N.K. Agarwal), pp. 57-65, Narendra Publishing House, New Delhi.

Pandey, B.N., Siddhartha, R., Tanti, K.D. and Thaku, A.K. 2013. Seasonal Variation in Zooplanktonic Community in Swamp of Purnia (Bihar), India. *Aquatic Biology Research* 1(1): 1-9.

Paria, Tapas, Chakraborty, Chinmoy and Roy Chayan. 2010. Freshwater Fish Diversity in India: Issues of Conservation and Management. In:

Aquatic Ecosystem and its Management (Eds. K. Vijaykumar and B. Vasanthkumar), pp. 1-70, Daya Publishing House, New Delhi.

Parihar, R.P. 1999. A Text Book of Fish Biology and Indian Fisheries, Central Publishing House, Allahabad, pp. 310-313.

Patalas, K. 1972. Crustacea Plankton and the Eutrophication of st. Lawrence Great Lakes. *J. Fish. Res. Bd. Can;* 29: 1451-1462.

Pathak, S.K. and Mudgal, L.K. 2004. Biodiversity of Zooplanktons of Virla Reservoir Khargore (M.P.), India, pp. 317-321. In: Arvind Kumar (Ed.) Biodiversity and Environment, A.P.H. Publishing Corporation, New Delhi.

Patil, B.V. 2013. Zooplankton Composition in Reservoirs of Buldhana District of Maharashtra. *Ecology and Fisheries.* 6(2): 99-112.

Patil, S. and Sahu, B.K. 2012. Studies on the Correlation between Rainfall and Phytoplankton in a Tropical Reservoir. *J. Zool. Res;* 5(1 & 2): 73-79.

Patil, S.G. 1976. Freshwater Cladocera (Arthropoda: Crustacea) from North East India. *Curr. Sci;* 45: 312-313.

Patil, S.G. 2002. Freshwater Ostracoda. Wetland Ecosystem Services No. 3, Fauna of Ujani, pp. 87-90, Zoological Survey of India, Kolkata, 196 pp.

Patil, S.G. and Talmale, S.S. 2005. A Checklist of Freshwater Ostracods (Ostracoda: Crustacea) of Maharashtra, India. *Zoo's Print Journal,* 20(5): 1872-1873.

Patra, C; Bandopadhyay, P; Tewary, A; Kar, A. and Sarkar, S. 2002. Participation of Rural Women in Aquaculture in Himalayan Darjeeling of West Bengal. *Fishing Chimes,* 22(9): 51-53.

Pau Biak Lun, K; Ajit kumar and Basavaraja, N. 2009. Status of Aquaculture and Fisheries in Manipur State. *Fishing Chimes,* 29(1): 102-104.

Pawar, Ashwini, P. and Mushan, 2012. Studies on Diversity of Zooplankton in Four Lakes of Solapur, Maharashtra. *Fishing Chimes.* 32 (3): 47-49.

Pawar, Sandhya and Pawar Sourabh, 2012. Ichthyofaunal Diversity of Kanher Dam from Satara District of Maharashtra State of India. *International Journal of Fisheries and Aquaculture Sciences.* 1: 15-19, Paper available on http://www.irphouse.com.

Pawar, S.B. and Shembekar,V.S. 2012. Studies on the Physico-chemical Parameters of Reservoir at Dhanegaon District, Osmanabad (M.S.), India. *Journal of Experimental Sciences,* 3(5): 51-54.

Pawar, S.K., Madlapure, U.R. and Pulle, J.S. 2003. Study of Zooplankton Community of Sirur Dam Water Mukhed in Nanded District (M.S.). *J.Aquqa. Biol.* 18: 37-40.

Pawar, S.K. and Pulle, J.S. 2005. Qualitative and Quantitative Study of Zooplankton in Pethwadaj Dam, Nanded District, Maharashtra, *J. Aqua.biol.* 20(2): 53-57.

Pawar, S.M. and Sonawane, S.R., 2011. Water Quality Index of Kanher Dam of Satara District (M.S.) India. *The Ecoscan*, 5(3 & 4): 199-202.

Payne, M.F; and Rippingale, R.J. 2001. Intensive Cultivation of the Calanoid Copepod Gladioferens Imparipes. *Aquaculture*, 201: 329-342.

Pejaver, Madhuri, Somani, Vaishali and Mangala Borker. 2002. Physico-chemical Studies of Lake Ambegosale, Thane, India. *J.Ecobiol.* 14(4): 277-281.

Pejaver, Madhuri, Somani Vaishali and Goldin Quadros, 2004. Physico-chemical Parameters of Two Quarry Lakes near Thane.

Pennak, R.W. 1978. Freshwater Invertebrates of the United States, 2nd Ed. John Wiley and Sons, New York, 803pp.

Pentewar, M.S. 2013. Physico-chemical Analysis of Dhanora Dam Water in Bhokar Tahsil of Nanded District. Proc. of National Conference on Global Environmental Problems: Impact and Solutions, Netaji Subhashchandra Bose Arts, Commerce and Science College, Nanded 22 & 23 February 2013, pp. 51-54.

Percy, Dawson. 2002. Trawling in Indian Reservoirs. In: Riverine and Reservoir Fisheries of India (Boopendranath, M.R; Meenakumari, B; Joseph, J; Sankar, T.V; Pravin, P. and Edwin, L. Eds.), p. 264-267, Society of Fisheries Technologists (India), Cochin.

Peter, T. and Mitrofanov., 1998.The Impact on Fish Stocks of River Regulation in Central Asia and Kazakhstan Lakes and Reservoirs: Research and Management, 3: 143-164.

Petters, G.E., 1988. Impounded Rivers, Chichester, U.K.: John Wiley & Sons Ltd. Publishers, 326p.

Phillipose, M.T. 1959. Freshwater Phytoplankton of Inland Fisheries. Proc. Symp. Algology, ICAR, 272-291.

Pillai, P.P. 2012. Erratic Monsoon, *Fishing Chimes*, 32(4): 36-37.

Piska, Ravi Shankar. 1998. Fisheries and Aquaculture, Lahari Publication, Hyderabad. Piska, Ravishankar. 1999. The Present Status of Fisheries of a Minor Reservoir Ibrahimbagh, Hyderabad. National Conference-cum-Workshop on Wetland Conservation, Washim.

Piska, Ravishankar. 2000. Impact of Stocking Densities of Major Carp seed on Fish Production in a Minor Reservoir. *Fishing Chimes*. 20(9): 38-41.

Piska, Ravi Shankar, B. Sarala Devi and Divakara Chary. 2000. The Present Status of Fisheries of Ibrahimbagh, a Minor Reservoir of Hyderabad. *Fishing Chimes*, 20(2): 41-43.

Piska, Ravishankar and Naik Jithender Kumar. 2000. Fresh Aquaculture, Lahiri Publications, Hyderabad.

Ponniah, A.G. and Sarkar, U.K. 2000. Fish Biodiversity of North-East India. National Bureau Fish Genetic Resources, 228p.

Prakash, Sadguru, Ansari Khalid K. and Sinha, Mukul, 2002. Seasonal Dynamics of Zooplankton in a Fresh Water Pond Developed from the Waste Land of Brick-Klin. *Poll. Res.* 21(1): 81-83.

Pramod Babu, K.R. 2006. A Study on the Ecobiology of Kuttanad with Reference to Fisheries, Ph.D. Thesis, Mahatma Gandhi University, Kottayam, 264p.

Prasad, B.N. and Saxena, M. 1980. Ecological Study of Blue Green Algae in River Gomati. *Indian J. Environ. Health.* 22(2): 151-168.

Prasada Rao, D.L. and Kumar, R.Y. 1984. Impact of Mechanization on a Traditional Economy: A Case Study of Fishermen in Vishakhapattnam. *Man and Life*. 10(1&2): 31-42.

Pravin, P; Meenakumari, B; Baiju, M; Barman, J; Baruah, D. and Kakati, B. 2011. Fish Trapping Devices and methods in Assam: A Review. *Indian J. Fish*. 58(2): 127-135.

Pulle, J.S. and Khan, A.M. 2003. Studies on Zooplanktonic Community of Isapur Dam Water, India. *Poll. Res*. 22(3): 451-455.

Purkayashta, Pinki and Gupta, Sushmita. 2014. Traditional Fishing Gears used by the Fisher Folk of Chatia Foodplain Area, Barak Valley, Assam. *Indian Journal of Traditional Knowledge*. 13(1): 181-186.

Purushan, K. 2001. To Empower the Fisherwomen to Avail the Immense a Vocational Avenues. *Seafood Export Journal*, 32(5): 19-23.

Purushothama, R., Sayeswara, H.A., Mahesh Anand Goudar and Harish Kumar, K. 2011. Physico-chemical Profile and Zooplankton Community Composition in Boahamana Kalasi Tank, Sagara, Karnataka, India. *The Ecoscan.*, 5(1&2): 43-48.

Qadri, M.Y. and Yousuf, A.R. 1980. Influence of the Physico-chemical Factors on the Seasonality of Cladocera in Lake Manasbal. *Geobios*. 7: 273-276.

Quiros, R. 1989. Structures Assisting the Migrations of Non-salmonids Fish: Latin America, FAO-COPESCAL Technical Paper 5, UN FAO, Rome.

Quiros, R., 1998, Reservoir Stocking in Latin America, an Evaluation. pp. 91-117. In: T. Petr. (ed.), *Inland Fishery Enhancement*. Papers Presented at the FAO/DFID Expert Consultation on Inland Fishery Enhancements. Dhaka, Bangladesh, 7-11 April, 1997. FAO *Fisheries Technical Paper*, 374. Rome, FAO. 463p.

Radhakrishnan, K.V. and Madhusoodana Kurup, B. 2002. Habitat Preference and Biodiversity Assessment of Potential Freshwater Ornamental Fishes of Kerala (Boopendranath, M.R; Meenakumari, B; Joseph, J; Sankar, T.V; Pravin, P. and Edwin, L. Eds.), p. 162-171, Society of Fisheries Technologists (India), Cochin.

Raghunathan, M.B. 1983. Studies on some Planktonic Cladocerans (Crustacea) of Tamil Nadu, Ph.D. Thesis Madras University.

Raghunathan, M.B. 1989. Indian Cladocera (Crustacea). *Indian Review of Life Sciences*. 9: 137-152.

Raghunathan, M.B. and Kumar, S. 2003. A Checklist of Indian Cladocera (Crustacea). *Zoo's. Print. J.* 18: 1180-1182.

Raheem, A. 2005. Women's SHG for Alleviating Poverty. *Kisan World*. 32(7): 37. Raj, Deleep Packia. 2010. Sediment Profile of Perumchani Reservoir of Kanyakumari District, Tamil Nadu. *Journal of Basic and Applied Biology*, 4(3): 174-180.

Raj, Deleep Packia and Beena Lawrence. 2012. Ecological Investigation of Water of Perumchani Reservoir, Kanyakumari District, Tamil Nadu, *Applied Research and Development Institute Journal*, 5(3): 23-30.

Rajashekhar, A.V., Lingaiah, A., Satyanarayana Rao and Piska Ravi Shankar. 2007. The Studies on Water Quality Parameters of a Minor Reservoir, Nadergul,Rangareddy Dist.Andhra Pradesh. *J.Aqua. Biol.* 22(1): 118- 122.

Rajashekar, M.,Vijaykumar, K. and Zeba Parveen. 2009. Zooplankton Diversity of Three Freshwater Lakes with Relation to Trophic Status, Gulbarga District, North-East Karnataka, South India, *International Journal of Systems Biology*,1(1): 32-37.

Rajasekhar, M; Vijayakumar, K. and Zeba Parveen. 2010. Seasonal Variations of Zooplankton Community in Freshwater Reservoir, Gulbarga District, Karnataka, South India. *International Journal of Systematic Biology*. 2: 6-11.

Rajkumar, B. 1984. Ecological Studies in the River Manjira with Special Reference to its Lithophytic Flora, Ph.D. Thesis, Osmania University, Hyderabad.

Rama Rao, S.V; Singh, V.P. and Mali, L.P. 1978. Biological methods for Monitoring Water Pollution Levels: Studies of Ujjain. In: Glimpses of Ecology, Inter. Sci. Publ. Jaipur, pp. 341-348.

Ramakrishna, N.R. 2008. Exotic Fishes in Karnataka: Their History, Status and Prospects. In: Fish Introductions in India: Status, Potential and Challenges (Eds. W.S. Lakra, A.K. Singh and S. Ayyapan), 249-254, Narendra Publishing House, Delhi.

Ramesan, M.P. 2006. Studies on Inland Fishing Gears of North Keralla, Ph.D. Thesis, Cochin University of Science and Technology, Cochin.

Ramkrishnan, Suja, 2003. Socio-economic Issues and Sustainable Fishery Management: A Case Study of Kerala, Ph.D. Thesis, Cochin University of Science and Technology.

Rane, Pramod. 1983. A New Species of the Genus *Latonopsis Sars*, 1988 (Cladocera, Sididae) from Madhya Pradesh, India. *Crustaceana*, 45(1): 82-84.

Rao, C.A.N., J. Deepa and M. Hakeel., 2011. Comparative Account on ichthyofauna of Pocharam and Wyra Lakes of Andhra Pradesh, India. *Journal of Threatened Taxa* 3(2): 1564-1566.

Rao, D.S.P. 1991. Taxonomic Revision of the Family Lecanidae (Rotifera), M.Phil. Dissertation Submitted to Andhra University, Waltair. 1-58.

Rao, K.S. and Choubay, Usha. 1993. Systematic and Ecological Studies on Central India Lentic Cladocera In: Recent Advances in Freshwater Biology (Edited by K.S. Rao).

Rao, L.M; Prasad, K.V.S. and Sivani, G. 1998. Ecology and Ichthyofauna of Freshwater Ponds of Amalapuram, Andhra Pradesh. *J. Aqua. Biol.* 13(1 & 2): 29-33.

Rao, R.J; Garg, R.K; Tigare S; Arya, M; Singh, H; Bidyalakshmi and K. Kushwah 2010. Status of Biodiversity in Inland Wetlands of Gwalior - Chambal Region in Madhya Pradesh. In: *Advances in Aquatic Ecology* (Vol. 3), Eds. VBS, pp.1-11, Daya Publishing House, New Delhi.

Rathod, S.R. and Khedkar, G.D. 2011. Impact of Elevation, Latitude and Longitude on Fish Diversity in Godavari River. *Journal of Research in Biology*. 4: 269-275.

Rawat, M.S., Sharma, R.C. 2010. Analysis of Zooplankton Population in Garhwal Himalayan Lake, Deoria Tal, Uttarakhand. In: Aquatic Ecosystem and its Management (Eds. K. Vijaykumar and B. Vasanthkumar), pp. 102-109, Daya Publishing House, Delhi.

Raymond, H.L.,1979. Effect on Dams and Impoundments on the Migration Rate of Juvenile Chinook Salmon and Steelhead Trout from the Snake River,1966-1975, In: Transcations of the American Fisheries Society, 108(6): 509-29.

Ridhi, Jha, B.C; Parashar, A; Das, A.K. and Bose, A.K. 2013. Fishes of Gobindsagar Reservoir in Madhya Pradesh. *J. Chem. Bio. Phy. Sci.* 3(1): 390-398.

Rowland, S.J. 1986. Site Selection, Design and Operation of Aquaculture Farms. *Freshwater Aquaculture in Australia,* Owen, P. and J. Bowden, eds. Brisbane, Australia: Rural Press Queensland.

Roy, Deepayan and Mandal, S.C. 2011. Rudrasagar Lake (Ramsar Site) in Tripura State Present Status of Fish Production and Suggestions for Future Development. *Fishing Chimes*. 31 (7): 38-40.

Roy, T. 1999. Copepoda: Calanoida and Cyclopoida, 2001. Surv. India, State Fauna Series 3: Fauna of West Bengal, Part 10: 287-313.

Rylov, V.M. 1922. Was ist unter "Plankton Organismus" zuverstehen. *Russ. Hydro. Biol.Zeit.*, 1: 241-247.

Sachidanandamurthy, K.L. and H.N. Yajurvedi. 2006. A Study on Physico-chemical Parameters of an Aquaculture Body in Mysore City, Karnataka, India. *Journal of Environmental Biology*. 27(4) 615-618.

Saha, L.C. and Pandit, B. 1988. Density of Zooplankton between Lentic and Lotic Ecosystems. *Geobios New Reports*, 7(1): 31-35.

Sahu, P. 2000. Marine Fishery and Sustainability of the Fishermen in Ganjam District, Ph.D. Thesis, Berhampur University.

Sakhare,V.B. 2001a. Reservoir Fisheries in Solapur District of Maharashtra. *Fishing Chimes*. 21 (5), pp. 29-30.

Sakhare, V.B. 2001b. Ichthyofauna of Jawalgaon Reservoir in Solapur District of Maharashtra. *J.Aqua.Biol.* 16 (1): 31-33.

Sakhare, V.B., 2005. Ecology and Fisheries of Manjara Reservoir in Maharashtra. *Fishing Chimes*. 25 (3): 42-45.

Sakhare, V.B., 2005. Water Quality of Hingni (Pangon) Reservoir and its Significance to Fisheries. In: Advances in Limnology (Ed. S.R. Mishra), pp. 231-235, Daya Publishing House, Delhi.

Sakhare,V.B. 2007. Reservoir Fisheries and Limnology, Narendra Publishing House, Delhi.

Sakhare,V.B. 2007.Wan Reservoir (Beed Dt., Maharashtra): Ecology and Fisheries. *Fishing Chimes*. 27 (6): 23-26.

Sakhare, V.B. 2008. Impact of Tilapia on Indigenous Fishes: A Case Study of Ramdara Reservoir in Osmanabad District of Maharashtra. Final Report of Minor Research Project, Western Regional Office, University Grants Commission, Pune 28pp.

Sakhare, V.B. 2012. Water Quality of Mamdapur Reservoir in Relation to Fisheries, *Ecol. Env. & Cons.*18(3): 547-549.

Sakhare, V.B. 2012a. Ecology and Ichthyofauna of Ekuruk Reservoir near Solapur City, Maharashtra. In: Perspectives in Ecology (Eds. V.B. Sakhare and J.S. Mohite) pp. 103-108, Oxford Book Company, Jaipur.

Sakhare, V.B. 2012b. Zooplankton Diversity in Udyan Sarovar Tank in Ambajogai, Maharashtra. In: Perspectives in Ecology (Eds. V.B.Sakhare and J.S. Mohite), pp. 152-158, Oxford Book Company, Jaipur.

Sakhare, V.B. 2014. Reservoir Fisheries of Satara District, Maharashtra. In: Advances in Aquatic Ecology (Vol. 8), (Eds. V.B. Sakhare and B. Vasanthkumar), pp. 159-171, Astral International Pvt. Ltd; New Delhi.

Sakhare, V.B. and Bidkar, A.R. 2001. Fisheries Status of River Godavari at Village Raher of Nanded District in Maharashtra, India. *Ecol. Env. and Cons.* 7(2): 151-153.

Sakhare, V.B. and Jetithor, S.G. 2009. Physico-chemical Limnology of Pathri Reservoir (Maharashtra) in Relation to Fisheries. In: Aquatic Biology and Aquaculture (Edited by V.B. Sakhare), pp. 147-163, Manglam Publications, Delhi.

Sakhare, V.B. and Jetithor, S.G. 2013. Crafts and Gears used in Reservoirs of Marathwada Region, Maharashtra. *Sustainability, Agri, Food and Environmental Research* 1(1): 40-45.

Sakhare, V.B. and Joshi, P.K. 2002. Ecology of Palas-Nilegaon Reservoir in Osmanabad District, Maharashtra. *J.Aqua. Biol.* 18 (2): 17-22.

Sakhare, V.B. and Joshi, P.K. 2002. Ecology and Ichthyofauna of Bori Reservoir in Maharashtra. *Fishing Chimes.* 22 (4): 40- 41.

Sakahre, V.B. and Joshi, P.K. 2005. Ichthyofauna of Reservoirs in Osmanabad District, Maharshtra. *Fishing Chimes.* Vol. 25 (9), pp. 43-44.

Sakhare, V.B. and Joshi, P.K. 2006. Plankton Diversity in Yeldari Reservoir, Maharashtra, *Fishing Chimes.* 25(12): 23-25.

Sakhare, V.B. and Joshi, P.K. 2011. Present Status of Reservoir Fisheries in Maharashtra, pp. 92-116. In: Applied Ecology (Eds. V.B. Sakhare and B. Vasanthkumar), Narendra Publishing House, Delhi.

Salasakar, P.B. and Yeragi, S.G., 2004. Primary Productivity of Powai Lake, Mumbai, Maharashtra. J.*Aqua.Biol.* 19 (1): 19-22.

Sampaio, E.V; Rocha, O; Matsumura-Tundisi, T. and Tundisi, J.G. 2002. Composition and Abundance of Zooplankton in the Limnetic Zone of Seven Reservoirs of the Paranapanema River, Brazil. *Brazilian Journal of Biology.* 62: 525-545.

Samul, Eddy. 1934. A Study of Fresh-water Plankton Communities, Contribution from the Zoological Laboratory of the University of Illinois No. 448.

Sanap, G.B; Haregaonkar, R.B. and Sakhare,V.B. 2012. Study on ichthyofauna of Waterbodies around Ambajogai, Maharashtra. In: Advances in Aquatic Ecology (Vol. 6), Edited by V.B. Sakhare and Patrico De los Rios, pp. 22-29, Daya Publishing House, New Delhi.

Santhi, D., 2012. Assessmet of Water Quality Parameters in Kodumudiaru Dam at Nanguneri Taluk of Tirunelveli District. *Poll. Res.* 31(1): 83-86.

Sarang, N.and Sharma, L. L., 2010. Length Weight Relationship and Harvestable Size of *Labeo Calbasu* from Jawahar Sagar Dam of Southern Rajasthan, India. *Journal of Inland Fisheries Society of India.* 42(1): 53-58.

Sarang, N.; Sharma, L.L. and Saini, V.P. 2009. Age, Growth and Harvestable Size of *Cirrhinus mrigala* from the Jawahar Sagar Dam, Rajasthan, India. *Indian Journal of Fisheries.* 56(3): 215-218.

Sarma, P.K. 2000. Systematics, Distribution and Ecology of Zooplankton of some Floodplain Wetlands of Assam, India, Ph.D. Thesis, Gauhati University, Assam.

Sarwade, J.P. and Khillare, J.K. 2010. Fish Diversity of Ujani Wetland, Maharashtra, India. *The Bioscan.* 1: 173-179.

Sathiadhas, R. and G. Venkitaraman. 1981. Impact of Mechanized Fishing on Socio-economic Conditions of the Fishermen of Sakthikulangara - Needakara, Kerala, *Mar. Fish. Infor. Serv. T.&E. Serv.* 29: 1-18.

Sawant, R.S., Desai, P.D. and Desai, J.S. 2011. Physico-chemical Properties of the Uttur Tank in Ajara Tahsil, Maharashtra. *J.Ecobiol.* 29(3): 205-211.

Sayeswara, H.A; Mahesh, A.G. and Manjunatha, R. 2011. Water Quality Evaluation and Phytoplankton Diversity of Hosahalli Pond, Shivamogga, Karnataka (India). *Int. J. Chem. Sci.* 9(2): 805-815.

Sayeswara, H.A., T. Vasantha Naik, H.S. Ravikumar Patil and K.M. Prashantha. 2012. Phytoplankton Diversity and Pollution Indicators of Purle Pond Water of Shivamogga, Karnataka, India. *Ecology, Environment and Conservation*, 18(3): 626-627.

Sayeswara, H.A., Naik, K.L., Naik, T.V., Sumanthrappa, D.B., Jeevan, E.N., Dhananjaya, S.G. and Asahshree, H.M. 2014. Diversity of Zooplankton in Nagathibelagalu Tank, Bhadravthi, Kumataka. In: Advances in Aquatic Ecology (Vol. 8), Astral International Pvt. Ltd., pp. 235-239, (Eds. V.B. Sakhare and B.Vasanthkumar).

Segers, H. 2007. Annotated Checklist of the Rotifers (Phylum Rotifera), with Notes on Nomenclature, Taxonomy and Distribution, *Zootaxa*; 1564: 1-104.

Sehgal, K., Phadke, G.G., Chakraborty, S.K. and Vijay Kumar Reddy, S., 2013. Studies on Zooplankton Diversity in Dimbhe Reservoir, Maharashtra, India, *Advances in Applied Science Research*, 4(1): 417-420.

Sehgal, K.L. 1983. Planktonic Copepods of Freshwater Ecosystems. Interprint, New Delhi, 169pp.

Sekharan, Mini, Pramod, P.K. and Ramacharan, A. 2002. Role of Chalakkudy Riverine Resource in the Ornamental Fish Marketing Sector of Kerala (Boopendranath, M.R; Meenakumari, B; Joseph, J; Sankar, T.V; Pravin, P. and Edwin, L. Eds.), p. 384-392, Society of Fisheries Technologists (India), Cochin.

Selot, M. 1977. Ecological Study of Dulhara Tank with Special Reference to Plankton Population and Physico-chemical Properties of Water. Ph.D. Thesis, Ravishankar University, Raipur.

Selvaraj, C; Murugesan, V.K. and Unnithan, V.K. 1997. Ecology based Fisheries Management in Aliyar Reservoir, Golden Jubilee Bulletin of CIFRI, Barrackpore, pp. 30.

Senthilkumar, R. and Sivakumar, K. 2008. Studies on Phytoplankton Diversity in Response to Abiotic Factors in Veeranam Lake in the Cuddatore District of Tamil Nadu. *J. Env. Biol.* 29(5): 747-752.

Shah, Javaid Ahmad and Pandit, Ashok Kumar. 2014. Taxonomic Survey of Crustacean Zooplankton in Wular Lake of Kashmir, Himalaya. *J. Evol. Biol. Res.* 6(1): 1-4.

Shailaja, K. and Johnson, Mary Esther Cynthia, 2006. Elemental Analysis of Certain Plants Growing around Osman Sagar Lake, Hyderabad, Andhra Pradesh, *J.Aqua. Biol.* 21 (1): 231-234.

Shanker, P.H. 2010. Phytoplankton Diversity in Lakes of Mysore District, Karnataka State, India. *The Ecoscan*, 4(1): 53-57.

Shardendu, and Ambasht, R.S. 1990. Variations in the Physico-chemical Characteristics of a City Pond Ecosystem at Varanasi, *Bio. Journal.* 11-18.

Sharma, A.P. and Das, M.K. 2012. Impact and Vulnerability of Inland Fisheries to Climate Change, *Fishing Chimes*, 32(1): 73-79.

Sharma, Archana and Mohan Devedra, 2010. Fish Faunal Diversity of Hemawas Dam, Pali, Rajasthan. *J.Aqua.Biol.*25(2): 37-40.

Sharma, B.D., 2008. Status of Exotic Fishes, their Introduction and Role in Himachal Fisheries, pp. 259-264. In: Fish Introductions in India: Status, Potential and Challenges (Eds. W.S. Lakra, A.K. Singh and S.Ayyapan), Narendra Publishing House, Delhi.

Sharma, B.K. 1978. A Note on Freshwater Cladocera from West Bengal. *Bangladesh J. Zool.* 6: 149-151.

Sharma, B.K. 1991. Rotifera: Animal Resources of India: Protozoa to Mammalia. State of the Arts: Zoological Survey of India, Calcutta. 69-88.

Sharma, B.K. 1981. Contribution to the Rotifer Fauna of Panjab State, India. 1. Family Branchionidae. *Hydrobiol.* 76: 249-253.

Sharma, B.K. 1996. Biodiversity of Freshwater Rotifera in India – A Status Report. Proc. Zool. Soc. Calcutta 49. 73-85.

Sharma, B.K. 1999. Rotifera. In: Faunal Diversity in India (Eds. J.R.B. Alfred, A.K. Das and A.K. Sangal), Zoological Survey of India, Calcutta: 57-70.

Sharma, B.K. 1999. Freshwater Rotifers (Rotifera: Eurotatoria), 2001. Surv. India, State Fauna Series 3, Fauna of West Bengal, Part II: 341-468.

Sharma, B.K. 2000. Synecology of Rotifers in a Tropical Floodplain Lake of Upper Assam (N.E. India). *The Indian Journal of Animal Science*, 70: 880-885.

Sharma, B.K. 2005. Rotifer Communities of Foodplain Lakes of the Brahmaputra Basin of Lower Assam (N.E.) India. Biodiversity: Distribution and Ecology, *Hydrobiologia*, 533: 209-221.

Sharma, B.K. 2010. Rotifer Communities of Deeper Beel, Assam, India: Richness, Abundance and Ecology. *Journal of Threatened Taxa*. 2(8): 1077-1086.

Sharma, B.K. and Michael, R.G. 1983. Redescription of Alona Taraporevalae Shirgur and Naik 1977(Cladocera:chyloridae: Aloninae). *Rec. Zool. Surv. India*; 81: 35-39.

Sharma, B.K. and Pachuau, L.2013. Zooplankton Diversity of a Sub-tropical Reservoir of Mizoram, Northeast India. *Opusc.Zool.Budapest*. 44(1): 47-60.

Sharma, B.K and Sharma, S. 2001. Biodiversity of Rotifers in some Tropical Floodplain Lakes of the Brahmaputra River Basin, Assam (N.E. India). *Hydrobiol.* 446/447: 305-310.

Sharma, B.K and Sharma, S. 2005. Biodiversity of Freshwater Rotifers (Rotifera, Eurotatoria) from North-Eastern India, *Zoosystematics and Evolution*, 81(1): 81-88.

Sharma, B.K. and Sharma, S. 2008. Faunal Diversity of Cladocera (Crustacea: Branchiopoda) of Deeper Beel, Assam (Northeast India)- A Ramsar Site, *Journal of Bombay Natural History Society*, 105(2): 196-201.

Sharma, Duyshant Kumar. 2001. Seasonal Variations in Different Physico-chemical Characteristics in Makroda Reservoir of Guna District (M.P.). *Ecol.Env. & Cons.* 7(2): 201-204.

Sharma, Dushyant Kumar 2007. Studies on the Ecology and Fish Fauna of Makroda Reservoir of Guna District (Madhya Pradesh). In: Advances in Aquatic Ecology (Vol. 1), Editor V.B. Sakhare, pp. 31-34, Daya Publishing House, New Delhi.

Sharma, Dushyant Kumar and Renu Jain. 2000. Physico-chemical Analysis of Gopalpura Tank of Guna District (M.P.). *Ecol. Env. & Cons.* 6(4): 441-445.

Sharma, Dushyant Kumar and Singh, R.P. 2012. Seasonal Variation in Zooplankton Diversity in Tighra Reservoir, Gwalior (Madhya Pradesh). *Indian J. Sci. Res.* 3(2): 155-161.

Sharma, K.K. and Chanderkiran. 2011. Comparative Analysis of Cladoceran Communities from Three Subtropical Freshwater Ponds of Jammu. Patterns, Composition and Diversity. *The Bioscan*. 6(2): 233-237.

Sharma, K.K; Kaur, S. and Gupta, S. 2005. Distributional Pattern of Cladoceran in Subtropical Lake, Mansar, *J & K. Nat. J. Life Sci.* 2(1-2): 23-26.

Sharma, K.K. and Kotwal, Sanjay 2011. Studies on Diversity and Dynamics of Cladocera in a Sub-tropical Sungal Pond, Akhnoor (J &K). *The Bioscan*, 6(4): 623-625.

Sharma, K.P. and Bharadwaj, R.S.,1980. Fisheries of Gudha Reservoir, Rajasthan. *India Today & Tomorrow*. 8(4):175-171.

Sharma, R. 2001. Traditional methods and Fishing Gears of Assam. *Fishing Chimes*, 20(12): 23.

Sharma, Rekha and Diwan, A.P.1993. Limnological Studies of Yeshwantsagar Reservoir I Plankton Population Dynamics, In: Recent Advances in Freshwater Biology (Vol. I), Edited by K.S. Rao, 199-211.

Sharma, Riddhi, Sharma Vipul, Sharma Madhu Sudan, Verma Bhoopendra Kumar, Modi Rachana and Gaur Kuldeep Singh, 2011. Studies on Limnological Characteristic, Planktonic Diversity and Fishes (Species) in Lake Pichhola, Udaipur, Rajasthan (India). *Universal Journal of Environmental Research and Technology*. Available online at: www.environmentaljournal.org.1(3): 274-285.

Sharma, S., Sharma, B.K. and Michael, R.G. 1984. The Biology of Daphnia lumholtzi Sars (Cladocera: Daphnidae) Laboratory Studies on Longenity, instar duration, Egg Production and Growth. Proc. Nat. Acad. Sci. India, 54: 306-314.

Sharma, S.S.S; Nandini, S. and R.D. Gulati. 2005. Life History Strategies of Cladocerans: Comparisons of Tropical and Temperate Taxa, *Hydrobiologia*, 542: 315-333.

Sharma, Sanjay; Mishra, Smriti R, Yadav, R.K. 1992. Diurnal Cycle of Physico-chemical Characteristics of Matsya Sarovar, Gwalior. *Env Eco*, 10 (1): 127-129.

Sharma, Vipul, Bhoopendra Kumar Verma, Ridhhi Sharma, Madhusudan Sharma and Kuldeep Sing Gaur. 2012. A Report on the Freshwater Cladocera (Crustacea: Branchiopoda) of South Rajasthan (India). *International Journal of Environmental Sciences*, 3(1): 275-296.

Sheeba, S; Ramanujan, N. and Santosh, S. 2004. Qualitative and Quantitative Study of Zooplankton in Ithikkara River, Kerala. *Ecology, Environment & Coservation*, 10(3): 249-292.

Sheshappa, D.S. 2002. Culture and Capture Techniques - An Engineering Approach. In: Riverine and Reservoir Fisheries of India (Boopendranath, M.R; Meenakumari, B; Joseph, J; Sankar, T.V; Pravin, P. and Edwin, L. Eds.), p. 218-224, Society of Fisheries Technologists (India), Cochin.

Shetty, H.P.C. 1990. Forward. Proc. of Nat. Workshop on Reservoir Fisheries, 3-4 January 1990. Spl. Publ. Asian Fisheries Society, Indian Branch, Mangalore, India.

Shiel, R.J. 1995. A Guide to Identification of Rotifers, Cladocerans and Copepods from Australian Inland Waters, Cooperative Research Centre for Freshwater Ecology Identification Guide No. 3, Murray Darling Freshwater Research Centre, Ellis Street, Thurgoona, P.O. Box 921, Alburg, NSW 2640.

Shinde, S.E. 2011. Studies on the Physico-chemical and Coorelation Coefficient of Harsool-Savangi Dam, Dist. Aurangabad, India. *Middle-East Journal of Scientific Research*, 8(3): 544-554.

Shinde, S.E; Pathan, T.S; Bhandare, R.Y. and Sonawane, D.L. Ichthyofaunal Diversity of Harsool Savangi Dam, District Aurangabad, (M.S.), India. *World Journal of Fish and Marine Science*, 3: 141-143.

Shinde,Y.S. 2012. Studies on Freshwater Ostracoda (Crustacea) of Pune District, Maharashtra. Ph.D. Thesis, Pune University, Pune.

Shinde,Y.S; Reginald Victor and Pai, Kalpana. 2014. Freshwater Ostracods (Crustacea: ostracoda) of the Plateaus of the Northern Western Ghats, India. *Journal of Threatened Taxa*, 6(4): 5667-5670.

Shive, S.E; Pathan, T.S, Bhandare, R.Y. and Sonawane, D.L. 2009. Ichthyofaunal Diversity of Harsool Savangi Dam, District Aurangabad, (M.S.), India. *World Journal of Fish and Marine Science*, 3: 141-143.

Shiyani, R.L. 2003. Socio-economic Profile of Fisherfolk in Gujrat. P. 123-140. In: A Profile of People, Technologies and Policies in Fisheries Sector in India. (Eds. Anjani Kumar, P.K. Katiha and P.K. Joshi), National Centre for Agricultural, Economics and Policy research, New Delhi.

Shrirame, N.V; Gyananath, G; Mulgir, M.T; Phartale, N. N. and Kanse, O.S. 2014. Diversity and Seasonal Fluctuation of Zooplankton in Ghagardara Pond, Taluka Kandhar Dist. Nanded. *International Journal of Aquaculture*, 4(3): 20-23.

Shukla, Suresh,C; Kant Rajani and Tripathi, B.D. 1989. Ecological Investigation on Physico-chemical Characteristics and Phytoplankton Productivity of River Ganga at Varanasi, *Geobios*. 16:20-27.

Siddamallayya, N. and Pratima Mathad. 2010. Impact of Physico-chemical Factors on Primary Productivity of Phytoplankton in Papnash Pond, Bidar (Karnataka). In: Aquatic Ecosystem and its Management (Eds.Vijaykumar and B. Vasanthkumar) pp. 298-304, Daya Publishing House, New Delhi.

Siddiqui, S.Z. and Chandrasekhar, S.V.A. 1993. New Distributional Records of Freshwater Cladocera from Hyderabad: A Taxo-ecological Profile. *Geobios New Report*, 12: 105-110.

Siddiqi, S.Z. and Khan, R.A. 2002. Comparative Limnology of Few Man-made Lakes in and around Hyderabad, India. Rec. Zool. Surv. India. Occ. Paper No. 203:1-64 (Published by the Director, Zool. Surv. India, Kolkata).

Singh, A.K. 1993. Pre Impoundment Studies on Sardar Sarovar Area of Narmada River (West Zone) with Special Reference to Fisheries, Ph.D. Thesis, Vikram University, Ujjain, India.

Singh, A.K. 2004. Aquaculture Diversification and Species Enhancement: Problems and Perspectives. In: Zoology and Human Welfare Edited by Dr.Ashok Verma, Published by University of Allahabad (Dr. S.P. Mukherji Government College, Phaphamaos), 252-261.

Singh, A.K. and Ahmed, S.H. 1990. A Comparative Study of the Phytoplankton of the River Ganga and Pond of Patna (Bihar), India, *J. Indian Bot. Soc*, 69: 153-158.

Singh, A. K. and Ahmed, S.H. 2006. Potential and Prospects of Fishery Development in Jharkhand State. *Fishing Chimes*. 26 (1): 192-203.

Singh, B.S. and Sahai, K, 1986. The Primary Production of Phytoplankton of a Tropical Shallow Water Body of Gorakhpur. *Tropical Ecol*. 27: 33-39.

Singh C.S., Sharma A.P. and Deorari B.P. 1993. Limnological Studies for Bioenergetic Transformation in a Tarai Reservoir, Nanak Sagar (U.P.). Proc. of Nat. Symp. on Advances in Limnology and Conservation of Endangered Fish Species; 23-26 (Ed.) H.R. Singh, Dept. of Zoology, H.N.B. Garwal University, Sri Nagar, India.

Singh, C.S., Sharma, A.P. and Deorari, B.P. 1993. Plankton Population in Relation to Fisheries in Nanak Sagar Reservoir, Nainital. In: Recent Advances in Freshwater Biology (Vol. I), Edited by K.S. Rao, 66-79.

Singh, D.N. 2000. Seasonal Variation of Zooplankton in Tropical Lake. *Geobios* 27(2-3): 97-100.

Singh, D.P. and Saxena, R.S. 2008. Diurnal Variations of Zooplankton in Daryabganj Lake of District Etah. *Int.J. Mendel.* 25(1-4): 39-40.

Singh, K.M.P. 1995. Final Project Report of Studies of Hydrobiology and Fisheries of Powai Lake, Mumbai.

Singh Kohili, M.P. 1991. Final Project Report of Studies of Hydrobiology and Fisheries of Powai Lake, Mumbai.

Singh, Meena and Sinha, R.K. 1995. Diel Variation of Water Quality and Zooplankton Community in a Freshwater Pond of Patna, Bihar. *Eco.Env. and Cons.* 1(1-4): 57-64.

Singh, Meera. 2011. Study of Plankton Abundance in Freshwater Fish Pond at Malwan, Etah (U.P.). *Ind. J. Biol. Stud. Res.* 1(1): 39-44.

Singh, P.P. and Tuli, R.P., 2006. Fisheries Development in Chattisgarh. *Fishing Chimes.* 26 (1): 214-217.

Singh, R.1991. Rotifer Fauna of Jamalpur, Munger, Bihar. *Journal of Current Biological Sciences.*, 8: 45-46.

Singh, R. and Mahajan, I. 1987. Some Physico-chemical Factors and Phytoplankton or Rewalsar Lake, Himachal Pradesh. *Geobios.* 14(1): 6-9.

Singh, R.K. 1986. Fluctuations in the Composition of Zooplankton Population in Relation to Hydrobiological Conditions of a Reservoir. *J. Hydrobiol.* 2(3): 37-42.

Singh, R.K., N.P. Shrivastava and Desai, V.R. 1980. Seasonal and Diurnal Variations in Physico-chemical Conditions of Water and Plankton in Lotic Sector of Rihand Reservoir (U.P.). *J. Inlad Fish. Soc.India,* 12 (1): 100-111.

Singh, R.P. and Mathur, P. 2005. Investigation of Variations in Physico-chemical Characteristics of a Freshwater Reservoir of Ajmer City, Rajasthan, *Ind. J. Env. Sci.* 9: 57-61.

Singhai, S; G.M.A. Ramani and U.S. Gupta, 1990. Seasonal Variations and Relationship of Different Physico-chemical Characteristics in Newly made Tawa Reservoir. *Limnologica* (Berlin)., 21(1): 263-301

Sinha, K.K. and Sinha, D.K. 1993. Seasonal Trends in Physico-chemical Factors and Zooplankton in a Freshwater Pond of Munger, Bihar. *J. Ecobiol.* 5(4): 299-302.

Siraj, S; Yousuf, A.R. and Parveen, M. 2007. Cladoceran Community in Sheshbug Wetland, Kashmir. *J. Res. Dev.* 7: 67-74.

Sivakumar, K. and Altaff, K. 2004. Ecological Indices of Freshwater Copepods and Cladocerans from Dharmapuri District, Tamil Nadu. 2005. *Print Journal*,19(5): 1466-1468.

Sivakumar, K. and Karuppasamy, R. 2008. Factors Affecting Productivity of Phytoplankton in a Reservoir of Tamil Nadu, India. *Am. Euras J. Bot.* 1(3): 99-103.

Smith, G.M.1920. Phytoplankton of the Inland Lakes of Wisconsin. Pt. I. Myxophyceae, Phaeophyceae, Heterokonteae, and Chlorophyceae Exclusive of the Desmidiacae. Wise. Geol. and Nat. Hist. Surv. Bull. 57, Scientific Series No. 12. 243 pp.

Solanki, Pradeep, Shiv Singh, I.V. Sharma and Mathur, R. 2011. Fish Fauna of Sanjay Sagar Reservoir of District Guna (M.P.). *Biological Forum.* 3(1): 44-45.

Somani, U.V. and Pejaver, M.K. 2003. Rotifer Diversity in Lake Masunda, Thane (Maharashtra). *J. Aqua.Biol.* 18(1): 23-27.

Somani, U.V. and Pejaver, M.K. 2004. Crustacean Zooplankton of Lake Masunda, Thane, Maharashtra, India. *J. Aqua. Biol.* 19(1): 57-60.

Sone, A.A. ad Malu, R.A., 2000. Fish Diversity in Relation to Aquaculture in Ekburjii Reservoir, Washim, Maharashtra. *J.Aqua.Biol.*15 (1&2): 44-46.

Soruba, R. and Sangeetha, B. 2011. Phytoplankton Diversity of the Temple Pond at Minjur, Tiruvalluvar District, *J. Ecobiol.* 29(4): 305-309.

Sreenivasan, A., 1967. *Tilapia mossambicus*: Its Ecology and Status in Madras State, India., *Madras J.Fish.*, 3:33-39.

Sreenivasan, A. 1984. Influence of Stocking on Fish Production Reservoirs in South India. FAO Fish. Rep. 312: 40-52.

Sreenivasan, A.1998. Integrated Development of Reservoir Fisheries of India: Production to Marketing. *Fishing Chimes.*18 (1): 60-63.

Sreenivasan, A.,1998. Fifty Years of Reservoir Fisheries in Mettur Dam, India: Some Lessions. Naga, The ICLARM Quarterly, October-December 1998: 4-7.

Sreenivasan, A. 2001. Stagnating Reservoir Fish Production of India. *Fishing Chimes*, 21(1): 39-42.

Sreenivasan,Y., 1980. Fishing Technology in the Development of Reservoirs. *India Today & Tomorrow,* 8(4): 171.

Srivastava, Neera; Agarwal Meena and Tyagi, Anupama. 2003. Study of Physico-chemical Characteristics of Water Bodies Around Jaipur. *J.Environ. Biol.* 24(2): 177-180.

Srivastava, S.K. 2013. Mothly Variations in the Occurrence of Zooplankton in a Freshwater Body, Ramgarh Lake, Gorakhpur, U.P. *International Journal of Applied Biosciences,*1(2): 23-27, online available at http://mutagens.co.in/ijab.html.

Srivastava, U.K., D.K. Desai, V.K. Gupta, S.S. Rao, G.S. Gupta, M. Raghavachari and S. Vatsala. 1985. Inland Fish Marketing in India - Reservoir Fisheries, Vol. 4 (A & B). Concept Publishing Co; New Delhi, pp (A) 403 & (B) 1184.

Subenthung, Odyuo N. and Nagesh, T.S. 2012. Fisheries and Management Status of Doyang Reservoir, Nagaland, North-east India. *Indian J. Fish.* 59(2): 1-6.

Sugunan, V.V. 1990. Reservoir Fisheries Management. Technologies for Inland Fisheries Development, Central Inland Fisheries Research Institute, Barrackpore, West Bengal, 153-163.

Sugunan, V.V. 1995. Reservoir Fisheries of India, FAO Technical paper No. 345, Daya Publishing House, Delhi.

Sugunan, V.V. and Katiha, P.K., 2004. Impact of Stocking on Yield in Small Reservoirs in Andhra Pradesh, India. *Fisheries Management and Ecology.* 11: 65-69.

Sukand, B.N. and Patil, H.S. 2004. Water Quality Assessment of Fort Lake of Belgaum (Karnataka) with Special Reference to Zooplankton. *J.Environ. Biol.* 25: 99-102.

Sukhija, L. 2010. Hydrobiological Studies of Foy Sagar Lake, Ajmer. *Nature Environment & Pollution Technology,* 9(3): 601-604.

Sukumaran, P.K. and Das, A.K. 2004. Distribution and Abundance of Rotifers in Relation to Water Quality of some Tropical Reservoirs, *Indian J. Fish;* 51(3): 295-301.

Suresh, V.R. 2002. Fishery Resources of Manipur Potential, Problems and Strategies for Development. In: Riverine and Reservoir Fisheries of India (Boopendranath, M.R; Meenakumari, B; Joseph, J; Sankar, T.V; Pravin, P. and Edwin, L. Eds.), p. 135-140, Society of Fisheries Technologists (India), Cochin.

Swingle, H.S. 1967. C. Biological means of Increasing Productivity in Ponds. FAO Fish. Rep. (44): 3: 416-23.

Szlauer, B., and Szlauer, L. 1980. The use of Lake Zooplankton as Feed for Carp (*Cyprinus carpio* L.) Fry in Pond Culture. *Acta Ichthyol. Piscat.* 10(1): 79-102.

Szlauer, L. and Szlauer, B. 1982. Utilization of Autumn Zooplankton in Carp Fry Rearing, *Acta Ichthyol. Piscat.* 12(2): 71-81.

Talwar, P.K. and Jhingran, A.G., 1991. Inland Fishes of India and Adjacent Countries, Vols. 1 and 2. Oxford and IBH Publishing Co. Pvt. Ltd., New Delhi.

Tapiadar, D.D; Henderson, H.P; Delmendo, M.N. and Tsutsui, H. 1977. Fresh Water Fisheries and Aquaculture in China. A Report of the FAO (Fisheries) Aquaculture Mission to China, FAO Fisheries Technical Paper No. 168: 20-28.

Tayade, S.N. and Dhabade, D.S. 2011. Checklist of Rotifers in Washim District of Maharashtra, India. *International Journal of Innovations in Bio-sciences* 1: 27-31.

Telkhade, P.M. 2007. Hydrobiology and Biodiversity of Tadiba Lake, Chandrapur. Ph.D. Thesis, R.T.M. Nagpur University, Nagpur.

Thakur, R.K; Jindal, R; Singh Uday Bhan and Ahluwalia, A.S. 2013. Plankton Diversity and Water Quality Assessment of Three Freshwater Lakes of Mandi (Himachal Pradesh, India) with Special Reference to Planktonic Indicators. *Environ. Monit. Assess.* 185: 8355-8373.

Thirumala, S; Kiran, B.R. and Kantaraj, G.S. 2011. Fish Diversity in Relation to Physico-chemical Characteristics of Bhadra Reservoir of Karnataka, India. *Adv. Appl. Sci. Res*; 2(5): 34-47.

Thirumathal, K. 2006. Cladocerans of Amaravathy Reservoir, Udumalpet, Coimbatore District, Tamil Nadu, India. In: Ecology of Lakes and Reservoirs (Ed. V.B.Sakhare) pp. 105-110, Daya Publishing House, New Delhi.

Thomas, R.K. 2002. Habitat and Distribution of Hill Stream Fishes of Southern Kerala (South of Palghat Gap), Ph.D. Thesis, Mahatma Gandhi University, Kottayam, 240p.

Thomas, Sabu and Abdul Azis P.K. 2000. Physico-chemical Limnology of a Tropical Reservoir in Kerala, S. India, *Ecol. Env. & Cons.* 6 (2): 159-162.

Tijare, R.V. and Thosar, M.R. 2008. Rotifer Diversity in Three Lakes of Gadchiroli, a Tribal District of Maharashtra (India). Proceedings of TAAL, 2007: The 12th World Lake Conference: 480-483 (Eds. Sengupta, M. and Dalwani R.).

Tijare, R.V. and Thosar, M.R. 2010. Studies on Ecology of Zooplankton found in Freshwater Lake of Gadchiroli City, Maharashtra. *J. Aqua.Biol.* 25(1): 20-23.

Tiwana, N.S., Jerath, Neelima, Sexena, S.K. and Sharma Vivek, 2008. Conservation of Ramsar sites in Punjab. In: Proceedings of TAAL - 2007: The 12th World Lake Conference (Sengupta M. and Dalwani, R.Eds.), pp. 1463-1469.

Tiwari, A. and Chauhan, S.V.S. 2006. Seasonal Phytoplanktonic Diversity of Kitham Lake, Agra. *J. Env. Biol.*, 27(1): 35-38.

Tonapi, G.T. 1980. Freshwater Animals of India (an Ecological Approach), Oxford and IBH, New Delhi: 341.

Tripathi, A.K. and Chishty Nadim. 2012. Rotifer Diversity in a Semiurban Shallow Perennial Water Body: A Case Study of Jalaser Tank Mandalgarh, India. I. *Res. J. Environmental Sci.* 1(1): 42-45.

Tripathi, A.K. and Pandey, S.N. 1990. Water Pollution, Ashish Publishing House, New Delhi, p. 326.

Trivedy R.K., 1993. Water Quality of Dhom Reservoir Maharashtra, India. In: Mishra P.C. and Trivedy, R.K. (Eds.), Ecology and Pollution of Indian Lakes and Reservoirs, Ashish Publishing House, New Delhi, pp. 347.

Trivedy, R.K., and Goel, P.K. 1986. Chemical and Biological Methods for Water Pollution Studies. Environmental Publication, Karad (India).

Tyagi, O.D. and Mehra, M. 1990. A Textbook of Environment Chemistry. Anmol Publications, New Delhi, India.

Ubharhande, S.B. and Sonawane, S.R., 2012. Study of Freshwater Fish Fauna and Water Quality at Paintakli Dam from Buldhana District, (M.S.) India. *Journal of Experimental Sciences*, 3(7): 4-8.

Uchchariya, D.K. and Saksena, D.N. 2012. Zooplankton Diversity of Tighra Reservoir of Gwalior, Madhya Pradesh. *Flora and Fauna*, 18(2): 233-242.

Ude, E.F., Ugwu, L.L.C. and Mgbenka, B.O. 2011. Evaluation of Zooplankton Diversity in Echara River, Nigeria. Conti. *J. Biol. Sci.* 4 (1): 1-5.

Uma Chandra, N., Revathi, K. and Rekha, V. 2014. Biodiversity of Ostracods in Ambattur Lake, Tamil Nadu, India. *Eco.Env. & Cons.* 20(1): 167-174.

Vaishnav M.M. and Dewangan S. 2013. Quality Assessment of Different Aquatic Systems in Balco and its Adjoining Area, Kobra (C.G.), India. *Poll. Res.* 32 (3): 543-550.

Valsangkar, S.V., 1993. Mahseer Fisheries of Koyana (Shivajisagar) in Maharashtra: Scrap to Bonaza. *Fishing Chimes.* 12 (10): 15-19.

Vanjare, A.I. and Pai, Kalpana. 2010. Rotifers from a Pond in Pune (India), with the Record of *Ptygura pedunculata* (Edmondson, 1939) (Rotifera: Monogononta) from the Oriental Region, *Turk. J. Zool.* 34: 417-419.

Vankhede, G.N. and Kulkarni, K.M. 1984. Physico-chemical Conditions and Plankton Population of Two Lakes near Amaravati (M.S.). *Env.Bio.* 2(2): 431-433.

Varghese, M.D; George, V.C; Khan, A.A. and Iyer, H. 1982. Shore Seines for Reservoirs, Part II, Studies on Optional Mesh Size, *Fish. Technol.* 20(2): 97-100.

Varghese, P.U. 2002. Sustainable Production through Riverine and Reservoir Fisheries Management, in: Riverine and Reservoir Fisheries of India (Boopendranath, M.R, Meenakumari, B; Joseph, J; Sankar, T.V; Pravin, P. and Edwin, L; Eds.), p. 91-96, Society and Fisheries Technologists (India), Cochin.

Vasanthkumar, B; Roopa, S.V. and Gangadhar, B.K. 2013. Fish Diversity of Tungabhadra Reservoir, Karnataka. *Ecology and Fisheries*, 6(2): 53-56.

Vasanthkumar, B. and Vijaykumar, K.2012. Limochemistry of Bennitura Dam Near Gulbarga, Karnataka. In: Advances in Aquatic Ecology, Edited By V.B. Sakhare and Patricio Rene De los Rios Escalante (Vol. 6), pp. 67-71, Daya Publishing House, New Delhi.

Velayudhan, T.D. and Sidharthan, T. 1998. Influence of Stocking on Fish Yield in Chulliar Reservoir and its Impact on Rural Economy. *Fishing Chimes*, 18(4): 17-20.

Venkataraman, K. 1993. Studies on the Morphology of Post Abdomen of Cladocera and Conchostraca (Crustacea) using Scanning Electron Micrographs. *J. Indian Inst. Sci.* 73: 253-258.

Venkataraman, K. 1999. The Freshwater Cladocera (Crustacea: Branchiopoda) Zool. Surv. India, State Fauna Series 3: Fauna of West Bengal, Part 10: 251-284.

Venkatesharaju K; Ravikumar.P; Somashekar. R.K. and Prakash, K.L. 2010. Physico-chemical and Bacteriological Investigation on the River Cauvery of Kollegal Stretch in Karnataka, *Journal of Science Engineering and Technology*, 6 (1): 50-59.

Venkateswarlu, V. 1969a. An Ecological Study of the Algae of the River Mossi, Hyderabad (India) with Special Reference to Water Pollution. I Physico-chemical Complex. *Hydro.Biol.* 33:117-143.

Venkateswarlu, V. 1969b. An Ecological Study of the Algae of the River Mossi, Hyderabad (India) with Special Reference to Water Pollution. III Algal Periodicity. *Hydro.Biol.* 34: 533-560.

Venkateswarlu, V. 2006. Algae in Aquatic Environments. *Indian Hydrobiol.* 9(1): 1-6. Verma, M.N. 1969. Hydrobiological Study of a Tropical Impoundment, Tekeapur Reservoir, Gwalior, India, with Special Reference to the Breeding of Indian Carp. *Hydrobiol.*34:358-368.

Verma, P.K. and Datta Munshi, J.S. 1987. Plankton Community Structure of Badura Reservoir of Bhagalpur (Bihar). *Trop. Ecol.* 28: 200-207.

Verma, R; Singh, U.B. and Singh, G.P. 2012. Seasonal Distribution of Phytoplankton in Laddia Dam in Sakar District of Rajasthan, *Vegetos.* 25(2): 165-173.

Vijay Anand, P.E. 1996. Fishing methods in Lakshadweep. *Infofish International*, 3: 57-65.

Vinod, K., Mahapatra, B.K. and Mandal, B.K., 2003b. Studies on the Growth of Stocked Indian Major Carps and their Impact on Fisheries in Umiam Reservoir, Meghalaya, *Aquacult*, 4(2): 247-252.

Vladykov,V.D., 1964. Inland Fisheries Resources of Iran, Especially of the Caspian Sea with special Reference to Sturgean, Report No. 1818, FAO, Rome, 51p.

Vyas, Vipin; Parashar, Vivek; Damde, Dinesh and Singh Satyendra. 2009. Fish Biodiversity of Narmada in Submergence Area of Indira Sagar Reservoir. *Journal of the Inland Fisheries Society of India.* 41(2): 18-25.

Wagh, G.K. and Ghate, H.V. 2003. Freshwater Fish Fauna of the Rivers Mula and Mutha, Pune, Maharashtra. *Zoos' Print Journal.* 18 (1): 977-981.

Wesenberg-Lund, C.1908. Plankton Investigations of the Danish Lakes. Copenhagen. 389 pp.

Yadav, Pradeep, K.,1983. Reservoir Fishery Management: Major Policy Issues for Government Intervention. In: Fisheries Development in India: Some Aspects of Policy Management (Eds.U.K. Srivastava and M. Dharma Reddy), Proceedings of National Seminar on Fisheries Development in India, April 9-11, 1982 at Ahemadabad, pp. 433-457.

Yousuf, A.R. and Quadri, M.Y. 1977. Cladocera of Malpur sar, Kashmir, *J. Sci. Univ. Kashmir*; 3: 87-92.

Yusuf Kamal, M. 2002. Effect of Impoundment on the Indigenous Fish Population and their Management, In : Riverine and Reservoir Fisheries of India (Boopendranath, M.R; Meenakumari, B; Joseph, J; Sankar T.V; Pravin, P. and Edwin, L; Eds.), p. 1-5, Society of Fisheries Technologists, (India), Cochin.

Zebek, E. 2004. Species Biodiversity of Net Phytoplankton as an Indicator of Trophic Changes in the Urban Lake Jeziorak Maly. Teka kom ochr kszt Srod Przyr. 1: 316-321.

Zhong, Y. and Power, G., 1996. Environmental Impacts of Hydroelectric Projects on Fish Resources in China. In: Regulated Rivers: Research and Management, 12: 81-98.

Index